Other Books by Edward N. Luttwak

The Pentagon and the Art of War
The Question of Military Reform

The Grand Strategy of the Soviet Union

Strategy and Politics
Collected Essays

The Grand Strategy of the Roman Empire
From the First Century A.D. to the Third

The Israeli Army
(*with D. Horowitz*)

The Political Uses of Sea Power

Dictionary of Modern War

Coup d'Etat

ON THE MEANING OF VICTORY

ESSAYS ON STRATEGY

Edward N. Luttwak

SIMON AND SCHUSTER *New York*

Published by Simon and Schuster
A Division of Simon & Schuster, Inc.
Simon & Schuster Building
Rockefeller Center
1230 Avenue of the Americas
New York, New York 10020
SIMON AND SCHUSTER and colophon are registered trademarks of
Simon & Schuster, Inc.
Designed by Rueith Ottiger/Levavi & Levavi
Manufactured in the United States of America
10 9 8 7 6 5 4 3 2 1
Library of Congress Cataloging-in-Publication Data
Luttwak, Edward.
    On the meaning of victory.
    Includes index.
    1. Strategy—Addresses, essays, lectures.   2. Military
art and science—History—20th century—Addresses,
essays, lectures.   3. World politics—1945—   —Ad-
dresses, essays, lectures.   4. Military history, Modern—
20th century—Addresses, essays, lectures.   5. United
States—Military policy—Addresses, essays, lectures.
I. Title.
U162.L868   1986   355'.02   85-26145
ISBN 0-671-61089-9

To my wife, Dalya

CONTENTS

7

PREFACE

The peculiar instability of world politics in our days has, no doubt, many causes but surely one of the greatest is the inconstancy of American conduct on the international scene. Small powers can change policies abruptly without causing any great disturbance, and they certainly need to be agile when threatened. A very great power such as the United States, by contrast, should not need to maneuver rapidly to preserve its security, and unless any major alteration is very gradual, in its course, it must cause great instability. There was much continuity in the substance of American policy, to be sure, but in the short span of seven years that passed between the resignation of President Nixon and the inauguration of President Reagan, the stance of the United States on the world scene underwent two great and contrary transformations.

In the first, the dissipation of military strength caused by the Vietnam War was compounded by drastic reductions in the armed forces to much below pre-war levels, by the mutilation and paralysis of the Central Intelligence Agency, and by the perceptible loss of nerve manifest in Congress as well as the Executive branch, in the quality media, and among the nation's academic and professional elites. The Soviet Union, in the meantime, preserved a most remarkable continuity of governance while accumulating military strength of unique dimensions.

The second transformation was just as profound, and just as abrupt. In place of willful disarmament, and the reductions of strength exacted by inflation, by 1980 a definite recovery of military strength was underway, which was destined to accelerate during the next six years until this writing. In foreign policy, the reversal was even more drastic, as the declared activism manifest from 1981 displaced the imposed passivity of the Ford interval, and ideological "non-power" politics of the Carter years. In comparison, Soviet military and foreign policies evolved at a positively glacial rate.

At the lowest point of those years of upheaval, it seemed only natural to a great many Americans, the President included, that the overriding goal of foreign policy should be to avoid the use of force at any price, as if American pledges of protection issued to allies large and small round the world would not be undermined as a result. When American diplomats with full rights of immunity were held captive in Iran, it seemed just as natural, at first, that the unprecedented outrage should become the subject of protracted negotiations, timid pleadings by way of dubious intermediaries, and pitiful ceremonies of remembrance, instead of evoking a drastic Great Power response.

Just as the vital connection between the readiness to use force, the validity of American alliance guarantees and the stability of world politics was disregarded, so also the danger to all diplomats everywhere caused by an exclusive concern for the safety of some was seemingly overlooked: the subsequent mass attacks against American diplomats in Libya and Pakistan actually came as a surprise. The inordinate delay, unrealistic planning, and clumsy failure of the rescue attempt finally made in 1980 to liberate the diplomats in Iran, was perfectly consistent with the image that America presented to the world by then.

The recovery of means and morale that was to follow was astonishingly rapid, and its impact on world politics was magnified by an accidental coincidence with the degeneration of Soviet governance, whose continuity had plainly become a fossilized inertia. In the new conjunction, the Reagan administration could ride the momentum of success scarcely embarrassed by occasional failure, in Lebanon, for example—just as during the previous years even the large success of Camp David could not remove the mark of failure from the Carter administration.

Now that the Reagan rearmament has peaked, while in Moscow a new leadership may at least repair if not reform a system in historic decline, another turning point is perhaps at hand—but this time from upheaval to stability, one may hope. It therefore seems fitting to review the questions of strategy and military policy that seemed most important during the turbulent years just passed, in the context of the wider political circumstances of their time—so near at this writing by the calendar, yet already so remote in spirit.

I

HOW TO THINK ABOUT NUCLEAR WAR

1

TEN QUESTIONS
ABOUT SALT II

As part of a campaign for ratification of the SALT II agreement, ten questions and answers pertaining to the treaty were sent by the Carter administration to all members of the United States Senate. These questions and answers appear below, followed in each case by my critique.

1. What specifically will the Russians have to destroy as a result of SALT II? Won't they destroy only their oldest launchers?

Administration: The emerging SALT II agreement will require the Soviets to reduce their force by more than 250 strategic nuclear delivery vehicles—over 10 percent of current Soviet force levels. This reduction is important militarily because of the destructive power these systems represent. It is important politically because it concerns an important political measure of strategic capability and the central goal of equality in numbers of systems mandated in the Senate resolution approving the SALT I agreement. Moreover, these reductions are symbolically important because they set a precedent for further reductions in the future.

As an example of the military significance of the systems to be reduced, they are capable of destroying the largest 250 cities in the United States. The launchers reduced will clearly be the older systems in the current Soviet inventory, but these systems are by no means decrepit. They include ICBMs that are the same vintage as our Minuteman II missiles and SLBMs that are newer than our Polaris. The bombers to be reduced include the only all-jet bombers in the Soviet force.

More important, without the ceilings provided by the treaty, the Soviets would not only maintain and probably modernize these delivery vehicles but, based on past performance, they would be likely to increase their force size by adding new systems. The resulting force would not only be substantially larger than 2,250—perhaps by a third—but would have far greater destructive power, throw-weight, and warhead levels.

Politically, the reductions achieve equality in numbers of strategic systems at lower levels. The Senate recognized the importance of this measure by mandating equality in numbers in approving the SALT I Interim Agreement. The value of these reductions cannot be depreciated. In their absence, it could be politically necessary for the U.S. to build up to projected Soviet force levels. This numbers race would cost billions of dollars—a major diversion of resources with no resultant increase in security.

Finally, a goal of the United States in SALT must be not simply to ratify the number of strategic delivery vehicles on the two sides, but to reduce these levels. The SALT II reductions are the critical first step in this process.

Luttwak: The SALT II agreement is advertised as imposing equal ceilings on intercontinental weapons of both sides. Since the United States has no more than 2,058 heavy bombers and ballistic missiles, while the Soviet Union has at least 2,504, a genuine equality would require the elimination of more than 400 Soviet weapons. In fact, a Soviet-desired ceiling of 2,400 units has been accepted, and various bookkeeping devices are now being used to justify the claim of equality. For example, some 220 old B-52 bombers in storage (some actually disassembled) are counted in the American total, even though they have no military value whatsoever.

Under the terms of the SALT II agreement, both sides are to reduce their overall forces to 2,250 weapons by the end of 1981. It will be noted that bookkeeping tricks aside, the United States is already below that ceiling. The Soviet Union, however, will have to eliminate some 250 weapons. The administration claims that this is a very important provision of the agreement. In fact, the Soviet weapons to be withdrawn consist of rather primitive ballistic missiles, comparable to U.S. Minuteman I ICBMs (*unilaterally* withdrawn a decade ago) and Mya-4 jet bombers built in the 1950s which are now quite decrepit. The Russians will certainly not lose any real military options: they have plenty of high-grade missile capability in their large new ICBMs, and to replace the antique Mya-4s they have brand-new Backfire bombers, which have artificially been excluded from the SALT II ceilings.

When the U.S. Senate in 1972 mandated an equality in numbers for any new SALT agreement, it could scarcely have expected that an American administration would join the Soviet Union in contriving arbitrary definitions of what is and what is not a "strategic" weapon in order to achieve a spurious numerical equality.

By linking the important and highly desirable principle of force reductions to grossly unbalanced definitions, the SALT II agreement perverts what could have been a useful precedent for the future. The Russians now know that if they keep obsolete and pratically worthless weapons in their nominal weapons inventory, the United States will sooner or later reward them by making real and painful concessions in exchange for their withdrawal.

2. Are multiple protective structure (MPS) mobile ICBM systems using vertical shelters permitted under SALT? What is the Soviet view of this issue?

Administration: The Soviet side and the U.S. side have agreed on language in the SALT II treaty that states explicitly that mobile ICBM launchers are permitted after the Protocol expires. We have made clear that this language includes the various basing concepts we have been considering, including those, such as the MPS systems, in which missiles with their canister launchers are moved among shelters which might themselves be hardened. The Soviets have expressed the view that they do not see how the number of launchers in an MPS-type system could be verified and suggested that such a system would appear to involve construction of additional ICBM silo launchers. We have made clear that we do not accept these objections as valid.

With regard to verification, we recognize that there are additional difficulties connected with the monitoring of numbers of deployed mobile launchers, compared with such monitoring of fixed launchers, and that any new U.S. or Soviet mobile ICBM systems are subject to the SALT ban on deliberate concealment measures which impede verification of compliance with the provisions of the agreement. As a consequence of this prohibition, we must ensure that any mobile ICBM system which we deploy will permit adequate verification of the number of launchers deployed, and we will insist that any Soviet system meet the same verification standards. (It is noteworthy that these same requirements apply to SLBM launchers where the location of deployed launchers is concealed and the sides depend on observation of submarine construction to determine the number of launchers.)

We are confident that the various mobile ICBM options we are considering would meet these verification requirements.

We do not accept the Soviet claim that the shelters in an MPS system would constitute additional ICBM silo launchers, since the MPS system we are considering employs a mobile canister launcher. The basis for classifying the MPS system as mobile is that essentially all the equipment required to launch the missile, as well as the missile itself, is moved together periodically from one shelter to another—with the shelter providing a protected launch location. (The hardened shelter alone cannot launch a missile.) This assessment would apply irrespective of the type or orientation of the shelters in which the launcher and its missile are deployed (horizontal, vertical, trench).

The United States has both publicly and privately made clear that the various mobile ICBM systems we are considering, including ones in which the launch point would itself be hardened, will be permitted to either side during the post-Protocol period. We accept the requirement that mobile ICBM deployment must permit adequate verification of the number of launchers deployed and have designed the MPS system accordingly. We do not plan to seek Soviet blessing of our designs and similarly are not asking the Soviets to submit their mobile ICBM designs for our review.

The responsibilities of both sides on this matter are clear. There can be no question on the part of either side as to the interpretation which will govern U.S. actions under the provisions of the SALT II agreement.

Luttwak: There is a fundamental difference between the two parties to the SALT II agreement: while the Soviet Union is a closed and unusually secretive society, the United States is virtually transparent. The Russians can easily find out exactly how many and what sort of strategic weapons the U.S. has, and will have, merely by reading the *Congressional Record*. By contrast, to keep track of Soviet weapons the U.S. must rely on the sometimes uncertain data of satellite and other remote sensors. Nevertheless, the fiction has been maintained that the two sides are in an equal position as far as intelligence is concerned. As a result, when the Soviets argued that the "multiple protective structure" (MPS) basing mode for MX would violate the SALT II agreement (on the grounds that they would not be able to determine the number of actual missiles involved), their objection was not rejected out of hand, as it should have been. Instead, the American side has apparently followed the discredited "unilateral statement" formula in claiming the right to deploy a new ICBM in the MPS (or now "sunroof") mode, subject to adequate verification rules. ("We accept the requirement that mobile ICBM's must permit adequate verification. . . .")

Having seen the B-1 program cancelled unilaterally, the Russians obviously hope that the administration will sooner or later abandon the MX program also. Their objection to MPS was a friendly contribution to the unilateralist faction inside the Carter administration.

3. Why are the Soviets permitted a 308-0 advantage in heavy ICBMs?

Administration: The U.S. gave up the rights to modern heavy ICBMs in the course of the SALT I negotiations and agreed to continue this situation in SALT II quite simply because our military planners have absolutely no interest in such missiles. By giving up our rights to modern heavy ICBMs, which we do not need and would not build, we were able to gain important concessions in other areas. In particular, this bargaining chip was used in the negotiations at Vladivostok in 1974 to get the Soviets to drop their insistence on limits on U.S. European-based aircraft and the nuclear systems of U.S. allies.

Furthermore, it is important to understand that the Soviet advantage in heavy ICBMs applies only to *silo-based* ICBMs. Neither side is permitted heavy *mobile* ICBMs or heavy SLBMs. We could have retained the option to deploy unlimited numbers of heavy *mobile* ICBMs since this option was still open in the treaty in the fall of 1978. We recognized that keeping this option would have been attractive politically in offsetting arguments about the Soviet advantage in *silo-based* heavy ICBMs. At the same time, it was possible that the Soviets might someday exercise this option. We weighed this issue and with the support of the Joint Chiefs of Staff proposed to the Soviets that heavy mobile ICBMs and heavy SLBMs be banned. The Soviets accepted.

Another important factor is that the treaty will allow us to build a missile of equivalent effectiveness to the Soviet heavy ICBMs. The Soviets will be permitted a maximum of 10 warheads on their heavy missiles, the same number we will be permitted on our MX missiles, which will have better accuracy. Thus, they will not be able to exploit the greater payload of their heavy missiles in any meaningful fashion.

Luttwak: Much of the destabilizing Soviet throw-weight advantage derives from the heavy ICBMs in the Soviet force. SALT II would allow the Soviet Union to deploy 308 heavy modern ICBMs (SS-18s) as against zero for the United States. Once fully deployed, the SS-18 force alone would have a throw-weight of more than *four-and-one-half-million pounds* (by the lowest estimate) as compared to *two million pounds* for the entire U.S. ICBM force; and then of course the Soviet ICBM force includes another 1,090 ICBMs (SS-11s, 17s, 19s) on top of that.

The administration claims that the 308-to-zero advantage in heavy ICBMs was exchanged for an important Soviet concession ("to get the Soviets to drop their insistence on limits on U.S. European-based aircraft and the nuclear systems of U.S. allies"). In other words, in Act I the United States freely agrees not to count Soviet medium-range ballistic missiles deployed against our allies; in Act II the Soviet Union extracts this major concession for the nuclear systems of U.S. allies which are deployed to match those same medium-range missiles. And again, in Act I the United States agrees that the Backfire is not a "strategic weapon"; in Act II the Soviets have to be given a major concession to "drop their insistence" that our F-111s (with less than half the range of Backfire) are strategic weapons. True, the F-111s are forward-based in the United Kingdom; equally true, however, is the fact that the Backfires do not need to be forward-deployed in order to reach the United States.

The administration points out that we have not built heavy ICBMs as a matter of choice. True. In fact, air force planners wanted a balanced force-structure, with a modern medium-sized MX missile and a modern and versatile B-1 bomber. The administration then proceeded to cancel the B-1 bomber without even trying to trade it for Soviet concessions, and it has delayed procurement of the MX till this day. In other words, the Soviet planners chose to invest in heavy ICBMs; ours chose to invest in the B-1 and the MX. *They* have their SS-18 heavy ICBMs fully operational, while *we* have only cancellations and endless reassessments.

The administration takes pride in having persuaded the Soviet Union to ban heavy *mobile* ICBMs and heavy SLBMs. In fact, a heavy missile as large as the 120-foot-long SS-18 can scarcely be made mobile at all anyway. As for heavy SLBMs, a definition of these is eagerly awaited, since the current Soviet SSN-18 SLBM is already very large indeed, and already has a throw-weight range greater than that of the future U.S. Trident C-4.

4. Since the Backfire bomber can reach targets in the continental U.S., why shouldn't it be included in SALT?

Administration: The Soviet Union is currently deploying Backfires in both their long-range air force and in naval aviation units. The Backfire bomber has been in production for several years, and current production averages two and a half aircraft a month. We continue to believe that the primary purpose of the Backfire is to perform peripheral attack and naval missions. Undoubtedly, this aircraft has some intercontinental capability in that it can surely reach the United States from home bases on a one-way, high-altitude, subsonic, unrefueled flight; with refueling and Arctic staging, it can probably, with certain high-altitude cruise flight profiles, execute a two-way mission to much of the United States.

The ability to strike the territory of the other side is not the criterion for determining whether an aircraft is a "heavy bomber" and, thus, subject to the limitations in the SALT II agreement. For example, the U.S. has 67 FB-111s which are part of our strategic bomber force and dedicated to attack on the Soviet Union. We also have over 500 aircraft deployed in the European and Pacific theaters which have the capability to strike Soviet territory. The Soviet Union at one time tried to get these latter aircraft included in SALT on the grounds that they could strike the Soviet Union. With the firm support of our allies, we adamantly resisted that position on the grounds that these aircraft, whatever their theoretical capability, are deployed for theater missions and, thus, not subject to SALT limitations. The Soviets have used this same argument with respect to the Backfire.

Nevertheless, the Soviets have agreed to furnish specific assurances concerning the Backfire. The U.S. regards the obligations undertaken by these assurances as integral to the treaty. These

assurances, which include a freeze on the current Backfire production rate, are consistent with the U.S. objective of constraining the
strategic potential of the Backfire force, while continuing to exclude
our own European and Pacific-based theater aircraft from SALT.
Those assurances also help to restrict the Backfire to a theater role.
In particular, limiting the numbers available means that Soviet diversion of Backfire from its theater and naval missions to a strategic
role would substantially reduce Soviet strength in these areas while
adding only marginally to overall Soviet strategic capability.

Luttwak: The Backfire bomber looks like a strategic bomber, flies
like a strategic bomber, and could definitely strike at targets in the
United States as a strategic bomber. Only in the text of the treaty
is the Backfire not a "strategic" bomber.

The administration asserts that it agreed not to include Backfires
in the overall SALT II weapon ceilings in exchange for Soviet agreement to a similar exclusion of the FB-111s on our side. The Russians
are producing some 30 Backfires a year with some 150 already built;
we have long since stopped building FB-111s and have a total of
only 67; the Backfire is also about three times as large as the FB-111
and has more than twice the range, with a larger payload.

More important still is the underlying inequality in air defenses.
To get through the 2,500 Soviet interceptor fighters and 12,000 Soviet anti-aircraft missiles, American bombers need special weapons,
large ECM payloads, lots of range (for evasion), and a great deal
of fortitude. To attack targets in the United States, Soviet bombers
need only to get here, since we have no deployed surface-to-air missiles at all and only 309 active interceptor fighters, a derisory force
by any estimate. As a result, while Backfire bombers would not perhaps be sufficiently capable for our own purposes against the Soviet
Union, they are definitely more than adequate for Soviet attacks
against us.

The administration stresses the fact that the Soviet Union has
given us verbal assurances that the Backfires would not be used in
a strategic role. This introduces a novel standard in arms control:
can anyone imagine a scenario in which the Russians would *want*
to bomb the U.S. targets with Backfires but would then refrain from
doing so because they had given such "assurances" in SALT? Verification is supposed to regulate concrete capabilities, not vapid
"assurances."

There is merit in the administration's claim that Backfires would be more effective in the theater role (against Europeans, Chinese, and U.S. forces overseas) than in executing attacks over intercontinental ranges. That is true of any aircraft, or indeed of any vehicle: the shorter the range of the mission, the easier to get there, and the greater the payload that can be carried.

The real issue is the very unsound precedent that would be created in our arms-control dealings with the Russians. They *know* that we know that the Backfires should in fact be counted under the overall SALT weapon ceiling; now they also know that we can be maneuvered into distortions of the criteria of definition, in their favor. This will confirm the Soviets in their judgment that in dealings with the U.S. a tough diplomatic stance sooner or later results in American concessions, no matter what the merits of the case might be.

5. Won't our Minuteman missiles be vulnerable to a Soviet first-strike under SALT II? What good is SALT if it couldn't solve this problem?

Administration: SALT did not produce the Minuteman vulnerability problem. With or without SALT, our Minuteman missiles will become increasingly vulnerable to attack by Soviet ICBMs. This situation is the result of Soviet advances in missile accuracy, coupled with the deployment of large numbers of MIRVed ICBMs. The issue of Minuteman vulnerability must be viewed in perspective. As Secretary of Defense Harold Brown has stated, the vulnerability of the Minuteman—a serious problem requiring corrective action by the U.S.—"would not be synonymous with the vulnerability of the United States or even of the strategic deterrent." Any Soviet planner must realize that even a successful attack on the Minuteman would still leave the Soviet Union vulnerable to massive response by our submarines and heavy bombers. The damage these remaining forces could do, to military, political, and industrial targets in the Soviet Union, would be devastating.

The inability of SALT to solve the Minuteman vulnerability problem, largely a consequence of substantial MIRV deployments on both sides and the infeasibility of formulating verifiable limits constraining missile accuracy, testifies to the fact that some strategic problems are not amenable to solution in SALT but must be solved by unilateral U.S. action under a vigorous strategic-forces modernization program.

SALT does make it more feasible, however, to consider mobile

ICBM systems as an alternative basing mode for ICBMs. Without the SALT II limits on MIRVed ICBMs and the number of warheads per missile, a multiple protective structure (MPS) mobile ICBM system would face much more serious feasibility problems from the standpoint of both cost and land availability. Similarly, the viability of the air-mobile ICBM basing mode is also improved through the limitations in the SALT II agreement.

Because we do maintain a balanced strategic-nuclear force of land-based ICBMs, submarine-launched missiles, and heavy bombers, we are in a position to take the time to evaluate judiciously and deliberately implement alternative, more survivable, ICBM basing modes to replace the increasingly vulnerable fixed ICBM.

Luttwak: The purpose of arms control is, or should be, to control arms. Since the United States has a comparative advantage in developing high-technology weapons, the only justification for accepting parity in strategic-nuclear forces would be to achieve genuine and substantial arms control. Thus, if the Soviet Union and the United States had reached an agreement which actually limited strategic arms, and if equality had truly been achieved, there would be equal ICBM throw-weights and the Minuteman vulnerability problem would have receded. The Soviets could not threaten our Minuteman force if they had only the same missile throw-weight that we have. What creates a problem now is the fact that the Soviet ICBM force is several times as large in throw-weight as the American, and this potential is increasingly exploited in the deployment of large numbers of accurate and very powerful warheads.

Under SALT II we get the worst of both worlds: there is no real control on the most important threat, and we must therefore undertake the great effort of protecting our ICBM force. On the other hand, a number of Soviet-desired restrictions have been imposed on our technological abilities, thus making remedial measures much more expensive and difficult than would otherwise have been the case. Without the SALT II restrictions, it would be much easier to cope with the Minuteman vulnerability problem.

As it is, we have to tread the thin (and very expensive) line between the demands of verification (which means that the missiles must be seen, in order to be counted) and the necessity of protection (which means that the missiles must be concealed).

An active defense of the missile silos would offer by far the most effective (and cost-effective) solution to the vulnerability problem.

This is now ruled out by the 1972 ABM treaty. But we signed that treaty in the *declared* presumption that the next SALT agreement would seriously limit Soviet ICBM throw-weights. If SALT II is ratified, we will not have controlled Soviet throw-weights, and we will still be prevented from defending the Minuteman silos by means of ABM weapons. This is doubly unfortunate, since nowadays ABM techniques are available to protect ICBM silos at a cost much lower than the mobility-and-concealment schemes being considered by the administration. For example, the "trench-and-sunroof" scheme, in which MX missile transporters would be placed in concrete trenches with sliding roofs, would cost some $30 billion; a silo-defense ABM would by contrast be available for one-third that amount.

6. How do our NATO allies feel about SALT? Aren't they concerned about the lack of limits on such Soviet systems as the SS-20 IRBM? Aren't they concerned about continued U.S. cooperation on theater systems?

Administration: Allied support of SALT was evidenced recently by the strong statements made by allied leaders at the Guadeloupe summit meeting. German Chancellor Schmidt has urged early ratification on several occasions, while former British Prime Minister Callaghan declared that it would be tragic if the SALT II treaty were not ratified. French President Giscard d'Estaing also noted the need to move quickly to a conclusion of SALT II. This allied support at the highest levels reflects the continuing and close consultation which the U.S. has had with the allies throughout the conduct of the SALT II negotiations in order to insure that SALT II will fully protect allied as well as U.S. security interests.

While the SS-20 and the Backfire bomber are part of the Soviet arsenal which unquestionably does threaten Europe, NATO is confident that the alliance spectrum of conventional, theater-nuclear, and strategic forces remains an effective deterrent to aggression. Nevertheless, Soviet deployment of the SS-20 and the Backfire is a cause for concern. As a result, NATO is currently conducting an in-depth review of the issue of long-range theater-nuclear force modernization in order to ensure that we can adequately respond to Soviet threats of both a military and political nature. This includes the possibility of new deployments of long-range theater-nuclear systems, as well as arms-control initiatives in this area, possibly within the context of SALT III.

We have assured our allies both privately and publicly that we will not permit the Soviets to use SALT as a vehicle for undermining continued close cooperation in the theater-nuclear area. The agreement will not affect existing patterns of collaboration and cooperation with our allies, nor will it preclude cooperation in modernization. We explicitly rejected a Soviet effort to prohibit the transfer of technology or systems in this area and have made clear to our allies that the non-circumvention provision in the agreement does not entail any additional obligations beyond those assumed in the agreement.

Luttwak: At a time when the Western world was being seriously threatened by multiple crises, including the troubles in Iran and Turkey, German Chancellor Schmidt, British Prime Minister Callaghan, and French President Giscard d'Estaing discovered that President Carter had called them to the Guadeloupe summit mainly to extract from them pro-SALT statements for the benefit of the TV cameras, and of Congress.

By now, only the naive remain deceived: it is plain that the European leaders must do business with the President of the United States, no matter who he is. They have urgent matters of their own to transact with the U.S., and they have powerful left-wing factions at home which are pressing for disarmament; both Schmidt and Callaghan must live with strong pro-disarmament factions within their own parties. As a result, if the President of the United States insists on parading their approval of SALT for the TV cameras, they will perform. But it is no secret that Chancellor Schmidt was dismayed by the fatal incoherence of the President's sense of priorities. As for President Giscard of France, he made his real opinion very clear indeed upon his return to Paris, when he flatly ruled out any French participation in SALT III.

A summit meeting can easily be manipulated, but the underlying strategic realities are not to be concealed: the Soviet build-up in "continental" weapons (notably the SS-20 missiles) presents a direct threat to NATO; the strategy of inaction followed by the Carter administration in the face of Soviet imperialism threatens the vital supplies of oil and scarce metals of the entire Western world; and the willful refusal to maintain the strength of U.S. strategic-nuclear forces undermines the credibility of the American guarantees on which the entire structure of the alliance is based. As far as Schmidt, Callaghan, and Giscard are concerned, those are the subjects which should have been raised at the Guadeloupe summit.

7. **Why did we accept the cruise-missile limits in the Protocol? Don't these limits affect only U.S. systems? Won't they set a precedent for follow-up negotiations?**

Administration: In the course of the SALT II negotiations, it became clear that, in order to get an agreement that contained limits on certain Soviet strategic programs of interest to us, we would have to accept some limitations on cruise missiles. For air-launched cruise missiles (ALCMs), we had a clear idea about what type of limits would be acceptable for the period through 1985 and were able to reach agreement with the Soviets on ALCM limits in the 1985 portion of the treaty, which do not, in any way, constrain the ALCM options of interest to us. However, for ground-launched cruise missiles (GLCMs) and sea-launched cruise missiles (SLCMs) (that is, surface ship or submarine-launched), we were not prepared to accept long-term limitations.

Early in SALT II, the Soviets proposed that the treaty contain a ban on the testing and deployment of SLCMs with ranges over 600 km and later adopted the same position for GLCMs. We took the position that consideration of restrictive long-term limits on these systems should be postponed to future negotiations. However, the Soviets insisted that SALT II contain some limits on SLCMs and GLCMs. When it became clear in the post-Vladivostok negotiations that an agreement could not be concluded without some SLCM and GLCM limits, the U.S. attempted to obtain Soviet agreement to a variety of packages limiting SLCMs and GLCMs. Eventually we agreed to accept some SLCM and GLCM limits in a short-term Protocol, not in the treaty itself. By this approach, we accommodated Soviet insistence that the agreement address SLCMs and GLCMs, while making certain that these limitations would have no impact on U.S. programs. The Protocol limits ban the deployment of SLCMs and GLCMs with ranges over 600 km but place no limit on development and testing, which can and are going forward.

Therefore, under the terms of the Protocol, the U.S. can continue its cruise-missile development program on schedule. We can test SLCMs and GLCMs to any range, while we have given up only the right to deploy such cruise missiles during the period of the Protocol—which we had no plans to do anyway. In the meantime, we can continue to analyze with our allies the potential role of SLCMs and GLCMs in long-range theater-nuclear force modernization and arms control. We consider this an acceptable outcome on this difficult issue.

Concerns about the precedential nature of the Protocol limits on SLCMs and GLCMs are totally unwarranted. The President would not accept any limits on SLCMs and GLCMs in future negotiations which were not in the interests of the U.S. and its allies. This means that any limitations on systems designed for theater missions would have to be accompanied by appropriate limitations on Soviet systems. Similarly, the United States Senate would have the opportunity to review and make their own judgments as to whether any future SLCM/GLCM limits that might be negotiated are in our national interest.

The history of SALT supports the conclusion that limits accepted in one agreement are not necessarily extended to another agreement unless they are judged to be in our national interest. For example, the original ABM treaty limited ABM deployments to two sites. This was later changed to one site. That agreement also contained a very restrictive limitation on the transfer of ABM systems and components; the SALT II agreement contains no such limits for offensive systems. The SALT I Interim Agreement provided for unequal aggregates of ICBM and SLBM launchers and unequal limits on ballistic-missile submarines, and some predicted at the time that these unequal limits would become a permanent feature of SALT. However, SALT II provides for equal aggregates between the United States and the Soviet Union and drops entirely the idea of numerical limits on submarines.

On the other hand, the two sides agreed to extend the SALT I freezes on building new ICBM silos and converting light ICBM launchers to heavy ICBM launchers. In the first case, we wanted the extension and, in the second case, the Soviets wanted it—which we accepted in return for Soviet concessions in other areas.

Moreover, both sides have made it clear in the negotiating record that the Protocol limits expire with the Protocol.

Luttwak: The Soviet system of government has a comparative advantage in allocating national resources to build up military power; the United States, being a creative, open society, has a *potential* advantage in science and technology for military innovation. The cruise missile (CM) is the current expression of this potential. Of low value on a unit basis, cruise missiles are of potentially very great value on a *force* basis. (A single cruise missile is worth much less than a single ballistic missile, but a billion dollars' worth of cruise missiles can provide a more powerful, and certainly more survivable, force than a billion dollars' worth of ballistic missiles.) The main advantage of the cruise missile is its small unit size and its potential for high accuracy. The first quality allows highly versatile deployments: CMs can be launched from many kinds of aircraft, from ships, submarines, or even from the back of ordinary trucks forward-deployed in Europe or the Far East. It was therefore a high Soviet priority in SALT to impose restrictions on the cruise-missile potential of the United States. The SALT II Protocol would now ban cruise-missile deployments of strategic value (by prohibiting sea-launched and land-based CMs with ranges in excess of 600 kilometers) except for air-launched CMs mounted on heavy bombers. As a result, only a fraction of the potential of CM technology will be realized if the SALT II agreement is ratified.

The goals of arms control are supposed to be, *first*, to ensure strategic stability; *second*, to limit destruction in war; and *third*, to limit military expenditures. The central fact that SALT obscures is that CM technology offers *in itself* the means to achieve these goals:

First, since they are so small and so versatile in deployment, CM forces are inherently very stable indeed: not even the most optimistic counter-force planner could hope to target a diversified CM force distributed among ships, submarines, aircraft of various kinds, and small ground vehicles.

Second, CMs are highly accurate and therefore need only small (and less destructive) warheads; a force of 100 current CMs would cause less fallout than a single Soviet SS-18 ICBM.

Third, since CMs are inherently cheap, a shift to CM forces would reduce expenditures as compared to an equivalent force of ICBMs, bombers, or SLBMs.

Genuine arms control could thus have best been achieved by leaving CMs entirely unlimited, to provide an incentive for a shift into these stabilizing, less destructive, and cheaper weapons. But arms control and SALT II parted company long ago, and the outcome is not surprising.

The administration claims that the SALT II Protocol limits only the *deployment* of CMs and only until the end of 1981; it also claims that ground-launched and sea-launched CMs could not have been deployed within that time anyway. That result was of course contrived by manipulating the scheduling of the CM program: we *could* have had CMS by 1980, given the will to acquire them. The administration states above:

In the course of the SALT II negotiations, it became clear that, in order to get an agreement that contained limits on certain Soviet strategic programs of interest to us, we would have to accept some limitations on cruise missiles.

One would like to know exactly what were those "limits on certain Soviet strategic programs" that the Russians accepted in exchange for the heavy restrictions on our CM technology. With no strategic sea-launched CMs in prospect, no submarine CMs, no ground-launched CMs, and air-launched CMs allowed only on "heavy bombers," it appears that in the end the only benefit which we will obtain from the entire CM technology will be to enhance the penetrability of roughly 120 of our old B-52s. That is certainly not what we expected when the B-1 was canceled. At that time, the White House spoke of the cruise missile as the great new weapon which had made the B-1 unnecessary, and there was talk of thousands of cruise missiles, deployed in all convenient modes.

8. It is claimed that SALT II will be adequately verifiable, but how will the U.S. make sure that the Soviets aren't cheating? Doesn't the loss of intelligence collection sites in Iran undermine our ability to verify the SALT II agreement?

Administration: The U.S. relies for verification on "national technical means" (NTM), which is a general term covering a variety of technical collection methods for monitoring Soviet military activities. As the President has publicly confirmed, these national technical means include photographic satellites. There are other collection methods as well. For example, we are able to monitor Soviet telemetry—that is, the technical data transmitted by radio signals from the Soviet missiles during tests—from outside Soviet territory. A further example of national technical means are the ships and aircraft which we also use to monitor Soviet missile tests. The sides have also acknowledged that large radars, such as the COBRA DANE radar at Shenya Island in the Aleutians, can be used as a form of national technical means.

This is not a complete list of the technical devices that constitute our NTM. Still less is it a complete list of U.S. intelligence resources. Many of our intelligence resources are very sensitive. Public acknowledgment of their existence, much less of their technical capabilities and details of how they work or what information they produce, would make it far easier for the Soviets to negate them. Therefore, what we can say publicly about the details of our intelligence facilities is very limited. Members of the Senate who will have to vote on the treaty will, of course, have full access to all the details.

However, there is no secret that our NTM enable us to learn a great deal about Soviet military systems, including the strategic-nuclear forces that are limited in SALT. We are able to monitor many aspects of the development, testing, production, deployment, training, and operation of Soviet strategic forces, despite the closed nature of Soviet society and Soviet concern with secrecy. A good measure of the capabilities of our systems of intelligence collection is the detailed information we publish on Soviet forces. For example, the Secretary of Defense's *Report for Fiscal Year 1980* lists the numbers of Soviet bombers and missiles, and gives estimates of the numbers of weapons carried on Soviet forces. We know that the Soviets have a "fifth generation" of ICBMs under development, and we know a good deal about their characteristics—this, before a single missile has been flight-tested. That this is by no means the full extent of our knowledge of Soviet systems is clear from the mass of un-official—but often all-too-accurate—leaks of detailed information on Soviet programs.

From these sources, then, we are able to assemble a detailed picture of Soviet forces, both overall and in terms of the characteristics of particular systems. No one source is essential; instead we rely on information from a variety of sources—for example, what we learn from photography can be checked against information from radar or telemetry monitoring. This means that loss of a particular source, though it can be important and can require replacement, does not "blind" our ability to monitor what the Soviets are doing. Moreover, the use of multiple sources complicates any effort to disguise or conceal a violation. The Soviets know we have a big intelligence operation and know a certain amount about how it works, from our official statements, from leaks, from spies, and from their own NTM. But we know they do not know the full capabilities of our systems—or, equally important, how we use the information we collect. The result is that efforts to conceal would have to be planned to cope with a number of U.S. collection systems, some of them entirely unknown. (The need to maintain this uncertainty is a major justification for continued secrecy about our intelligence systems and methods.)

As for the loss of the intelligence-collection sites in Iran, we are proceeding in an orderly fashion to reestablish that capability. As Secretary of Defense Harold Brown pointed out in his April 5 speech in New York, the issue is not whether the capability will be reestab-lished but rather how, where, and how quickly. There are a number of alternatives available to us for recovering the capability. Some can be implemented more quickly than others. Some involve consultations with other countries, some do not.

Intelligence of the kind obtained from the Iranian sites provides information on Soviet strategic systems, including some of the aspects of the strategic systems which are limited by SALT. For this reason, we will be moving with all deliberate speed to reestablish the capability. However, as noted above, we have a large number of other technical intelligence-collection sources which collect intelligence on Soviet strategic systems. As a consequence, it is not imperative that the Iranian capability be immediately established to ensure that the emerging SALT agreement is adequately verifiable, i.e., that any Soviet cheating that could pose a military risk be detected in time for the U.S. to respond and offset the threat. As long as the capability is reestablished on a timely basis—as we plan to do—there will be no impact on SALT verification. We estimate that regaining enough capability to monitor adequately these tests for SALT purposes will take about a year.

The principal information at issue is the nature and characteristics of new or modified Soviet ICBMs. Each such Soviet program will require about 20 flight tests over a period of years. We would be able to monitor testing and detect violations well before the testing programs were complete. On this basis, we are confident that we will be able to verify adequately a SALT agreement from the moment it is signed.

Luttwak: The fundamentals of verification are not in fact a matter of satellite technology, telemetry, and so on. The crucial facts of the matter are political. We have a virtually transparent society; the Russians are entirely secretive. We publish masses of hard data on our military forces; they publish only vague boasts. As a result, when we obtain a satellite photograph of a missile-like object on a Soviet test-range, all we know is just that. When the Russians get a similar photograph, they can immediately find out from published evidence whether it is an experiment or a prototype, if there is a production program and how large, what is its range and payload, what is the intended mission, and more.

This long-standing intelligence imbalance has become much worse of late. We have lost critical observation facilities in Iran, and some of our most important satellite systems have been fatally compromised. (The Russians now know exactly how the devices work; they therefore know how to fool them.) Beyond that, we have virtually eliminated the CIA's ability to collect intelligence overseas by covert means.

We can still identify and count large, fixed objects of classic form such as uncamouflaged ICBM silos. Beyond that, everything is a matter of relative uncertaintly and claims to the contrary are either dishonest or ill-informed. Stansfield Turner, the director of Central Intelligence, did his honorable duty when he testified before Congress that the SALT II agreements could not be verified reliably at the present time, and that it would take five years to acquire the necessary capabilities. Others, much closer to the politics of the White House, more remote from the realities of the trade, and free of the special responsibilities of the director of Central Intelligence before the nation, have claimed that we could verify SALT II within one year. It is evident that Turner deserves our respect for his civic courage in telling the truth in the face of extreme political pressures.

9. If this SALT agreement is so much in the national-security interests of the United States, why does the Soviet Union want it?

Administration: Before examining possible reasons for the Soviets' concluding that this agreement is in their national interest, it is important to note that there is nothing inconsistent in the agreement's being in the interests of both the United States and the Soviet Union. As in any agreement voluntarily signed by two independent parties, whether it be a business deal, a labor contract, or an international treaty, the incentive for signing and adhering to an agreement is that both parties find it beneficial, even though it is less than their maximum desires.

There are several possible reasons for the Soviet interest in this agreement. First of all, it should not be surprising that they, like us, believe that an unconstrained strategic-arms competition could increase the risk of nuclear war, while at the same time not enhance the security of either nation. This is not to imply that they view the U.S. as any less of a competitor—or that they would expect to lose such a race—but only that they realize that it is safer, and more in their interest from the viewpoint of national survival, if that competition is limited in the area of strategic weapons.

A second possible reason concerns the allocation of resources within the Soviet economy. While there is no question that they will spend on military systems whatever they think they need to, or could get an advantage from, it is well known that their economy is not in good shape. They have chronic problems with their agricultural production, technology lag, a shortage of skilled labor, a very cumbersome system of production and distribution, and the possibility of an energy shortage sometime in the next decade. With these problems, Soviet defense spending becomes a very great burden. The Soviet Union spends about 12 percent of its gross national product on defense, while we spend only about 5 percent.

Another reason for Soviet interest in SALT II may be that they see the equality in the SALT limits as confirming equal superpower status with the United States. The Soviets might well find it ironic that there are those in the U.S. who tend to regard them as ten feet tall, since that is their general attitude toward us—particularly where technology is concerned. Even though the Soviets have had a larger overall number of strategic delivery vehicles than the U.S. for several years, they have lagged behind the U.S. in the most modern of strategic systems, MIRVed missiles, and could feel that they were viewed as second best.

Finally it is clear that the current Soviet leadership has invested considerable personal prestige in the SALT negotiations. Thus, they probably want SALT to succeed so that their view of détente and the utility of cooperation with the West in some areas can be vindicated over the views of others in the Kremlin who may not be so enthusiastic about the SALT process.

Luttwak: Unlike the United States, the Soviet Union has a strategy. As a result, for Soviet planners arms control is a tool of policy instead of being a policy goal in itself. It is self-evident that the goal of Soviet strategy over the long term is to maximize the relative power of the Soviet Union.

In the past, the Soviet superiority in ground forces was diminished even within the sphere of land combat by the Western advantage in tactical air power; beyond that, any Soviet advantages in land strength (ground and air) were contained by the Western advantage in naval power. In the still broader frame of overall military strength, any Soviet advantage in conventional military forces would have been offset by the net advantage of the United States in strategic-military capability.

In the past, therefore, the Soviet Union was unable to use military force or the threat of force to impose its will upon other nations beyond the boundaries of the empire it had already conquered by 1945. Offsetting Western advantages checkmated every major Soviet military option.

Over the last two decades, the Soviet Union has worked with extreme tenacity to remove one by one the Western military counterweights to its strength. In tactical air power, a broad development effort has by now produced a Soviet tactical air force much larger than the American, and it has greatly narrowed the gap in quality. At sea, the Soviet Union now has a large oceanic navy that has definitely ended the period of U.S. naval supremacy.

The Soviet effort in building tactical air and naval forces has been impressive, but there is no doubt that the finest achievement of Soviet strategy has been the skillful combination of arms-control negotiations with a most energetic build-up program in the realm of long-range nuclear weapons. This combined policy now promises to eliminate the last of the counterweights—American nuclear deterrence of Soviet military pressures against NATO and other U.S. allies. By using SALT as a tool of policy (while the United States allowed the SALT process to usurp the proper place of strategy), the Russians have managed to stimulate American unilateralism (e.g., the B-1 cancellation, MX and cruise-missile delays) even while they themselves were building ICBMs, SLBMs, and bombers by the hundreds. Even better, they have been able to use SALT as a way of overcoming the most difficult of all the obstacles in their path, American technological creativity.

At first, the Russians were unhappy with discussions of *qualitative* limits in SALT, so long as negotiations focused on heavy ICMBs and such; but they soon realized that the Americans in their unstrategical innocence were willing to give up their only real card in the power competition across the board: technological innovation. This of course was the key to the implementation of Soviet strategy, since in the natural course of things they could never have hoped to defeat the creativity of American society.

It is not surprising, therefore, that the Russians should greatly desire SALT II. As far as they are concerned, the treaty is a most important achievement, a critical element in a broader strategy designed to eliminate the one residual American military advantage, so that Soviet strength can at long last be brought to bear with full effect on the world situation. If SALT II fails to be ratified, if a great national debate ensues on the purposes and content of U.S. strategy, the Soviet Union would have a great deal to lose. A key ingredient in Soviet success to date has been the American enthusiasm for arms control for its own sake. This would not survive a clear-sighted reappraisal.

The administration's spokesmen like to explain Soviet enthusiasm for SALT as due to a putative desire to reallocate resources within the Soviet economy. It is true of course that the Soviet Union allocates 12 percent of its gross national product to military outlays (as compared to 5 percent for the U.S.). Nevertheless, the administration's theory reveals a touching innocence, or perhaps a fatal credulity: the Russians have *never* allowed civilian priorities to get in the way of their strategic goals. And if they did want to reallocate resources, why not simply slow down by a little the frenetic pace of their buildup? After all, even if they were to stop the SS-17 and SS-19 ICBM programs, they would still have two other healthy ICBM programs as against our single MX project (still in its research-and-development phase). Why pursue multiple SLBM efforts with such drastic urgency? The fact is that the Soviet Union is building in accordance with a strategy, and SALT II will in no serious way reduce Soviet efforts. If the precedent of SALT I is any guide, Soviet strategic expenditures will not go down by a single kopek.

10. Did the Soviets violate the SALT I agreements?

Administration: No. We have closely monitored Soviet strategic forces limited by SALT I for over six years. During this period on several occasions we have observed ambiguous situations or Soviet activities which were of concern to us. In each instance, we have promptly raised our concerns in the Standing Consultative Commission, a special body created in SALT I to deal with questions of implementation of the agreements, including questions which might arise concerning compliance and related situations which may be considered ambiguous. In each instance, the questionable activity ceased or additional information has clarified the situation and allayed our concern. In no instance did we find any grounds for charging the Soviets with a violation of the SALT I agreements.

The Soviets, for their part, have raised questions about U.S. activities which they considered of concern. These questions have also been satisfactorily resolved.

The record of exchanges by the parties on these issues has been provided to the Congress by Secretary of State Vance in February 1978. This report is available to the public (Department of State Publication 8930).

The record of the SALT I agreements demonstrates both the ability and willingness of the U.S. to object to questionable practices and the commitment of both sides to ensuring the viability of the SALT agreements by using effective procedures for resolving compliance questions when they arise.

Luttwak: The administration's answer is a flat no. That is a true, but grossly incomplete, answer. It *is* true that the Soviet Union did not violate the strict letter of the SALT I agreed texts. But the Soviet Union made nonsense of the whole meaning and purpose of the SALT I agreements by exploiting every significant loophole and by violating the entire spirit of the accords.

Actually, in a way, it is the United States that has violated its own undertakings: the loopholes in the agreement were obvious enough, and were clearly pointed out at the time in the open literature.[1] We were told, however, that there was nothing to worry about, since a series of "unilateral statements" issued by the United States had fully covered all the loopholes. We were told that the U.S. would terminate the agreements if these restraints were ignored by the Soviet Union.

In reality, since 1972 the Soviet Union has ignored the unilateral statements while the United States has failed to enforce them by appropriate remedies. For example, the whole rationale for the American acceptance of the unequal limits on ICBMs in the 1972 SALT accords (1,608 for the USSR versus 1,054 for the U.S.) was that the Soviet Union would limit the overall throw-weight of its ICBMs by not building any more "heavy" ICBM (SS-9/SS-18) silos—otherwise, we were told, the U.S. Minuteman ICBMs would be endangered. To obtain the 308-unit limit on "heavy" ICBM silos in SALT I, the United States agreed to the higher overall ceiling for Soviet ICBMs of all types. Obviously the presumption was that those ICBM silos which were *not* for "heavy" missiles would be used for "light" ICBMs. As we now know, the Soviet Union was even then building SS-19 ICBMs, which are not "light" by any imaginable definition: their throw-weight is more than *three times* as great as that of the "light" SS-11s or Minuteman IIIs. Each SS-19 carries up to six large warheads of half-a-megaton yield (as against three 0.17 megaton warheads for the Minuteman III); two SS-19s are therefore more of a threat to U.S. ICBM silos than one SS-18 would have been. In 1972 it was commonly understood that the So-

---

[1] See *Edward N. Luttwak*, The Strategic Balance, *CSIS Washington Paper No. 3, 1972.*

viet Union would not be allowed to replace "light" ICBMs with heavy ones. By replacing SS-11s (no threat to Minuteman) with SS-19s, the Soviet Union has in effect done just that.

More generally, the Soviet Union has violated the whole purpose of the SALT I accords. An arms-control agreement is supposed to control arms, but since 1972 we have witnessed the deployment of no fewer than four new Soviet ICBM types (SS-16, SS-17, SS-18, SS-19), three types of SLBM submarines, two new SLBMs (SS-N-17 and SS-N-18), and the Backfire bomber. All but one of these weapons (the SS-16) have been produced in generous quantities. Had the Soviet Union shared a genuine interest in arms control, it would surely have taken care to exercise at least a modicum of restraint. Why not have, say, only *two* ICBM types to match each American project instead of four? Why all the urgency and costly multiplicity of types?

There is no reason to believe that SALT II will serve the interests of the United States, *or* the disinterested purposes of arms control, any better than the SALT I accords did.

2

IS THERE AN ARMS RACE?

*A*lthough both the superpowers have been deploying new weapons and modifications of older weapons, there is no "arms race," and the "action-reaction" phenomenon that dominates popular perceptions and—less excusably—much comment that passes for expert is nowhere in evidence. The United States embarked on a large buildup during the 1957–63 period, whose results became manifest in the 1961–67 period. Since then, only one truly new weapons system has been put into production, the Trident ballistic missile on board the Ohio-class submarine. Otherwise, we remain with the B-52 bombers of 1950s vintage, and with ICBMs that reflect the deployment decisions of the early or mid-1960s. The United States certainly has not been "racing": note the evident reluctance with which the cruise-missile technology is being exploited for the construction of actual weapon systems.

On the Soviet side, efforts were limited and deployments slow until 1960 or so. They then gradually accelerated, and they have continued to accelerate ever since. No fewer than seven different Soviet

ICBM types have been introduced in service since 1965, the SS-9, SS-11, and SS-13 between 1965 and 1970, and the SS-19, SS-18, SS-17, and SS-16 during the post–1972 period. Since 1967 we have seen three basic submarine-launched ballistic missiles entering service on board as many new Soviet submarine types (Y-class, D-I, and D-II), and in addition the Backfire long-range bomber is also being deployed. One side is certainly running, but that does not make it a race. There is, by the way, no evidence that the Soviet buildup was triggered by the Cuban Missile Crisis; the time-phasing is actually inconsistent with that theory, now endlessly repeated without scrutiny of the evidence.

In examining the factors that drive the deployment decisions of the United States and the Soviet Union, we can see that on the American side there was until the Cuban Missile Crisis a manifest intention at the political level to overcome any possible "missile gap" and to establish an ascendancy in strategic nuclear power; this was communicated downwards to the military services, which naturally responded with enthusiasm. But immediately after the Cuban Missile Crisis there was a loss of faith in the value of strategic nuclear strength at the highest political level. Thereafter, it was only with the most evident reluctance that approval was given for any innovation or addition to the strategic arsenal. Since then, every new weapon system has been examined and reexamined *ad nauseam* inside the executive branch, only to become the target of concerted opposition on the outside. Service advocacy is now virtually the only engine for innovation, and this of course has resulted in systematic bureaucratic distortion.

In the absence of strategy formulated at the national level, programs have been shaped by scientific ambitions, engineering perfectionism, and the narrow "mission" goals of military men; the result has been that the only weapons system now actually being produced, the Trident/Ohio combination, bears all the marks of these unstrategical urges. More commonly, the outcome has been the unguided growth of weapon programs, followed by their cancellation, the latest victim being the B-1 bomber.

The fate of the B-1 is one more indication that far from there being an "action-reaction" phenomenon at work, there is merely a willful inadvertence: the B-1 was canceled at a time when the overall deficiency in projected strategic nuclear capability was becoming steadily more evident, and when Soviet air defenses were becoming more effective against the B-52s. In addition to those politico-strategic and reactive motives, there was also a powerful competitive motive in the deployment of the new Soviet Backfire bomber. Even so, dubious and unstrategical bookkeeping considerations sufficed to sink the project.

As for Soviet deployment decisions, there has been a tendency of late to explain them as bureaucratic phenomena, with the implied suggestion that this somehow makes the Soviet build-up less threatening. To the present writer it seems, on the contrary, that Soviet defense decisions reflect a purposeful strategic goal: the *neutralization* of American strategic nuclear capabilities.

American nuclear guarantees continue to offset the local military advantages of the Soviet Union vis-à-vis Western Europe and Japan, and Soviet diplomacy would have much to gain if the credibility of these guarantees could be destroyed. The imposed reduction of American strategic nuclear forces to a strike-back-only/self-defense-only capability is the natural counterpart to the establishment of a Soviet military ascendancy at the theater level. It appears that the Soviet Union has made much progress towards both these goals.

On a more detailed level, geographic and military considerations make an "artillery" model valid for the Soviet Union. Accordingly, its forces contain both Eurasian-range and fully intercontinental weapons, in three classes: heavy, medium, and light. The characteristic function of heavy artillery is of course counterbattery fire, and indeed the new heavy ICBMs of the SS-18 type are well suited to threaten the Minuteman silos. That is not to say that the actual execution of a "counterforce" strike is the desired end-result of Soviet development strategy; the latter is purposeful and not romantic-adventuristic, and its goal is not a nuclear Pearl Harbor but rather the political neutralization of our strategic nuclear forces. This is to be achieved by persuading both the American people and those who seek security from the United States that the latter can no longer offset local Soviet military advantages by strategic nuclear guarantees.

The Soviet Union has been moving rapidly toward this goal, which it will attain by the mid-1980s, unless the United States reacts very energetically indeed, and begins to do so very quickly. Only those who continue to argue that strategic nuclear power is of no consequence in the affairs of the world can disagree with the contention that a crash effort has now become necessary.

STRATEGIC STABILITY

Because strategy is not physics, there can be no single definition of "strategic stability." For the United States, "strategic stability" is a good in itself; it is a most important component of overall military stability, which in turn serves to promote the status quo in international politics.

For the Soviet Union, which still seeks to extend its influence, the status quo is not a desirable state of affairs, and "strategic stability" is thus a frustrating obstacle.

American policy has long been guided by a one-sided search for "strategic stability" on the presumption that it is also a Soviet goal. If it were, it would be a goal inexplicably out of phase with (1) the general character of Soviet strategy and (2) the actual Soviet weapons deployments that have been observed over the last decade or so. The persistent claim that "strategic stability" is also the goal of Soviet policy reveals an obdurate provincialism, perhaps most explained by the cultural inability of much of the American policy elite to comprehend classical strategy: having long since abandoned *American* strategic decisions to civil and military bureaucrats, bookkeepers ("system analysts"), engineers, and natural scientists, the members of our policy elite cannot apparently recognize the lineaments of a purposeful strategy in Soviet conduct. In the 1960s, we had the confident assertions of the annual "posture" statements of Defense Secretary Robert McNamara predicting that the Soviet Union would not seek to build ICBM forces as large as those of the United States, since he himself had discovered and told the world that such force levels were "wasteful and useless." Nowadays, we have the confident assertion that Soviet programs are evolving of their own momentum, while Soviet policy really seeks only "parity."

It is doubtful whether one could nowadays construct a stable strategic equilibrium with two forces of similar capabilities owing to the MIRV "multiplier" of counterforce incentives. But in any case "strategic parity" is not a definable point on any scale of capabilities; in fact, it is not a strategic concept at all. For those who seek to conserve the status quo (and who also happen to be legalistic), "parity" has all sorts of desirable connotations. To American ears, "strategic parity" suggests an equitable arrangement whose 50/50 simplicity and evident fairness has an irresistible appeal. But for the Soviet Union, still intent on increasing its influence worldwide, "parity" may only define a transitory moment in time, during which the ascending curve of Soviet military capabilities intersects the declining curve of our own. Strategic stability is thus threatened by its chief exponents. Owing to the refusal of the United States to react in adequate degree, the steady increase in Soviet capabilities is on the verge of destabilizing the strategic balance. Accordingly, one should not focus on specific military threats; they are much less important than the overall trends, and the perceptions of these trends worldwide. It is no longer sufficient, and it may even be unnecessary, to "fix the Minuteman problem." What must be "fixed" is the American problem, i.e., the overall deficiency in strategic nuclear power that is projected for the mid-1980s.

The United States now has strategic forces that reflect the technological standards of the 1960s and the optimistic threat assessments of a decade ago. If technology is indeed the strong suit for the United States, it must be applied in actual weapons; it is no longer sufficient to reiterate generalized claims of technological superiority while concurrently refusing to deploy new weapons. A broad effort of innovation would now serve to render obsolete the results of the Soviet buildup rather than compete with it; only in this manner can the overall military balance be re-equilibrated across the board. For both political and operational reasons, attempts to correct the NATO balance itself cannot contend with the Soviet buildup: the linear array of a multinational coalition can hardly provide a credible defense against the surprise-attack/deep-penetration capabilities of the Soviet Union. The United States must therefore acquire once again the ability to neutralize the theater-level threat by nuclear guarantees. These, in turn, cannot become credible until American strategic nuclear power is fully rehabilitated by extensive moderation.

AN EQUITABLE AGREEMENT?

The equity of a SALT II agreement is not the issue; international politics is not governed by jurisprudential rules. Rather we may ask: Is a SALT II treaty advantageous? Not now. A SALT II treaty would serve only to freeze a strategic nuclear balance that cannot be satisfactory to the United States. Given the Soviet operational advantages in theater capabilities (both nuclear and conventional), and the Soviet ability to interdict important sea lanes of essential transit for the alliance, any "equitable" SALT II treaty could offer only a meaningless *partial* equilibrium in a wider context characterized by an adverse relation of forces. The watertight distinction between strategic nuclear and all other forms of military power common in our own discourse is merely the crystallized product of an obsolete bureaucratic distinction: in the real world of international politics, alternative forms of military power merge into one another and belong to the same spectrum, within which they interact. An "equitable" SALT II would be fully acceptable if there was also an "equitable" theater balance, but not otherwise.

OVERALL POLITICAL CONSEQUENCES OF NO AGREEMENT

If, on the other hand, no agreement is reached, or if the Senate rejects an agreement, the moderates in Soviet policy circles will accuse the "hardliners" of having spoiled a good thing by pushing too hard in the growth of armaments and in their foreign adventures (the Horn of Africa, etc.), as well as in domestic affairs. If an agreement is reached and if it is then ratified, the moderates will lose ground and the hardliners will have been confirmed in their belief that the West will in the end swallow all their domestic brutalities, all their foreign adventures, and also their massive military buildup, rather than pay the costs of competing with the Soviet Union in adequate degree. A SALT II treaty would be the final proof that a wealthier and more advanced West is unwilling to uphold the balance of power, being too far gone in decadence and self-delusion to make the required effort—which it can certainly well afford.

Approval of a SALT II treaty at this juncture would thus tend to reinforce the negative trends in Soviet governance and Soviet external policy that have emerged over the last decade.

U.S. DEFENSE PROGRAMS WITHOUT SALT

Since a SALT treaty could only serve to register and freeze a Soviet advantage in potential capabilities (throw-weight, weapon numbers, etc.), it could hardly remedy the current inadequacy of American strategic nuclear strength. By the same token, nonsignature, or nonratification, would not in itself intensify this inadequacy. In either case, the same scale of effort is now needed. There is clearly little to be gained by weapons programs that would simply emulate Soviet efforts. Large fixed-site ICBMs would be as vulnerable as the small, static ICBMs the United States has already; an intermediate-range bomber such as the Backfire (the FB-111 is being proposed) is ill-suited to American strategic needs; nor would it be prudent to increase American reliance on submarine-based weapons, especially since the sea-based ballistic missiles are concentrated in a very small number of hulls. Instead, the United States should exploit the potential of the cruise missile in programs that would make full use of the basing versatility of these weapons by building land-based *and* sea-based cruise-missile forces, as well as an air-launched force. To retain its advantages of accuracy, responsiveness, and rapid reaction, the ICBM force should be modernized, but only with *mobile* ICBMs; in practice this must mean deploying the MX ballistic missile—although a smaller weapon (in larger numbers) would offer obvious physical advantages in a mobile deployment. A long-range bomber force offers important qualities that missiles lack, since it can both be launched and be recalled, and is also altogether more versatile than other strategic nuclear weapons, having both naval and non-nuclear uses. Perhaps the easiest short-term option would be to revive the B-1 program in a more austere form (e.g. with electronic countermeasure provisions rather than actual fittings, etc.). Better still, the new possibilities opened by recent scientific advances—lasers for example—should be developed into actual weapon systems, with more limited interim efforts in the established weapon types.

In engineering, one may seek finite solutions but in a strategic relationship each effort naturally sets in train countering efforts which will sooner or later erode its results; it is therefore particularly important to resist the short-term attractions of a submarine-only solution, now once again being offered as the complete substitute for the diverse nuclear forces still being maintained. If the United States continues to allow its old bomber force to decay (it is now down to 330 operational aircraft) and should it abandon the ICBM component, the Soviet Union would then be free to devote all its research and production efforts to antisubmarine warfare. Sooner or later, even the peculiar difficulties of underwater detection would then be overcome. There is no substitute for a broad effort, and neither can the competition for strategic power simply be abandoned, for the first rule of strategy is that one may not leave the game without paying the fullest penalty.

3

A NEW ARMS RACE?

*T*oo late to avert the predicament of weakness now upon us, the great debate over the facts of the military balance is finally over. At the outset of the Carter presidency, we were still being told that there was room for cuts in the defense budget, and that America was and would remain "number one." And as late as last year, the chairman of the Joint Chiefs, General David Jones—a man finely attuned to the prevailing political currents—endorsed the claim of military primacy by saying that he would not exchange our forces for those of the Soviet Union. Now, by contrast, it is only the grossly ill-informed, the self-deceived, and the willfully deceiving who will still argue the point. Otherwise the great majority of the voices in our public life have come to agree that the armed strength of the United States has been allowed to decline well beyond the limits of tolerable risk, and certainly to a level of net inferiority vis-à-vis Soviet military power in its totality.

Since the United States remains superior by far over the Soviet Union in both economic capacity and technical advancement, one might presume that the diagnosis having been agreed upon, the remedy would follow automatically by common agreement also, in the form of a broad and most energetic rearmament. The effort would have to be broad, since it is no longer merely one or two categories of military power that we have to worry about, but rather the whole spectrum of capabilities with only a few exceptions. And, characteristically, even the last remaining areas of American military advantage are greatly affected by the general impoverishment of the armed forces.

Thus, for example, the very wide theoretical advantage of the United States in the air power of the navy, provided by the globally maneuverable aircraft carriers, is greatly undermined by a lack of spare parts and by a crippling shortage of technicians, now driven by low wages to seek civil employment (the comparison between their earnings and those of "baggers at supermarket checkout counters" threatens to become proverbial).

Similarly, the one remaining strategic nuclear advantage we retain, in the number of bomber-delivered weapons, while itself quite inadequate to offset the Soviet superiority in missile weapons, is also devalued by the venerable age of the vast majority of those bombers, B-52s, designed thirty years ago and last produced in 1962.

More generally, the widespread presumption that the quality of American equipment is significantly higher than that of its Soviet counterparts is no longer justified in most cases. There are two major exceptions: tactical aircraft; and a variety of highly technical ancillary capabilities, such as night-vision devices and various kinds of guidance electronics. Once again, however, shortages of spare parts and even more of modern ordnance (very few of those fancy precision weapons are actually deployed) greatly diminish the true combat value of our superior combat aircraft. As for the ancillaries, the situation is even worse. We are supposed to rely on these fruits of our scientific and technical superiority to mitigate in some degree the Soviet advantage in major weapons and gross numbers overall. Unfortunately, a military establishment starved for funds sacrifices the present for the future, and tends to buy only sample numbers of those devices to save funds for yet more research and development. As a result, the fact that, for example, we have a much better night-vision technology than the Soviet Union possesses does not mean much, since only a few of our troops are actually issued with the equipment.

A net majority in Congress, belatedly reflecting mass opinion, has come to terms with the magnitude of the effort now required, and also appreciates the urgency of action; there has even been some talk of "mobilization." But so far not much has been done. Certainly President Carter and his administration are resisting anything more than merely cosmetic increases in overall spending—increases that are quite easily nullified by slight fluctuations in the inflation rate—and doing so with the powerful support of a significant slice of elite opinion, as well as that of the entire left wing of the Democratic party at large.

Since even those who oppose anything more than small percentage increases in the defense budget now mostly agree with the rest of us on the facts of military weakness, how is it that they reject what would seem to be the only logical conclusion?

• • •

It appears that two major arguments now stand in the way of translating the consensus on the military balance into a consensus on rearmament. The first begins by making two highly significant admissions: that the Soviet Union has indeed become the world's strongest military power (a thing vehemently denied until quite recently); and that this is indeed a dangerous development (another thing categorically denied in the past, on the ground that military power itself was of diminishing consequence in the modern world). But what follows then is not a call for action, to confront the danger belatedly recognized. Instead, quite contrary advice is offered: to reject all congressional attempts to achieve major increases in defense spending, to revive the arms-limitation efforts now in abeyance, and above all to ratify the SALT treaty still now before the Senate.

Thus the remedy for a weakness caused by too much emphasis on arms control and too little spending is more of the same. The paradox is explained by the central contention of this school of thought: that the people of the United States will not in fact sustain the prolonged sacrifice that a serious rearmament effort would require.

While it acknowledges that it is precisely mass opinion that is now inducing Congress to allocate more for defense, this school of thought argues that what we are witnessing is merely a transitory exasperation which will soon pass, and would do so all the sooner if there were serious spending increases and if conscription were to be introduced to make the effort count.

The Soviet Union, we are told, is by contrast in a wholly different position. Its policies, unaffected by the vagaries of public opinion, will maintain a steady course, most especially in the relentless accumulation of military power. If we provoke the Soviet leaders by increasing our military outlays, our own resolve to keep up the effort would soon evaporate, while the Soviet reaction would be long-lasting. In other words, the consequence of a one-time increase on our part might be to push up the Soviet effort to a permanently higher plateau, thus causing a further deterioration in the long-run military balance.

Hence we should instead hasten to ratify SALT II (if the Soviet leaders will still accept it) and then try to obtain any other arms limitations we can. Even if the actual constraint on Soviet armaments thus obtained must be feeble, it would still be better than nothing, while the attempt actually to compete would be downright self-defeating.

Presented in the form of analysis rather than advocacy, often in tones that are calculated to suggest that its exponents would dearly like to see the restoration of our power, if only the fickle American public would allow it, the argument attains respectability. But is it valid?

• • •

Certainly it is all too evidently true that the Soviet leadership has long pursued a fixed course of military accumulation, increasing its expenditures steadily year by year and from decade to decade regardless of whether the United States was also spending more (the Vietnam years), cutting back sharply (the early 1970s), or maintaining a level course through minor ups and downs (the last five years). But the undeniable fact of Soviet relentlessness only validates one half of the argument, while being the very source of the entire problem. The other half—the claim that the American public lacks the resolve to correct the balance and reverse the unfavorable drift—is unproven, and the record of thirty years would suggest that it is false.

To be sure, a graph of American defense outlays in real terms would show a number of high peaks, each short-lived and followed by valleys correspondingly deep. But once the matter is examined in terms of the *results* of these oscillations, it is not evidence of weakness in American resolve that we discover but rather evidence of the great potential strength of the country. The peak efforts of the Korean War rearmament (1951–53) and the lesser increases of the missile-gap period (1959–63) were not kept up, but that was because the results were so massive that there was no *need* to keep them up.

At the beginning of the Korean War, the arsenal of American military power consisted of a mass of leftovers from World War II, of some prototypes whose further development could not be funded, and of several hundred atomic weapons. With a budget of $13.5 billion in 1950 (even General Omar Bradley, then chairman of the Joint Chiefs, had been induced to declare that anything more would "bankrupt" the nation), there was no question of innovation. Indeed, there was not even enough money to keep the inherited World War II equipment in good repair: the first U.S. troops sent to resist the North Korean invasion of the South went into action with broken-down radios, worn-out trucks, and weapons already obsolete in some cases (such as anti-tank rockets that could not pierce the armor of North Korean tanks.)

This dismal picture was utterly transformed by a few years of $50-billion defense budgets, which provided funding not only for the war but for a comprehensive rearmament. The navy was endowed with a fleet of carriers (still the core of what we have), the nuclear submarine and other critical development programs were launched, and the fleets were re-equipped with new warships and aircraft across the board. During that same brief surge, the Air Force was given the means to develop the "century" series of fighters, on which we relied until quite recently, and also the B-52 bomber, which is to serve into the 1990s if the administration continues to block innovation in the form of a B-1 or similar new aircraft. As for the army, which entered the Korean War as little more than an occupation constabulary for Germany and Japan, with scarcely a handful of combat formations, it very quickly acquired fourteen well-armed divisions—the kind of strength that might have served to deter that war in the first place had it been available in time. (Korea was at first excluded from our strategic perimeter precisely because there were no forces for its defense.)

It is true that the effort was not kept up, Nevertheless, the one great surge had sufficed to change the military balance quite drastically, capturing a general superiority over the Soviet Union that was to last through the rest of the 1950s—and which no doubt played a role in bringing the sequence of Soviet postwar adventures to an end.

• • •

The pattern was repeated a decade later. The Soviet Union had capitalized on the shock of the Sputnik launch to support a great strategic deception—the famous "missile gap" still cited by the ill-informed as evidence of the Pentagon's deceit. On the basis of some real ICBM firings and the false claim that a vast force of those weapons was being built—a claim that could not be checked in those pre-satellite days—the Soviet Union attempted to extract real political advantage from nonexistent forces, using the status of Berlin as its pretext. As in our own days, it was Congress that pressed for a rapid rearmament, in the face of a reluctant Eisenhower administration whose greater concern was to balance the budget.

By the time the Kennedy administration took over in 1961, a large effort was under way to develop workable ICBMs (American boosters had a distressing tendency to explode on their launching pads), to build nuclear-powered submarines for what was to become the Polaris force, and to deploy continental air defenses. Simultaneously, in the heated atmosphere of the Berlin *ultimata* periodically issued by Moscow, there were increased expenditures for the conventional forces also.

This time, too, the surge did not last long; by the end of 1963, when Kennedy died, his administration had lost all enthusiasm for accumulating more strategic-nuclear weapons, and was pursuing economy in general. But once again the brief but intense effort had sufficed to correct the balance of power, and more. In fact, the 1959-63 surge was sufficient to gain for the United States a position of very wide advantage in strategic-nuclear capabilities, manifest in the Minuteman force of ICBMs (1,000 having been built), in the Polaris submarine-missile force (41 boats and 656 missiles), and in the formidable force of 600 B-52 heavy bombers. The Soviet Union thus found itself swiftly overtaken by ratios of 10-to-1 or more, in a devastating response to the empty boasts of strategic-nuclear superiority issued by its leaders.

Simultaneously, much was also done for the non-nuclear forces until the new economy wave set in. By 1965, the army had received many new tanks, guns, and troop carriers, while the navy obtained modern escorts and the air force a new generation of combat aircraft and tactical missiles. To this day, we are still living off the capital of military power accumulated in those few years of special effort; and indeed, in the strategic-nuclear arena it took a full fifteen years of unilateral arms control to lose the superiority so rapidly gained, and first revealed, in the Cuban missile crisis of 1962.

• • •

In both the Korean and the "missile-gap" surges, the ultimate secret of our ability to transform the balance of power so quickly was the very low level of antecedent effort. Today, we are relatively much worse off than in either 1950 or 1960, for the Soviet buildup has proceeded for well over a decade without a corresponding American response, and the sheer volume of Soviet resources allocated to military purposes is very much larger in absolute terms.

Once again, however, the level of the pre-surge effort is very low. We are now spending roughly 5 percent of our gross national product on military power—and wasting much of that because low-grade manpower is being asked to operate and maintain equipment of high sophistication. The Soviet Union, by contrast, is spending much more than 10 percent of its gross national product for military purposes (figures ranging from 11 to 15 percent are variously quoted), and the Soviet forces obtain the bulk of their manpower by conscription. Both in the Korean and the "missile-gap" surges, the draft was an indispensable part of the overall American response. So it must be again, preferably in the form of a system of general rather than selective conscription. Once that is achieved, and once the level of spending reverts to 10 percent or so of the GNP, the Soviet advantage could once again be overcome—and rather quickly.

There is, admittedly, a real problem of supply, caused by the erosion of the industrial base in the military segments of production. While clichés about the "fat profits" of defense contractors continue in circulation, those directly involved—the "vested interests" of today's rhetoric—know better. Private industry has been doing its level best to find civilian alternatives to military business, being driven out of military contracting by small profit margins as well as by an erratic pattern of contracting. Particularly damaging has been the flight of the subcontractors, whose specialized production is much more difficult to replace than the integration and assembly work done by the large companies of familiar name.

But in spite of these difficulties, which in some cases are indeed severe, a sharp increase in military purchasing would soon enough elicit a corresponding industrial response, and would in particular reverse the vicious cycle which is now giving us fewer and fewer weapons for higher and higher unit costs. At present, low budgets result in a pattern of contracting in which such things as combat aircraft are being bought in no more than sample numbers. This in turn naturally drives unit costs upward, and often enough the remedy is to cut further the number of items bought, thus once again increasing the overhead burden on each unit.

The ultimate impact of this self-defeating mechanism is manifest most strikingly in the case of naval fighters, where we are now buying fewer replacement aircraft than are being lost in training accidents, and doing so at exceedingly high prices. If more money were available to buy more aircraft each year, we would soon see the end of the $30 million fighters, whose high prices in fact reflect the total costs of research, development, administration, and factory overhead that are now being charged to the handful of aircraft purchased within each fiscal year.

From the viewpoint of economics one may deplore the inefficiency of sharp oscillation in our military outlays, which cause a wasteful industrial instability. But even so, it remains true that the United States could once again overcome the steady Soviet effort by an enhanced effort of its own, even if short-lived.

Defense outlays set at, say, 10 percent of the gross national product (still much less than the Soviet fraction and entirely tolerable), even if kept up for only three years, would amount to roughly $700 billion. To visualize what such a sum could achieve, assume that only a third could be spent on actual equipment, and then compare that $200 billion or so with the unit cost of an aircraft carrier fully equipped with aircraft ($4 billion); with the cost of a 200-aircraft B-1 bomber force ($30 billion or so); and with a division's worth of XM-1 battle tanks (roughly $500 million).

These costs are, of course, high, and yet what a surge effort could achieve is still most impressive. Certainly once the economies of series production are counted in, and once the higher quality of a conscript-sustained force is obtained, it becomes clear that even if the limits of sacrifice are set at 10 percent of the GNP and even if the surge lasts only three years, we could still go a long way toward that rehabilitation of our military power that has now become necessary.

Of course this does not mean that the military balance could be restored so quickly. Given the long intervals between the purchase of weapons and their actual combat-ready deployment, it would take a good deal longer than three years to re-establish a tolerable balance of forces. But that is not the point. What the argument being considered here maintains is that we are unfit to compete with the Soviet Union because we are unable to maintain a steady level of effort. That argument stands disproved, even if several years must intervene before the surge of expenditure yields its full result in increased military power.

We may now contemplate more dispassionately the moral status of this school of thought. Without apology and without retraction, the very people who did everything they could to discourage the upkeep of our defenses now emerge to denounce the unwillingness of the American people to do that very thing. The same people who relentlessly argued that the Soviet Union was only seeking "parity," that military power was in any case of little use in our days, and that arms-control negotiations would dispose of our major security problems, now accuse the people of this country of being too willing to accept their opinions.

More simply, we may also reflect on the sheer defeatism of this school of thought, which has such great respect for totalitarian continuity, and which overlooks the superior productive energies and greater inventive talents of a democratic America.

• • •

A second objection to increased military appropriations is not so easily dismissed. Expressed in more or less identical terms by all manner of people from Ambassador Andrew Young to any number of retired colonels, this argument questions the professional capacity of the armed forces to make worthwhile use of the weapons and the manpower that a rearmament effort would provide. It is the military conduct of the Indochina war that is cited as evidence, as well as the lesser episodes thereafter—and most recently, the Iran rescue debacle.

There is little doubt that in retrospect the American record in Vietnam has been largely vindicated, both in its political and in its humanitarian aspects. It is now a commonplace that Hanoi's policies were those of regional imperialism rather than nationalist unification; and it is equally evident that the totalitarian order which has descended on Vietnam is indeed very much more sinister than Saigon's authoritarianism ever was. As for Cambodia, those who held that a suspension of war would self-evidently improve the circumstances of the Cambodian people have now had full opportunity to appreciate the oceanic depth of their error. Even the corrupt logic and false evidence of a William Shawcross can only serve to attribute blame to some Americans for a genocide that undeniably followed upon the *suspension* of American intervention rather than its continuation.

But the return to reason that allows all but the outer fringe to see the nature of the antagonists as it always was, does nothing to redeem the character of our own military conduct of the war. Standing back from the details of single operations, discounting those lesser phenomena of error and evil that must attend all armed conflict (and which the critics of course wildly magnified), making full allowance for the persistent misdirection of war operations emanating from the White House, American warfare in Indochina still emerges in broad perspective as an essentially bureaucratic phenomenon, scarcely responsive to the real modalities of that conflict.

The artillery fired its ammunition, even if the enemy consistently refused to assemble in conveniently targetable mass formations; the armor maneuvered, even if there were no linear defenses to pierce and no flanks to turn; the air force bombed in close support, in interdiction, and in retaliation against North Vietnamese cities and infrastructures, even if only the last of these missions could find stable and worthwhile targets. Otherwise much of the air war was simply futile for reasons entirely fundamental: the tactical logic of close air support is to combine air strikes with ground combat against enemy forces that will not or cannot disperse, and this was a condition rarely satisfied in Vietnam; the strategic logic of interdiction is to diminish the flow of supply to an enemy who requires absolutely a certain quantum of supplies to sustain operations which cannot be deferred and this too was a condition mostly absent. Nevertheless, thousands and thousands of missions were flown month after month, year after year.

As the war progressed, almost every component of the American armed forces—coast guard included—found a satisfactory role for itself in the war, a role, that is, which allowed funds to be claimed for expansion, *without* changes of structure or function disturbing to the hierarchical or organizational order of things.

Thus the army retained its preferred style of warfare, based much more on the systematic application of firepower than on maneuver; it retained a structure of forces based on extra-large and logistically very heavy divisions; and it retained elaborate headquarters at battalion, brigade, and divisional echelons, these last under the command of officers of general rank—even if there were very few targets for the mass application of firepower, little need for the elaborate logistics, and hardly any valid operational functions for all those headquarters in a war of squad and platoon skirmishes. (It is notable that the one clear American victory, the utter defeat of the Vietcong in the Tet offensive, was won largely by scattered groups of men fighting with little central direction against an enemy that at last came out in force, thus presenting a stable target.)

The navy similarly could have taken care of all opposition afloat with a small destroyer flotilla and a few shore-based patrol aircraft, but instead found full employment for its aircraft carriers in flying attack missions of all kinds by day and by night. Only the submariners were left out in the cold.

As for the air force, every single type of squadron was seemingly needed: fighters; light and heavy bombers; tactical and strategic reconnaissance, both photographic and electronic; as well as transport squadrons, light, medium, and heavy.

In their hundreds of thousands, servicemen worked hard and a good many lost life or limb to operate all those forces. But unfortunately much of all this activity had little to do with the true phenomena of the war through most of its stages: the terrorism and propaganda that subverted the authority of the government in each small locality to extract recruits, food, and intelligence; the guerrilla that was thus manned, fed, and informed and whose own opportunistic attacks served to maintain the insecurity in which subversion could progress still further; and then the worldwide propaganda assault on American confidence and morale.

Even when, after Tet 1968, North Vietnamese regular forces largely took over the fighting, the fit between the combat actions performed by the American forces and the nature of the enemy was only very slightly improved. For North Vietnamese regulars still fought as irregulars, that is elusively. It was only late in the war that the fighting assumed the conventional form of large-scale European-style warfare, complete with sustained artillery barrages and tank assaults by the North Vietnamese. But by then almost all the American forces—structured precisely to prevail in that kind of fighting—had been withdrawn (and, of course, the North Vietnamese only went over to conventional war operations precisely because the American troops had been withdrawn).

• • •

Hence the peculiar nature of the American defeat. The United States was undone in a protracted political struggle waged all around the world, but most importantly in the United States itself, for the very soul of the policy and media elites, while all the action of the American armed forces themselves remained mostly quite tangential to the real phenomena of the war.

This absurd and tragic irrelevance was dictated by the simple fact that American military organizations structured, equipped, and trained for warfare on a large scale against regular forces did not adapt to entirely different circumstances by evolving appropriate small-unit structures. Nor did they develop operational methods related to the context, or tactics responsive to those of the enemy, of necessity radically different from traditional structured methods and tactics.

Those in charge at all levels can claim with full justification that there was continuous interference from Washington in the conduct of the war at the most detailed level, inevitably much of it ill-informed. They can claim with equal justification that the media were systematically ill-disposed, and indeed functionally structured to denigrate all that the South Vietnamese did and to criticize all that the Americans were trying to do. But responsibility for the utter failure to adapt structures, methods, and tactics to the terrain and to the nature of the enemy must rest squarely and exclusively upon the American officer corps. It was as if there were no body of staff and command officers willing and able to learn the facts of the conflict as it evolved and who could then tailor force-structures to suit combat needs, evolve relevant methods, and develop suitable tactics.

And indeed there was no such body of officers ready to perform the purely professional function of studying the war itself. All the hard work, all the undoubted technical and managerial expertise, were fully absorbed by operation of the military organizations themselves, which were shipped *en bloc* from the United States to Vietnam. Once there, all the highly complex weapons and ancillary equipment needed much maintenance, elaborate logistic systems had to be operated, and the whole intricate structure had to be supervised at each level, with a great deal of paper work being involved.

With so many different branches and sub-branches all engaged in war operations in circumstances of luxuriant bureaucratic growth, just the coordination of the different organizational bits and pieces absorbed the work of thousands of officers, especially senior officers. With so much inner-regarding activity, it was all the easier to ignore the phenomena of the war, which were in any case elusive, given the evanescent nature of the guerrilla element and the natural secrecy of subversion.

But for the tactical and operational realities of war to be so largely ignored by tens of thousands of military officers supposedly educated and trained to understand war and fight it, there had to be further and deeper causes of inadvertence, and indeed there were.

First, officers posted to Vietnam commands were rotated in and out of the country at short intervals, of one year or less. This meant that officers arrived in the country and then left it again before being able to come to grips with its complex situation. Characteristically, the first few months of a posting were a period of acclimatization and adjustment. Then the newly arrived officer could start to gather in the reins of command, and could begin work to rectify the deficiencies he uncovered within his unit. Often he would find that his predecessor had swept problems under the rug in the last phase of his posting, since by then he was already preoccupied with his next assignment. And then, by the time the officer was finally ready to look beyond the limits of his unit and its routines to focus on the tactical and operational problems of the war itself, the moment would be at hand to prepare for the next posting, almost invariably a desk job back in the United States.

This fatal lack of continuity (which also did great damage inwardly, since fighting units had no opportunity to develop their *esprit de corps* under the impulse of sustained leadership) denied to the United States all the benefits of a cumulative learning experience in the overall conduct of the war. As the saying went among the cognoscenti, the United States was not in Vietnam for ten years but rather for only one year, ten times over. Of the Romans it has been said that they made all manner of mistakes but never made the same mistake twice. In Vietnam, by contrast, the same tactical mistakes were repeated over and over again. Since officers were promptly sent off outside the country as soon as they began to acquire some experience of war leadership and combat operations, the American forces in Vietnam had no collective memory and the systematic repetition of error was inevitable.

• • •

Why was such a devastatingly harmful bureaucratic procedure tolerated? Certainly this was not one of the malpractices imposed by the interference of civilian policy officials but entirely willed by the military services themselves. The motive, once again, was innerregarding and exquisitely bureaucratic. Since the leadership of combat operations and indeed any service at all in a war zone would confer a great career advantage, it would not have been "fair" to allow some officers to remain in Vietnam year after year, thus depriving others of critical career-enhancing opportunities.

That people who run bureaucracies are apt to use them in a selfserving fashion to some extent is a thing inevitable, understandable, and even reasonable within limits. But in the case of officer rotation as practiced in Vietnam, we encounter a gross deviation from efficacy, with enormously damaging consequences.

How could it be that the desiderata of career management were allowed to prevail over the most essential requirements of effective warfare? Though it is true that reserving troop command and staff posts for the few would have caused much resentment, it would also have resulted in a much better conduct of the war. After all, it is no secret that troops cannot coalesce into cohesive fighting units under leaders constantly changing; and it is only slightly less obvious that the cumulative learning yielded by trial and error can scarcely be achieved by staff officers and commanders coming and going on short duty tours. Since we must assume the good intentions of those involved, it is ignorance of the basics of the military art that we must look for rather than a conscious, collective selfishness.

But the hypothesis of ignorance encounters an immediate and formidable objection. How is ignorance compatible with the high standards of the contemporary American officer corps? It is after all full of Ph.D.s and officers with M.A.s are quite common. The officer corps also contains many highly competent engineers and even scientists, not to speak of very large numbers of skilled managers of all kinds, and in all specialties.

As the list of qualifications lengthens, we begin to glimpse the answer to the riddle, and the source of the problem: only one subject of expertise is missing and it is warfare itself. There are plenty of engineers, economists, and political scientists in the officer corps—but where are the tacticians? There are the many skilled personnel managers, logistical managers, and technical managers—but where are the students of the operational art of war? And at the top, there are many competent (and politically sensitive) bureaucrats—but where are the strategists?

And where would these tacticians and strategists come from? Certainly not from the military schools which teach all manner of subjects—except those essentially military. At West Point, at Annapolis, and at the Air Force Academy, future officers receive a fairly good all-around education, but they do not study the specifically military subjects. Military history—the only possible "data base" for those who would understand war—is treated in a perfunctory manner as one subject among many.

At the opposite end of the hierarchy of military schools—at the war colleges of each branch and the National Defense University, which are meant to prepare mid-career officers for the most senior ranks—there too management, politics, and foreign policy are taught, but no tactics and little strategy. And in between, at the staff and command colleges, there also military history is treated as if it were a marginal embellishment instead of being recognized as the very core of military education, the record of trial and error on which today's methods can be based.

No wonder that the distinguishing characteristic of American officers is their lack of interest in the art of war. No wonder that "military strategy" is a phrase that refers only to budgets and foreign policy in the discourse of senior officers—men who think that Clausewitz was a German who died a long time ago.

• • •

The proximate causes of this extraordinary drift from military professionalism into so many other professions are obvious. The low quality of many of the recruits absorbs a great effort of personnel management, and stimulates the promotion of officers who know how to recruit and retain scarce manpower, rather than officers seriously interested in warfare as such. Similarly, the development and absorption of a mass of highly complex and very advanced equipment creates a great demand for officers who understand science and engineering. Equally, the need to coexist with civilian defense officials who impose economic criteria of efficiency, and who use mathematical techniques of "systems analysis," creates a demand for officers who understand fancy bookkeeping, and who can beat the mathematical models of civilian budget-cutters with models of their own. And so the list goes on and on.

From all these different streams of specialized expertise, officers are promoted stage by stage by way of "ticket punching" assignments to staff or command positions. But since duty tours are so short, the experience counts for little. In the present atmosphere of the officer corps, it is the desk jobs in the Pentagon, the assignments to high-prestige outside agencies (the National Security Council is a well-known launching pad to high rank), and high-visibility managerial positions that are most attractive. Staff posts, where war operations are planned, and unit commands, where there is no better company than more junior officers, are seen largely as obligatory stages to better things.

If the ambitious officer becomes too interested in the essential military functions of studying the enemy, of inventing suitable tactics, of developing war plans, and of inspiring and commanding men, a glance at the official biographies of the service chiefs will soon show him the error of his ways. It was not by allowing themselves to become bogged down in such things that those men reached the top, but rather by being good managers and smooth bureaucrats.

And what of the deeper causes of this state of affairs? Was the "civilianization" of the officer corps driven by the desire to avoid accusations of militarism? Did education in civil subjects displace the study of war because science and corporate business have had more prestige in America than the military profession? Or is it perhaps that the "up or out" rule (where those not promoted are forced out of the career) induces officers to focus on expertise which is of value on the civilian marketplace? Quite other causes also suggest themselves, notably the great shift in the balance of control, which nowadays places civilian defense officials in charge of essentially military decisions.

• • •

When the objection is thus made to a serious rearmament effort that, the need notwithstanding, more resources should still be denied since they would be ill-used in any case, one cannot simply dismiss the argument on its merits. And if the more general facts and broader assessments are disputed, then a close scrutiny of the details of the Iran rescue debacle certainly reveals the workings of a managerial-bureaucratic approach to the planning and execution of a commando operation, with disastrous consequences.

Commando operations are like all other infantry operations, only more so. They do, however, have their own rules, which the rescue attempt seems to have violated in every respect. No doubt the planners involved were good managers, economists, engineers, or whatever. But they must also have been quite ignorant of the military history of forty years of British, German, French, and Israeli commando operations. Otherwise they would not have sent such a small force into action. Here the rule is: "a man's force for a boy's job." Deep in enemy territory, in conditions of gross numerical inferiority, there must be a decisive superiority at the actual point of contact, since any opposition must be crushed before others can intervene, eventually submerging the commando force; there is no time for a fair fight. The ninety commandos were too few to do the job by this criterion.

If they had not been ignorant of the history of commando operations, they would not have had three co-equal commanders on the spot, and then a "task force" commander back in Egypt, not to speak of the Joint Chiefs, the Secretary of Defense, and the President—all connected by satellite. Here the rule is that there must be unity of command, under one man only, since in high-tempo commando operations there is no time to consult anyway, while any attempt at remote control is bound to be highly dangerous given the impossibility of knowing the true facts of the situation deep within the enemy's territory.

If they had not been ignorant of the history of commando operations, they would not have relied on a few inherently fragile helicopters. Here the rule is that since the combat risks are, by definition, very high, all technical risk must be avoided. If helicopters must be used, let there be twenty or thirty to carry the payload of six.

If they had not been ignorant of the history of commando operations, they would not have assembled a raid force drawn from different formations and even different services. Here the rule is that commando operations, being by definition exceptionally demanding of morale, must be carried out by cohesive units, and not by *ad hoc* groups of specialists. That indeed is why standing units of commandos were established in the first place. If the suspicion is justified that the fatal accident was caused by a misunderstanding or worse between Marine helicopter pilots and Air Force C-130 pilots—and procedures, technical jargon, etc., *are* different—those involved carry a terrible responsibility. For there is much reason to believe that all four services were involved in the raid precisely because each wanted to ensure a share of any eventual glory for its own bureaucracy.

• • •

Having gone so far to justify the second objection to rearmament, does one leave it at that? Surely not, since there can be no satisfactory equilibrium of power in world politics without strong American military forces placed in the balance. But how can American military strength be restored if the resources devoted to the national defense are apt to be misused?

In the first place, we must recognize the limits of the argument of military incompetence: it does not apply to the whole realm of ballistic-missile forces, where tactics and the operational art of war are very simple, and where the problems of force have a stable and known character, by now well understood. This is of course a very important exception, essential to the highest level of deterrence. It is also one of the several areas where the engineering, scientific, and managerial expertise of the American officer corps is highly useful, while its lack of specifically military competence is of little consequence.

Secondly, there are healthy components within the military machine, even if its ailments are indeed systemic. At the tactical level, at least, the marines are still reportedly pretty good, and so are a good many of the fighter forces of the air force, navy, and Marine Corps. In the surface and submarine navy also, high competence is still found in several components. As for the army, there too some exceptions survive.

But the real answer to the objection is not a list of exceptions. It is, rather, the recognition that we do indeed need fundamental military reforms. The most important of the congressional advocates of stronger defenses (notably Senator Sam Nunn) have explicitly recognized the need for basic reforms of the military institutions, along with the major increases in funding which they advocate. Some who hold a middle position on the defense budget, most importantly Senator Gary Hart, have also become persuasive advocates of reform.

These reforms would range from measures of long-term effect, such as drastic changes in the curricula of the military academies and the war colleges (with lesser changes in the schools and courses in the middle) to immediate moves designed to change career incentives to encourage the selection of officers for the top positions who are fighters, leaders, tacticians, or strategists rather than engineers, managers, bureaucrats, or office politicians. The hope would be to encourage a general takeover of the key positions by those many middle-ranking officers now in the services who already have the qualities needed but who are systematically being excluded from the most senior positions precisely because of the ascendancy of the wrong type of officer.

It must always be the human factor that is most important, for war after all is decided to a far greater extent by the moral and intangible factors than the material. Nevertheless, the reform of education and of officer selection would be undertaken in the presumption that the reformed military institutions would then move energetically to change a great deal of the material element as well. After all, officers whose minds are on the tactics, operations, and strategies of war are scarcely likely to be seduced by the unguided engineering and scientific ambition that yields the hyper-complex, very expensive, and often fragile major weapons that are being developed and fielded nowadays. And officers so inclined would also reject the mechanistic, heavy, and heavy-handed attrition tactics so greatly favored by our managerially-minded officer corps.

In the present climate of the armed forces, marked by acute financial stringency and pervasive shortages, one can neither innovate nor reform. On the other hand, if the nation does finally give the armed forces the better men and the additional money that they so badly need, then there will be both the opportunity and the obligation to carry out major reforms aimed at refocusing the military profession upon the military arts it has for so long now neglected.

4

CHAPTER

HOW TO THINK ABOUT NUCLEAR WAR

*N*ow that the United States is belatedly acting to restore a tolerable balance in forces nuclear as well as conventional, a vast chorus of protest has been heard from those who hold that deterrence is a policy not merely dangerous but irrational, and who therefore demand an immediate "freeze." Others have made a narrower protest, against the reliance of the United States and its allies on nuclear deterrence to dissuade a Soviet invasion that might be accomplished by the great non-nuclear forces of the Soviet army. And then there has been the broadest of claims, in which pastors and priests, rabbis and bishops, have been most prominent: that nuclear deterrence, and indeed nuclear weapons as such, are in themselves immoral.

Along with the arguments and the claims there has been a great outpouring of horrific imagery of Hiroshima and its victims, of mushroom clouds and radiation burns—imagery abundantly relayed in the complaisant press and in the visual media. The purpose has been to frighten those whom the arguments have not persuaded, so that the electorate which deliberately rejected Carter's strategy of weakness might now be terrorized into repudiating Reagan's strategy of strength.

Yet instead of reaffirming its strategy, the Reagan administration has for the most part responded to the arguments and the claims, to the words and the manipulative imagery, by appeasing the protesters, the churchmen, and the media. From those who once could explain quite lucidly the fundamental and unchanging reasons for the inevitable failure of arms control, we now hear much talk about the virtues of that very process. From those who started off resolutely determined to explain strategic realities, we now hear only great declarations of their love for peace, their revulsion against war, and their sincere dislike of nuclear weapons. Outside the administration, too, all manner of people once very attentive to the delicate texture of strategy have now come forward to mollify protest by offering schemes and plans designed to reduce the role of nuclear weapons in our defense, sometimes offering a non-nuclear substitute, and sometimes not.

And yet every one of the claims which sustain the protests large and small is false; each of the arguments, both strategic and moral, can be utterly refuted. The most respectable promoters of the "freeze" who claim that deterrence is irrational are guilty of a crude logical fallacy of composition; the four eminent retired officials who have called for NATO's renunciation of nuclear deterrence against a conventional attack reveal one more time their own peculiar lack of strategic understanding; and the churchmen who hold that nuclear weapons are *ipso facto* immoral are guilty of a crude ethical illiteracy. That is the charge sheet; the justification follows.

• • •

The "front" that the North Atlantic Treaty Organization sustains against the Soviet Union and its client-states divides not nations but political systems. On the one side there is the system of production, of individual welfare and social amelioration, while on the other side there is a system that proclaims those same goals very loudly, even while subordinating them to the preservation of totalitarian control and the accumulation of superior military power.

If nuclear weapons were now disinvented, if all the hopes of the nuclear disarmers were fully realized, the Soviet Union would automatically emerge as the dominant power on the continent, fully capable of invading and conquering Western Europe and beyond if its political domination were resisted.

But why should that be so in a non-nuclear world? After all, our side has all the men and all the means that would be needed to out-match the conventional forces of the other side. Already now, by the storekeeper's method of making up an inventory, the forces of NATO can appear as strong as or even stronger than those of the Soviet Union and its not-necessarily-reliable client-states.[1] Compare, for example, total manpower in uniform, on active duty: 4.9 million for NATO and the United States versus 4.8 million for the Soviet Union and its client-states (and remember that out of that total the Soviet Union must provide the large forces deployed against the Chinese). Compare total manpower in ground forces: 2.7 million for us versus 2.6 million for them (with the same Chinese qualifica-tion, to make us feel even better). Compare total ground forces in Europe itself: 2.1 million on our side and only 1.7 million on the other (and one must make allowance for Polish, Hungarian, and other client-state troops that prudent Soviet military planners would not want to rely upon except to add sheer mass to a successful of-fensive). In naval forces, the U.S.–NATO advantage is large in al-most every category, even if ships are counted by the prow as in Homer and not by tonnage (in which Western superiority is still greater).

If one delights in these comparisons, one can come up with more numbers that are comforting. But there are also some other numbers that are less reassuring. Tanks: 17,053 for NATO in Europe (U.S. included) versus a total of 45,500 on the other side, including 32,200 in reliable Soviet hands (Hitler had only some 3,000 in 1941 for "Barbarossa," the German invasion of Russia); artillery pieces: 9,502 versus 19,446; surface-to-surface missile launchers: 355 versus 1,224 for the Soviet camp (all the nuclear warheads are in Soviet hands exclusively); antitank guns (a rather antique category by conven-tional wisdom): 964 versus 3,614.

As for combat aircraft in Europe, the numbers go the same way: 2,293 fighter-bombers for NATO–Europe versus 3,255 in Soviet and Warsaw Pact air forces (but predominantly Soviet); fighters: only 204 on the NATO side (the U.S. air force believes in heavier multi-purpose aircraft) versus 1,565 on the other side; interceptors (an-other depreciated category): 572 on the part of NATO versus 1,490 in Pact air forces.

Each set of numbers means little in itself. But ignoring all the de-tails, there is one very striking fact that emerges—a fact that begins

---

[1] *All the statistics following are from the 1982 edition of the* Military Balance, *published by the International Institute for Strategic Studies.*

to tell us the real story about the "military balance" on which there is so much controversy now that McGeorge Bundy, George F. Kennan, Robert S. McNamara, and Gerard Smith have jointly proposed in an article in *Foreign Affairs* (spring 1982) that NATO should renounce the "first use" of nuclear weapons to deter a nuclear invasion. That fact, indeed very remarkable, is that the rich are seemingly armed as poor men are armed, with rifles, while the poor are armed as rich men, with heavy weapons. Recalling that comparison of "total ground forces in Europe" in which NATO is shown with 2.1 million troops on active duty versus a mere 1.7 million for the Warsaw Pact—a ratio of 1.27 : 1 in favor of our side—we now discover that the ratios for the major weapons which modern ground forces need go the other way, in favor of the Soviet side: 2.65 : 1 for tanks; 2.05 : 1 for artillery; 3.45 : 1 for missile launchers; and so on.

More remarkable still, the poorer and less advanced have more combat aircraft, by ratios of 4.5 : 1 (bombers), 1.4 : 1 (fighter-bombers), 7.67 : 1 (fighters), 2.61 : 1 (interceptors), and so on. Never mind that on each side one should sort out old aircraft in each category, and never mind also that Soviet aircraft are judged inferior to their U.S. counterparts (though to take Israeli-Syrian combat outcomes as an index is totally misleading, since Soviet aircraft would do very nicely in Israeli hands, just as they performed quite well against our own fighter-bombers in Vietnam, and also in Indian hands against the Pakistanis). In spite of all qualifications large and small, the fact stands, and it is a great fact: the poor are far more abundantly armed, even in air power, which is the quintessential arm of the rich.

• • •

How can this be? What does this mean? How and why have the rich come to be poorly armed as compared with the Soviet Union (whose gross national product is now 60 percent of the American and a mere 25 percent of the U.S.–NATO total)? There is, of course, a very simple answer revealed by the statistics themselves. That famous number, the count of NATO ground forces in Europe in the amount of 2.1 million (as compared to 1.7 million for the Pact), is actually made up of 980,000 men in the armies of Western Europe and another 922,000 men in the Greek, Italian, and Turkish armies which mainly consist of lightly armed infantry, disqualified by location, training, and equipment from fighting seriously against Soviet-style armored divisions.

But that too is no more than a circumstantial fact: it is not the ineluctable consequence of unalterable limits. NATO *could* have forces much larger *and* better equipped *and* in the right places, for it has a much larger population than the Pact, and also a far greater production. Why then do our richer allies in Western Europe fail to remedy the imbalance? Is it greed that dissuades them from spending enough, or is it perhaps defeatism? Both are in evidence in some degree. But the decisive reason is strategic: those in Europe who understand such matters know that an increased effort would not improve the balance unless it were truly huge, because there are two fundamental military factors at work which make NATO weak and the Soviet Union strong—and these are of such powerful effect in combination that they would nullify the benefits of any marginal increase in defense spending, just as they already outweigh every one of the disadvantages that afflict the Soviet Union, including the unreliability of some of its East European subjects, the hostility of China, and the technical inferiority of some Soviet weapons. Much more than the numbers, it is these two factors that truly determine the present military imbalance in non-nuclear strength, which is very great, and not at all the small matter that Messrs. Bundy, Kennan, McNamara, and Smith suggest (". . . there has been some tendency, over many years, to exaggerate the relative conventional strength of the USSR. . . .").

The first of the two fundamental military factors is, quite simply, that NATO is a defensive alliance—not just defensive in declared intent, as all self-respecting alliances will claim to be, but rather in actual military orientation. Specifically, the forces of NATO on the "central front"—the 600-kilometer line running from the Baltic Sea to the Austrian border—are incapable of offensive operations on a large scale. There are no plans for a NATO offensive against East Germany, there has never been suitable training, or any army-sized exercises for offensive action in spite of the abundant claims to the contrary in Soviet propaganda at its most implausible. Soviet military planners must know that NATO could not launch an offensive against their front. The notion that Belgian, Dutch, British, German, and U.S. forces would suddenly march across the border to invade is quite simply fantastic.

This means that the Soviet high command can concentrate its own forces for offensive action without having to allocate significant strength for defense. To be sure, many Soviet divisions are either deployed on or assigned to the very long Chinese border. But there too the Soviet Union need not disperse its forces to provide a territorial defense, since the Chinese, for all their millions of troops and tens of millions of rifle-armed militiamen, have no real capacity to mount significant offensive operations. At the very most, at a time of great opportunity such as a Soviet attack upon the West might present, the Chinese could mount a very limited and very shallow move against some segment of the Trans-Siberian railway where it runs near their territory.[2]

The Soviet army, which was greatly diminished in size during the 1950s but which has grown again during the last two decades, can now mobilize so many divisions that it can cover the Chinese border very adequately; provide more divisions to maintain a threat against Iran, Eastern Turkey, and Pakistan; keep the forces now in place in Afghanistan; and still send more divisions against the "central front" than NATO could cope with.

Not counting at all the divisions of the East European client-states (even though some at least could in fact be used), the arithmetic runs as follows: if 10 more Soviet divisions are added to the Chinese "front" (in addition to the 46 stationed there already); and if a further 18 divisions are kept in reserve to deal with all the contingencies that a prudent and well-provided military leadership can imagine; and if there is no reduction in the generous allowance of 26 divisions now deployed on the Soviet Union's "southern front" (opposite the underequipped Turks, the chaotic Persians, and in Afghanistan); then, finally, the Soviet Union, upon mobilization, could launch 80 divisions against NATO in Central Europe—that is, against the West German border. And since NATO is a defensive-only alliance, the Soviet army could concentrate its forces in powerful offensive thrusts aimed at narrow segments of that front.

By another estimate, produced by the International Institute for Strategic Studies—nowadays a great favorite of Messrs. Bundy et al. owing to its far from hawkish positions—the Soviet army could send a total of 118 divisions against NATO, the greater number being obtained by assuming that no central reserve is maintained at all (the Soviet Union does after all keep 500,000 KGB and MVD troops, which are heavily armed) and that no reinforcement would be made to the Chinese "front."

As against this, NATO can claim a total of 116 divisions, only two fewer than the higher estimate of the Soviet divisions that could be sent against it—and actually 36 divisions more than the Soviet total estimated more conservatively.

[2] *That, incidentally, sets a firm ceiling to the strategic value of a U.S.–China alliance.*

But that is truly a hollow number, since NATO's 116 divisions include more than 16 American National Guard divisions that would have to be mobilized, remanned, reequipped (with what?), trained for weeks or months, and then transported to Europe by way of ports and airfields benevolently left intact by Soviet forces. The 116 divisions include more than 29 Italian, Greek, and Turkish divisions that are stationed far from Central Europe and are neither trained nor equipped to fight on that front. And they include 9 other divisions of foot infantry of various kinds. Once all these make-weights are removed from the count, we discover that against 80 Soviet divisions, NATO might field no more than 58 divisions of its own, including more than 12 French divisions whose participation in a fight is uncertain but whose scant armament for such combat is unfortunately not in doubt.

In fact, we might estimate even more truly by measuring NATO forces in terms of *Soviet* division-equivalents, whereupon we obtain 35 divisions upon full mobilization and with the transfer of all earmarked U.S. forces. The numerical imbalance thus finally emerges as a sharp one indeed: 80 Soviet divisions versus 35 for NATO. And then the defense/offense asymmetry intervenes to make the true combat imbalance even greater, since the Soviet divisions can be concentrated during an offensive against a few narrow segments of the front while NATO's divisions must defend all along a 600-kilometer border.

• • •

Under any circumstances, the numerical imbalance in real capabilities would make things very difficult for NATO. But it would not be decisive were it not for the second great factor that makes NATO weak, which arises from the very nature of armored warfare. Nowadays, there is only one army in the world that has actual hands-on expertise in the reality of armored warfare, in the combined use of large numbers of tanks, troop carriers, and self-propelled artillery to stage offensives of deep penetration, whereby enemy forces are not merely destroyed piecemeal by firefights but are defeated by being cut off and forced into surrender—and that, of course, is the Israeli army. But if there is one army in the world that seriously strives to overcome its lack of recent and relevant combat experience, it is the Soviet army. It is the only one which stages vast army-sized exercises to educate its officers and men in the broad art and the detailed craft of armored warfare.

One reason Messrs. Bundy *et al.* are not much impressed by the strength of the Soviet army is that they simply do not understand the meaning of armored warfare in a setting such as the NATO central front. The Soviet army would not be lined up unit by unit along the 600 kilometers of the German frontier, there to fight it out in head-on combat with the forces of NATO similarly arrayed (hence the worthlessness of inventory comparisons which imply such front-to-front combat). Instead, its 80 divisions would be formed into deep columns and multiple echelons poised to advance by swift penetration of narrow segments of the front. Having learned the art of armored warfare in the hard school of war itself, at the hands of the best masters, and having made the method at once simpler and much more powerful by employing the sheer mass of great numbers to relieve the need for fancy German-style maneuvers, the Soviet army would not employ its forces to launch a set-piece offensive on a preplanned line of advance (which would be detectable and vulnerable), but would instead seek to advance opportunistically, just as water flows down a slope, its rivulets seeking the faster paths. Initially, the advance regiments would probe for gaps and weak sectors through which a swift passage might be achieved. Any Soviet forces that could make no progress would be left in place, to keep up the threat and prevent the NATO commands from switching their forces to strengthen the front elsewhere. But Soviet reinforcements would be sent only where successful advances were being achieved in order to add to the momentum. First more regiments, then divisions, then entire "armies" would thus be channeled forward to keep up the pressure and push deep into the rear of the NATO front.

By feeding reinforcement echelons into avenues of penetration successfully opened, the Soviet high command could obtain the full effect of the classic *Blitzkrieg* even without having to rely on the skill and initiative of regimental officers, as the Germans once did. Instead of a fluid penetrating maneuver obtained by free improvisation, theirs would be an advance just as fast, achieved by mass and momentum directed from above.

Soon enough, advancing Soviet columns would begin to disrupt the entire defensive structure of NATO, by cutting across roads on which Western reinforcements and resupply depend, by overrunning artillery batteries, command centers, supply depots, and finally airfields—until the very ports of entry on the Atlantic shore would be reached. With NATO's front cut in several places, with Soviet forces already in their deep rear, the choices open to NATO formations in such non-nuclear combat would be either to stand and fight for honor's sake even without true military purpose, or else to retreat—

thus opening further gaps in the front. In any case, the relentless advance would soon enough impose a broader choice at a much higher level of decision, for the Germans first and the others not much later: capitulation or military destruction.

Thus in the absence of nuclear weapons, it is not the numerical imbalance in itself that would bring the dismal results, but rather the fact that the Soviet army has a valid method of offensive war, while NATO for its part has no valid method of defense. For obviously the envisaged attempts to block Soviet advances by switching defensive forces back and forth along the line (right in front of Soviet forces which would have every opportunity to disrupt such lateral movement by fire and by their own thrusts) must fail. Indeed, it can be said that even if NATO had a perfect numerical equality, it would still find it impossible to match Soviet concentrations with its own, in order to block their advance right at the front line itself. The reason for this inherent defect is not any lack of military expertise on the part of NATO commanders and planners (although their unfamiliarity with modern armored warfare does show when some pronounce on the military balance by the bookkeeper's method). The defect rather is caused by the combination of NATO's defensive-only orientation and the character of large-scale armored warfare.

• • •

In the face of an offensive threat by an armored-mobile army (unless the defenders are *vastly* superior in sheer strength), one of two conditions must obtain to make a successful defense possible: either the defenders must be ready and willing to attack first, in order to disrupt an offensive preemptively; or else the defense must have considerable geographic space in which to maneuver and fight in a defense-in-depth strategy. If NATO had the political will, the training, and the organization to strike first in the face of massing Soviet forces, the latter could not safely form up in deep columns for the attack and would instead have to dilute their strength to form a defensive array of their own.

This option is purely theoretical in NATO's case. It is impossible to imagine that so many diverse governments would agree to let their national forces engage in a preemptive attack to anticipate a Soviet invasion before the outbreak of war. More likely, in the face of a Soviet mobilization and a buildup of divisions opposite NATO, there would be demands for negotiations to settle the crisis by what would no doubt be called "political means," i.e., eager concessions.

As compared with a wholly unrealistic strategy of preemptive attack, the second option, a defense-in-depth, may seem a feasible alternative; and it would offer the possibility of a very powerful defense indeed for NATO. Under such a strategy, Soviet invasion columns would *not* be intercepted by NATO's main defensive forces right in the border zone. Instead, advancing Soviet forces would encounter only a mere border guard along the frontier itself, thereafter being harassed, delayed, and clearly revealed by light and elusive forces as they continued to advance, being steadily weakened by the loss of momentum imposed by time, distance, breakdowns, mined barriers, multiple obstacles at river crossing points, canals, and towns—and also by successive battles with strongholds along the way. Then too, NATO air forces operating quite freely over their own territory, where Soviet air defenses would be very weak, could attack advancing Soviet forces heavily and frequently. Only then would the major combat on the ground finally take place, with fresh NATO divisions maneuvering to strike at the stretched-out and by then ill-supplied Soviet columns (air strikes would do much more damage to supply vehicles than to the Soviet armored forces themselves).

In such a setting, with a thin line of NATO covering forces on the border itself, with multiple barriers and strongholds in depth, and with the main line of resistance 100 or 200 kilometers to the rear, NATO could indeed have a very solid non-nuclear defense, and one which could moreover deter non-nuclear invasion all by itself—since any competent Soviet planner would have to estimate that defeat would be the most likely outcome. And that, of course, would be a defeat which would deprive the Soviet army of one-half of its divisions, and thus the Soviet empire of much of its gendarmerie as well as all its prestige, no doubt triggering unrest at home and perhaps outright insurrection in the client-states.

But to imagine such a defense in depth for the NATO central front in Germany is not to consider a live option. It is, rather, to indulge in sheer fantasy—and malevolent fantasy at that. For that zone of deep combat happens to correspond to the territory where tens of millions of Germans live. Quite rightly, what the Germans demand is not merely an eventual ability to defeat an aggression at some ultimate point in time and in space, but rather an actual provision of security for themselves, their families, their homes, and their towns. The British, French, or Americans might obtain satisfaction from the defeat of an invading Soviet army in the depth of West German territory, but such a victory would be of little worth to the Germans themselves. What the European system of peaceful construction needs is a preclusive method of protection, not ultimate victory after much destruction and millions of deaths.

• • •

In the absence of an offensive capacity by NATO and a lively willingness to preempt invasion, such protection can only be assured by nuclear weapons—or more precisely, by the architecture of nuclear deterrence which is now in place. If the Soviet Union does attack, its offensive would be met in the first instance by a non-nuclear defense of the forward areas close to the border. If NATO could not hold the front by non-nuclear combat, it would warn the Soviet Union that (small-yield) nuclear weapons would be used to strike at the invading Soviet forces. And then it would strike with such weapons if the warning went unheeded.

At that point the Soviet Union would realize that the alliance was standing up to the test, that it did have the will to defend itself in its moment of truth. One Soviet reaction might be to call off the war—a quite likely response if the invasion had been launched out of some hope of gain, but much less likely if it were the desperate last act of a crumbling empire.

Another Soviet reaction might be to respond to the threat by a wider threat against the cities of Europe, or else—and more likely—to reply in kind. With its own forces weakened by nuclear attack, it might employ nuclear weapons to make its invasion easier, by blasting gaps through the NATO defenses. Or else, the Soviet Union might want to avoid the intermediate steps, and try to impose a capitulation by threatening to attack European cities if any more battlefield nuclear weapons were used.

Such a verbal threat might in turn be averted by being answered in kind, in the first instance perhaps by the British and the French—assuming that their cities had also come under the threat. But a better response to such a Soviet threat would be possible if by then NATO had acquired its own theater nuclear forces which, like the Soviet forces that already exist in considerable numbers, would be suitable to threaten not merely cities indiscriminately, but rather such specific targets as political and military command centers, airfields, nuclear storage sites, and even large concentrations of ground forces—that threat being all the more credible for being less catastrophic.

Much more complex exchanges and many more variations can be envisaged. But by far the most likely outcome is that a war would end very soon if any nuclear weapons, however small, were actually to be detonated by any side on any target. The shock effect upon leaders on both sides—but especially on the Soviet leaders who had started the war—and also the devastating psychological impact upon the forces in the field, would most likely arrest the conflict there and then. It is fully to be expected that military units whose men would see the flash, hear the detonation, feel the blast, or merely hear of such things, would swiftly disintegrate, except perhaps for a handful of units particularly elite, and also remote from the immediate scene. The entire "software" of discipline, of morale, of unit cohesion and *esprit de corps* and all the practices and habits that sustain the authority of sergeants, officers, and political commissars, are simply not built to withstand such terror as nuclear weapons would cause—even if at the end of the day it were to be discovered that the dead on all sides were surprisingly few.

• • •

To believe—as Jonathan Schell insists in *The Fate of the Earth* and as Messrs. Bundy, Kennan, McNamara, and Smith imply—that the firing of small-yield nuclear artillery shells against an invasion force, or even the launch of some short-range battlefield missiles with kiloton-range warheads, would lead more or less automatically to successive nuclear strikes from one side and then the other, on a scale larger and larger, until finally European, Russian, and American cities would be destroyed, one has to believe that the instinct for survival would have been utterly extinguished in political leaders, and also that the armies in the field and their commanders, the air forces, the missile crews, and all the rest of mankind in uniform would behave as robots throughout. Just as a Roman legion trained to withstand all the terrors of the ancient world would surely break up and run if it came under machine-gun fire, so too a Soviet division that might otherwise fight and advance through artillery fire and close attack would almost certainly fall apart and retreat if its men came under nuclear attack. As for the politicians and the generals (who begin to resemble politicians when they reach the highest ranks), are we to believe that they would become so absorbed in the conflict-as-a-game that they would reply tit for tat, move by move, instead of stopping the war as soon as it had become nuclear, before it could destroy their own cities and their own families?

It is precisely this quality of nuclear weapons, their awesome, sinister, and only dimly known character, that makes them the fitting tools of deterrent protection in Europe. And yet Messrs. Bundy *et al.* hold that NATO should surrender its deterrent, except to deter a Soviet *nuclear* attack. They argue that NATO should renounce the first and by far the most important layer of deterrence, by repudiating its current and long-established policy whereby the alliance reserves the right to use nuclear weapons against a conventional invasion that could not be stopped by non-nuclear forces alone.

As we have seen, without a policy of "first use" there would no longer be a deterrent against a non-nuclear invasion and Western Europe would remain with only a dubious war-fighting defense which, even if greatly strengthened, could only yield at best some sort of ultimate victory—after much devastation and death.

But of course Messrs. Bundy, Kennan, McNamara, and Smith deny the bleak alternative. They do not believe that there is a gross imbalance, and indeed they confess that they have no sense of how one might estimate such a balance. Perhaps the four are too elevated to concern themselves with such lowly matters as the current Soviet method of armored warfare. And yet oddly enough a very specific technical suggestion is suddenly offered in the midst of the carefully crafted and indeed evasive political prose of their article. They suggest that the advent of "precision-guided weapons" might be weakening the Soviet army.

What Bundy *et al.* will only allude to most prudently others have proclaimed in black and white. The Soviet army, they say, is almost entirely made up of armored formations, and with the arrival of anti-armor missiles on the scene, its strength could now be nullified by the large-scale deployment of those cheap weapons—especially if the United States and NATO stop wasting their own funds on expensive and complex major weapons.

The prospect is most attractive: let the Soviet Union misuse its scant wealth on expensive tanks, obsolete playthings for nostalgic generals, since NATO can defeat their tanks, and their combat carriers too, and indeed all that relies on armor for its immunity, with cheap precision-guided weapons. Of late such things have been said or written by all manner of odd people, from a *New York Times* columnist who had never previously claimed the tactician's mantle, to that part-time physicist and full-time arms-control promoter Hans Bethe—who has for so long used his Nobel Prize to demand authority on things very much larger than the very small particles which he has investigated. And then, of course, there is the usual array of congressmen and assorted publicists who so readily assume that every military practice and every military choice must be the wrongheaded product of inert tradition and childish preference for large, and costly, weapons.

• • •

Reinforced by the sinking of British warships by "cheap" Exocet missiles, still sustained by lingering memories of the shell-shocked misreporting of the first days of the Yom Kippur war, hardly deflated by the outcome of that same war (decided by Israeli armor, inexplicably), or indeed by other experiences of missile combat before and since (the first use of anti-ship missiles dates back to 1943), the cheap-missile delusion lives on. In the new controversy over NATO's nuclear "first-use" policy, this delusion has attained an unprecedented currency by seemingly offering an alternative to the nuclear deterrence of invasion.

Imagine a Soviet tank approaching. A NATO soldier with his anti-tank missile can launch his weapon from three or four thousand yards away, he being well hidden in the undergrowth while the tank stands clear as a very vulnerable target. The missile duly strikes and destroys the tank. That is the technical level of warfare—the only level that many scientists and all "tech-fix" enthusiasts readily comprehend.

But now broaden the picture somewhat. In a larger view we see more tanks and more NATO missile crews, but we also see the gathering of Soviet artillery—as concentrated as the Soviet armored columns themselves, to pound not all along the front but only those of its segments where breakthroughs are being attempted. Now the missile crews must see their targets through much intervening smoke (and when they cannot see them—if only for a second or two—their missiles will go off-course). But under the heavy artillery barrage many missile crews will be driven to seek refuge in the ground, or in the rear, and if not, they will be wounded or killed. They, after all, are entirely unprotected, unlike the advancing Soviet armor, which can still move forward under artillery fire because of all that expensive armor protection. Now the weapon that had a 90 percent "killprobability" in a technical estimate is revealed as much less powerful, and perhaps a 9 percent kill-probability becomes the more realistic estimate.

This is the tactical level of warfare, and one that quite a few believers in the missile illusion can still comprehend. Accordingly, they accept the analysis and merely point out that even if ten or more missiles must be purchased for each tank to be destroyed, the missile solution would still work—and would still obviate the need both for large budgets and for the "first use" of nuclear weapons. It is a matter of simple arithmetic. Armored vehicles are expensive, and even the Soviet army could scarcely have more than 40,000 or 50,000 for an invasion against NATO's central front (that being a huge number

indeed, ultimately constrained by road capacities). Let NATO therefore deploy half-a-million missile launchers if need be—an enormous
number (now there are 5,000) and yet still easily affordable, since
for every planned $2.7-million tank that we give up we could obtain
instead some 150 missile launchers (and we are planning to build
thousands of those tanks).

But now finally broaden the picture still more, to embrace the full
width of that 600-kilometer NATO front. Let the half-a-million missile launchers be deployed, and now finally at the strategic level of
war we discover the true strength of offensive armored warfare:
while the Soviet army would attack the front here and there at
places of its own choosing in deep columns of concentrated strength,
the infantry's missile launchers would be unable to move about to
match the concentration. For even if some vehicles or other might
be found for the weapons and crews, they would be kept from reaching the places of need by Soviet artillery fire—against which they
would lack any armor protection. Now the arithmetic is suddenly
overturned. Where it really counts, at the unpredictable places
where the breakthrough battles would actually take place, the expensive and scarce armored vehicles would be many (because that
is where they would be concentrated), while the antitank missiles
would be few indeed once the initial array were scattered, suppressed, or destroyed by the devastating barrages of the abundant
and concentrated Soviet artillery.

Just as at sea the cheap missile can destroy the expensive warship
only so long as the latter's space and weight, crews and power
sources are not properly used to accommodate countermeasures and
counterweapons, so also the cheap missile can destroy armored forces
successfully only if it is used against the unprepared and the under-
concentrated. Otherwise it can only serve as one more weapon on
the battlefield, undoubtedly useful, but not a substitute for large defense budgets, and still less for the necessity of nuclear deterrence.

• • •

One can be certain that Jonathan Schell and all the marching and
chanting thousands would remain quite unmoved by the revelation
that "precision-guided munitions" will not evade the rules of strategy, that they will not offer a non-nuclear solution and a cheap one
to boot. Schell's formula for security in our age of conflict is very
simple: universal disarmament under the aegis of world government.
But of course that is not a proposal seriously meant, and in fact
Schell does not even bother to outline for us, not even briefly, any
scheme of action whereby those great results might be achieved. The

proposal that he does put forward in all seriousness is that we should immediately stop all work on the development and construction of nuclear weapons.

Now as it happens Schell knows quite well that the ability of the United States to avert war by deterrence requires on the contrary that we proceed, and rapidly, to improve our nuclear forces, in order to make up for the entire decade of the 1970s when the Soviet buildup was not offset by any adequate American response. But Schell is not concerned with the needs of deterrence because he holds deterrence to be too dangerous, and indeed irrational. The nuclear war he imagines is made of thousands of warheads unleashed upon our cities to burn, to blast, to irradiate. In such circumstances, the use of nuclear weapons for retaliation would indeed serve no purpose. From this Schell concludes that *all* retaliation must be purposeless, and thus all deterrence must be irrational.

Now it was always very clearly understood that if for some inexplicable reason the Soviet Union were to launch large numbers of intercontinental nuclear weapons upon our cities, then our own use of surviving nuclear weapons to destroy the Soviet population would serve no rational strategic purpose, and no moral aim. But the workings of deterrence are in no way governed by that theoretical and ultimate extreme, any more than the poisonous quality of many medicines denies their beneficial use against disease. Schell's argument that retaliation in planetary doses deprives deterrence of its purpose is of the same intellectual quality as the objections once heard against the use of fluoride in the water supply, which were motivated by the discovery that the chemical in question can kill—in large doses.

Deterrence does not rest on the theoretical ultimate of all-out population destruction. Whether nuclear or not, the workings of deterrence depend on threats of punishment that others will find believable. This requires that the act of retaliation be in itself purposeful, and less catastrophic rather than more. And indeed, contrary to what Schell and many others believe, the nuclear arsenals have become steadily *less* destructive than they used to be, as weapons have become more accurate. The total megatonnage of our strategic nuclear forces is nowadays perhaps one-tenth of what it was twenty years ago.

Thus, the entirety of Schell's argument rests on a logical fallacy. But what in a moral context is a good deal more serious is that Schell and his followers are in practice indifferent to the prospect of a large and very destructive non-nuclear European war. For such a war is the likely outcome of any prolonged "freeze," because a decline in nuclear deterrent forces would be inevitable, as worn-out weapons are not replaced; and without nuclear deterrence, great-power politics would resume as before 1945. Looking back on the events of the last generation, with its many and dangerous crises, it is impossible to believe that another world war could have been avoided had it not been for the terror that nuclear weapons inspire. Thus in practice Schell is ready to see untold numbers of Europeans suffer and die in countries ruined by the smashing advance of Soviet armor and by the blasting of great artillery barrages, just so long as those barrages remain non-nuclear.

In the crowds that march behind Schell's banner, many know so little of all such matters that their views do not warrant serious discussion. Many others will candidly acknowledge the abstract merit of the counterarguments, but will nevertheless assert that they have made their own incontrovertible choice. Rather than *risk* in any smallest way their own lives and those of their children in a nuclear conflict, however improbable, they are in fact prepared to see others and their children die in large numbers and by a certain outcome.

Those who thus frankly admit that they would abandon all the nations that now rely on our nuclear enhancement for their security, even if much war and much death would inevitably result, are the more honest members of the anti-nuclear camp. They have no moral pretensions and no shame to drive them into hypocrisy and false argument. But what are all those rabbis and priests, pastors and bishops, doing with them, standing in their crowds singing their songs? By what doctrine of theology, by what theory of morality, by what rule of ethics is it decreed that the small risk of nuclear war is a greater evil than the virtual certainty of the large-scale death in great-power wars no longer deterred?

The offense of the anti-nuclear churchmen is not strategical error but rather a brutal attack upon the most elementary principle of morality, the most basic of religious prescriptions, by which Rabbi Hillel once summarized the entirety of the Bible: what is hateful to you, do not do unto others. The intellectual terrorism of Jonathan Schell's book notwithstanding, nuclear weapons have no special quality, either in morality or in theology, that would invalidate the elementary calculus of good and evil.

• • •

The time has come to deal forthrightly with the anti-nuclear agitation. To do as the Reagan administration has done, to concede and appease, is highly dangerous. Because if the false argument is admitted, sound strategy is thereby delegitimized and then in due course policies of weakness will inevitably follow through congressional decision and public pressure.

If, for example, the Bundy-Kennan-McNamara-Smith proposal is accepted on the argument that it is good public relations to do so, and that only a verbal change would be involved, it will soon be discovered that once NATO's "first-use" policy is renounced it will be impossible to obtain approval for the upkeep of battlefield nuclear weapons. Why, it will be said, should we keep those nuclear-capable guns so near the border if we no longer seek to deter a non-nuclear invasion by nuclear deterrence? Thus the nuclear shells of the artillery will be withdrawn—they being the smallest of our nuclear weapons, and yet very likely the most powerful for deterrence because of their immediacy and the circumscribed effect that makes use credible.

Similarly, if the principle of arms-control negotiations for this or that class of weapons is once accepted, actually for purposes of public relations but ostensibly for the sake of peace and survival, how will the demand for more concessions be resisted? After all, it will be said, what petty diplomatic concern, what minor strategic advantage, is more important than peace and survival? Not to stand and assert the truth in the war of ideas means to suffer delegitimization now, and then eventual defeat in the practical realms of policy and strategy.

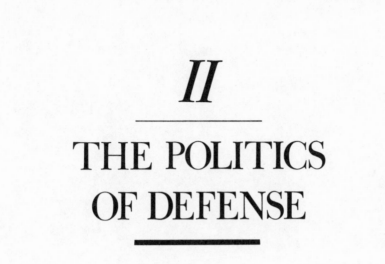

II

THE POLITICS
OF DEFENSE

5

C H A P T E R

WHY WE NEED MORE "WASTE, FRAUD & MISMANAGEMENT" IN THE PENTAGON

*I*n its revised budget the Reagan administration requested $214.1 billion for defense in the current (1982) fiscal year. Among those who object, some columnists and many TV personalities, full-time defense critics, disarmers, isolationists, and "concerned" churchmen and academics remain blessedly ignorant of the full dimensions of the Soviet military upsurge and of our own weakness. Others, who do have some fair notion of how the military balance stands, simply believe that the United States should be content with weakness, for that too can ensure a kind of peace. And then there is the George F. Kennan school of thought, which still refuses to recognize the profile of a classic military empire in the Soviet Union of our days, and which holds that we should not oppose Soviet aims because they are merely "defensive," as in Afghanistan for instance (Kennan's own chosen example).

Of all the odd spectacles of our intellectual scene none is so dispiriting as the widespread respect still accorded to Kennan's view, for it is the theory of a historian and yet one which can be persuasive only to those who are wholly ignorant of history. *All* great empires expand "defensively," their last conquest being necessary to shield their penultimate acquisition. That Roman aims were always defensive, from the first conquest of the Latium (to protect Rome itself) until the final sallies into Scotland and eastern Mesopotamia, is a mere commonplace; and it was the same "defensive" necessity that induced the British to expand their Indian empire, with the North-West Frontier being reluctantly occupied to protect the Punjab, just as the Punjab had been regretfully annexed to shield Rajaputana and the Sind, and they in turn had unwillingly been taken earlier, to provide defensive depth for what had been occupied earlier still.

Exactly the same sequence of defensive expansion has brought the Russians to invade Afghanistan—and now the Russians find their latest conquest insecure because of trouble that comes from across the frontier . . . just as, before the invasion, the violent popular resistance to the Russian-made Communist government in Kabul was making Soviet Central Asia insecure. This "defensive" expansion of the one great military empire of our days—which also happens to be the largest empire of all history—will quite obviously leave no country in a state of safety, except possibly New Zealand (and perhaps not even it, there being a latent territorial dispute over the Antarctic).

For practical politicians who must seek electoral support and who also oppose a serious level of defense spending, neither an obstinate denial of the need—against all the evidence—nor elegant obfuscation in the Kennan style will do the trick. Unlike many would-be experts, and the "concerned" this-and-that, a net majority of the American voting public understands far too much about the military balance and its consequences to tolerate an overt refusal to restore our strength before it is too late. The electors who replaced Jimmy Carter with Ronald Reagan did not do so for the sake of supply-side economics, but rather because having once known an America that was strong, and having seen the bitter consequences of a foreign policy of weakness, they decided that strength was after all far better than weakness.

Few indeed are the voters who can knowledgeably compare the intercontinental nuclear forces of the two sides, or those of continental range for that matter. But many can sense that Soviet conduct nowadays has become much more daring and more dangerous, because our long-standing superiority in those forces has been lost. Only the expert can estimate in detail the implications of a conventional balance in which the Soviet Union can spare as many as forty divisions for offensive war on a new front—*after* securing both its European and its Chinese frontiers—while we for our part would have no more than four or five divisions that could be sent to stop them. But again, the public understands what it must, namely, that the Soviet Union can now change the world map by war, and that we would have great difficulty in doing anything to stop its expansion, even if it happened to be vitally necessary to do so. Similarly, one does not need high skills in operational research to evaluate what the Soviet navy's 110 nuclear attack submarines and 198 diesel boats could do to our diminished fleet, and what that in turn means for our power—which must reach across the oceans to be effective at all.

Since the public understands so much about our military predicament and its broad meaning, the politicians who still desire to oppose our belated rearmament must now do so in camouflage. Hence their pious insistence that they fully support a strong national defense, and that they merely object to "waste, fraud, and mismanagement" in the Pentagon.

There is no doubt whatever that some defense spending is wasted, and that there is some mismanagement—and it would be astonishing if there were no fraud at all when so many billions change hands for the purchase of a million different things. Nevertheless, when a politician nowadays wants to cut the defense budget on the ground that it is the waste, fraud, and mismanagement that he really wants to cut, an informed public should see through the deception easily enough.

In the first place, the necessary detail is missing. We are not told where the waste and the rest occur—something that would be of great interest to the secretary of defense and his men, to Congress, to the General Accounting Office, and to the Office of Management and Budget.

Secondly, we have every reason to believe that the total amount of money that is wasted, mismanaged, or defrauded is very small— that is to say, it is small by the standards of government.

As numerous investigations have shown, the Defense Department and the armed forces are already subject to much tighter financial controls than the various health and welfare programs that nowadays account for a much larger share of the federal budget. (Defense now accounts for *one-fifth* of total public spending.) Contractors who sell products or services to the Pentagon are subject to the relentless scrutiny of an army of accountants and investigators, both civilian and military. Even in contracts that run to the billions, each outlay of a few hundred dollars will promptly be investigated if ground for suspicion arises. Nothing of the dimensions of the various medical-aid scandals would be possible, and such cases of fraud as have been uncovered are mostly very minor affairs involving marginalia like PX outlets and sergeants' messes. Thus it is not by accident, as *Pravda* would put it, that all the loose talk about fraud in defense spending is rarely decorated with any case histories.

• • •

Mismanagement, of course, is another matter, a question of opinion rather than law. When is it sensible to call off a development program for a new weapon that will not work? When should a shipyard be written off as unfit to do its work? When should an aircraft project whose cost keeps growing be stopped? In retrospect, to be sure, the answer is easy. A certain project having failed, one can go back a long way in its history to detect the point when the inevitability of failure should have been recognized. But that is not how matters would have looked at the time, when one could easily believe that a little more effort would cure the problem.

If one surveys, for example, the prolonged agonies of the first *Ohio*-class ("Trident") missile submarine which the Electric Boat Division of General Dynamics has finally managed to complete in its Groton, Connecticut, shipyard, years behind schedule, it seems obvious that the navy would have been better off in financing the creation of a whole new shipyard somewhere else, and under different management. But when the "Trident" submarine program was first started, the Electric Boat shipyard at Groton was the obvious, indeed inevitable, candidate for the job, since the only other shipyard with recent nuclear-submarine experience was already fully employed. Certainly the navy could not have anticipated the many problems that were to arise in the future, and all the many technical obstacles that would be encountered in the attempt to build the largest submarine ever, which was also supposed to be the quietest, and very fast too.

What happened at Groton during the years when the *Ohio* was being built has provided material for a number of major investigations by Congress, and for several journalistic exposés. The episode is indeed deserving of much scrutiny because it seems that all the dysfunctions of our society were visited upon the unfortunate shipyard: the overall decline in educational standards, which produced young workers with high-school diplomas but no literacy or numeracy; the influx of inexperienced women and minority workers that federal regulations imposed on the shipyard; the further decline in the quality of our industrial manpower brought about by the "dropping out" syndrome, and the furious quest for "meaningful" jobs; the deindustrialization caused by the inadequacy of savings and investment, and by clean-air and other novel restrictions which have forced hundreds of small casting and forging shops out of business; and finally the fiscal and legal complexities created by a legislative process itself dominated by lawyers and accountants, which favors the large multipurpose conglomerate with its own full staff of lawyers and accountants as opposed to the smaller specialized company with real industrial expertise—for one aspect of the whole sad story was that the Groton Yard passed from the control of shipbuilders (Electric Boat) to that of a conglomerate (General Dynamics) whose managers applied business-school techniques where craft and experience were needed.

The fact remains, however, that as the literature on the affair itself testifies, the *Ohio* case is more exception than norm in our defense purchasing, the result of a rare conjunction between the most complicated weapon ever built and an exceptionally troubled contractor.

What passes for mismanagement in the common discourse of our press is often nothing more than inflation. Those who indulge their eloquence so greatly in mourning the "cost overruns" that have attended virtually every major weapon procurement of the last decade make great play of the combat aircraft that was supposed to cost $10 million and which comes in at $20 million, and point to the $2-million battle tank that was originally presented to Congress as an "austere" design for half that price—as if our grocery bills and our houses had not undergone a similar explosion in price over the same span of years.

• • •

There is, of course, the entirely distinct complaint that even without any irregularities to add to the bill, our weapons simply cost too much because their design is overambitious (or "gold-plated," as the jargon goes). Some in the "military-reform" movement, a loose gathering of strategic and technical experts as well as a number of congressmen specializing in defense issues, have a straightforward solution for this problem. They advocate a general return to simplicity on the grounds that in real-life combat, sheer numbers count for more than unit quality, and that in any case the complexity of many weapons has become so great that they will not function properly in the harsh conditions of a real war.

Hence these "reformers" call for the production of small, one-seater fighter aircraft without radars or other complicated devices, which might cost $4 million each instead of $20 million; tanks that would be much lighter than the 50-ton M-1 and correspondingly cheaper; 2,000-ton destroyers in lieu of the 8,000-ton ships now being built; smaller non-nuclear carriers for vertical takeoff aircraft instead of the 90,000-ton nuclear-powered supercarriers of the *Nimitz* class that cost more than $2.5 billion apiece; 1,000-ton diesel-electric submarines in place of the very large nuclear submarines now being built at a cost of almost $1 billion each; and so on.

What makes the argument for simplicity so powerful is that the real difference between the simpler weapons that the reformers advocate and the more complicated weapons now being built is very much greater than mere arithmetic would suggest. In the first place, at any one budget level one can obviously buy many more of the simpler weapons; with more units being produced, industry can then have long production runs so that great economies can be achieved in fabrication and assembly; and then in turn, a much higher proportion of the simpler weapons will actually be maintained and available at any one time, and thus ready for combat when they are needed.

For example, a billion dollars spent on a complicated fighter will pay for, say, forty aircraft, and in war one may obtain from them at most, say, eighty combat sorties a day (often fewer). But the same amount spent on a very simple jet fighter might purchase 200 aircraft; with maintenance being correspondingly easier, that second force could provide as many as 800 combat sorties a day. And it is obvious that in equal combat (i.e., in daylight and at close range) the force of complicated fighters would be easily defeated, since it would have to fight under a crushing numerical inferiority of one to ten in actual sorties flown—and then all its advantages would count for nought.

On the other hand, the great weakness of the "simplicity" argument is that against worthy opponents and in demanding circumstances, fighters that are blind in the dark and have only visual-range missiles, tanks that are too lightly armored to withstand the pounding of the enemy's fire, warships that lack electronic brains, eyes, and ears for long-range surveillance and strike, as well as aircraft carriers that cannot launch powerful aircraft and submarines that lack endurance, will all fail to meet the test of combat.

In some war situations, the 800 sorties of the "cheap" fighter force would indeed be much more useful than the 60–80 sorties that the long-range, multipurpose fighters could provide. This would be so, for example, in a Battle of Britain setting, featuring the large-scale encounter of hundreds of aircraft all flying from bases nearby, and all fighting in confused daylight mass engagement. In such conditions, the ability of the heavyweight high-cost fighter to make long transits to battle would count for nothing, and equally its ability to fire radar-guided missiles would be useless, since the impossibility of identifying friend and foe would impose the need for visual combat. But as soon as we change the setting and demand long-range transits to the area of combat (as in the case, for example, of a war in the Persian Gulf), or if advanced weapons are needed to shoot down Russian bombers a long way away before they can launch their own missiles, the "cheap" fighter is revealed as almost enti ely useless.

The same is true of all other manifestations of the simple weapon in whatever form. There is bound to be much overlap between the abilities of the complicated and costly weapon and those of its simple counterpart. If the specific form of combat corresponds to that area of capability where both kinds of weapons can be used, then the larger numbers of simple weapons will indeed prevail, as the "reformers" claim. But then there are the further areas of capability that only the more complicated weapons can offer. At that point there is no longer a contest to be evaluated at all, since the simple weapon is totally outmatched.

It might therefore seem that both kinds of weapons should always be bought, and there is even a phrase in the jargon for such a practice, the "high-low mix." But the question cannot be resolved on technical and economic grounds alone, weapon by weapon, except in extreme cases—such as the weapon too complex to work at all, or too weak to survive in any combat whatever. The question is in fact strategic and one must begin at the beginning, in a consideration of national strategy. The right "high-low" mix for, say, Korea will not do for the United States, and vice versa, if only because American forces would almost everywhere fight alongside allies who are in place (often with large conscript forces), so that in general it is the allies who can best provide the numbers, while what they need from us is precisely the smaller high-quality force of special capabilities.

If this particular issue in our defense is pursued at all seriously, we find that only a fully strategical appraisal can yield a valid answer. Beginning at the level of *national* strategy, one must proceed level by level to the intended theater strategies, to the operational methods that are envisaged (do we fight the enemy in air combat, or do we attack the enemy's air power at its source, by attacking his airfields?), all the way down to the tactics of specific forces in particular situations. And the same, of course, is true of every other issue of significance, from the proper role of the Marine Corps to the proportion of our defense budgets that should be spent on intercontinental nuclear weapons.

• • •

This leads us to the third and most compelling reason for ignoring the politicians who campaign against "waste, fraud, and mismanagement." For there is indeed something wrong with our defense policy and with the workings of our armed forces, and what is wrong is very serious indeed. But far from being a failure to hunt out irregularities and waste, it is the very opposite. The obsessive attention now being devoted to micro-management is the root cause of an evil far greater than any marginal inefficiency or any thievery could possibly be. For it leads to the neglect of strategy, of the operational art of war, and of tactics. Our civilian defense leaders and our senior officers alike are systematically distracted from the pursuit that should be their dominant business by a wrongheaded quest for paper efficiencies and marginal savings.

Since too many of our military leaders share the national passion for technology and delude themselves that there is a "technical fix" for every tactical problem; since social pressures have forced the officer corps into a civilian mold, with the prescribed model being that of the bureaucrat-in-uniform; since antique fears have prevented the formation of a "general staff" dedicated to the serious planning and study of war; and since it remains the national illusion that smart lawyers and problem-solving pragmatism can do anything, circumstances are in any case most unfavorable for the serious pursuit of strategy. But it is the compulsion exercised upon the whole defense structure in the name of efficiency that finally strangles what potential there is for the pursuit of strategic wisdom, operational ingenuity, and tactical art.

Was it more important that the French before 1940 save 10 percent in building the fortifications of the Maginot Line, or would it have been more useful to consider—at the level of national strategy—whether a defensive orientation for the French army was compatible with a policy of alliance with the small powers around Germany—countries which would need the active protection of an offensive French army to protect France in turn? Was it more important to make sure that the most cost-effective of all guns were chosen for the forts of the line, or would it have been more productive—at the operational level—to consider what Panzer divisions, i.e., small groups of tanks spearheading truck columns, could do to French defenses if they found a gap to penetrate in depth? Was it more important that some Monsieur Dupont or other not steal a few bags of cement from the depot, or would it have been more fruitful to study—at the level of tactics—the problem of antitank defense, and to discover perhaps that antitank guns will destroy single tanks but will not defeat tank *forces* (the illusion of the 1930s) any more than the antitank missile can do so now (the illusion of the 1980s, and just as widely shared)?

Similarly, is our taxpayer better served by a saving of a few million dollars in the purchase of a particular kind of helicopter for the marine corps, or would the citizen in him benefit more from the development of an up-to-date operational method for the employment of our intervention forces as a whole? If so, perhaps we might win the next encounter, instead of staging a large-scale repetition of the Iran hostage-rescue attempt ("Desert One") with the Rapid Deployment Force. And so one could go on, in example after example, since the domination of micro-management is pervasive, and pervasively debilitating.

• • •

An objection will undoubtedly arise at this point. Why should proper bookkeeping detract from strategy? Why should the necessary management of our budget preclude the study of the different operational methods to be used in war? And why, finally, should the praiseworthy effort to minimize fraud interfere with the development of good tactics? After all, junior officials, clerks, accountants, bookkeepers, and investigators should take care of that sort of work, leaving all the higher civilian officials and the senior military officers free to attend to the strategical purpose of our forces and weapons.

Those who are spared from the knowledge of the real conditions under which the Department of Defense must operate, will find this objection compellingly plausible. From those who know better, it will evoke sardonic laughter or pleasurable fantasy. For the sad truth is that the attention of the senior figures in the Pentagon is monopolized by the mass of detail of the budget-making process itself, which runs right through the year in a perpetual cycle.

Each year by late January the budget must be presented to both houses of Congress; then the most senior civilian officials and many military officers will have to justify each item in elaborate presentations and argue many points in detail before the two major committees of each house and numerous subcommittees, in a process that continues for months. To prepare that January budget, each service branch and defense agency must sort out its own priorities several months in advance, and then present its budget proposal for detailed review again and again, before a multiplicity of internal authorities culminating in the Secretary of Defense himself. For each item requested, fully detailed justifications have to be prepared complete with the cost figures, the fullest possible exploration of all other possible alternatives, and detailed evaluations of the performance expected from whatever is being bought—and these justifications must themselves be reconciled and amended step by step going up from the branch or department level to the service or agency level, and then through the scrutiny of the Pentagon's "systems analysts," engineers, comptrollers, and lawyers. As this process unfolds, the Secretary of Defense, his deputy, and their staffs will be called upon to intervene at various levels before presiding formally over the final decision—when each major item must be reviewed once again if internal disagreements persist, as they often do.

Since Congress will eventually examine each line of the budget in great detail with its own very large staff of experts, lawyers, analysts, and accountants (with major items being further investigated by the General Accounting Office, the Congressional Budget Office, and even the Office of Technology Assessment), there is a most powerful pressure on the Pentagon to pursue efficiency, and to minimize "waste, fraud, and mismanagement" by the most minute scrutiny of every single item.

Congressional oversight there must be, but as it now operates, Congress offers no rewards whatever for tactical or operational innovation or for the development of a better strategy, while it penalizes most severely any error in micro-management. By the logic of the situation, and also because of the personal inclination of most congressmen and their staffs, the whole focus of the review to which the Pentagon's budget is subjected in the Armed Services and Appropriations Committees of each house (and their numerous subcommittees) is on the cost-accounting and legal details rather than on the purpose and meaning of our defense decisions. Five minutes of desultory conversation on the role of destroyer-sized warships in the present era of seapower may be followed by hundreds of hours of discussion on the merits of purchasing some weapon or other that is to be aboard a particular class of destroyers.

It is the great peculiarity of strategy that its issues can only be understood as a whole, that is, when matters are viewed in the broadest possible perspective—even if thereby the lesser detail is overlooked. But the nice young men and women who fill the greatly enlarged committee and personal staffs are not strategists, and they have found employment for themselves in arguing chosen points in minute detail and in trying to impose their own pet ideas, so that the Pentagon's senior officials, military officers, and civilian experts must be in attendance at hearings that go on for weeks on end, and sometimes for months. Even so, the Pentagon's decisions are not infrequently rejected, with staffs imposing their own judgments even in matters exceedingly technical.[1] Inevitably, the knowledge that all these courts are waiting to judge its work affects the Pentagon most profoundly, and indeed it has been the decisive impulse in the gradual absorption of all energies in the budget-making routine itself.

• • •

The Pentagon's priorities are certainly "distorted," then, just as the critics claim, but not in favor of waging war, preferably nuclear, at the slightest excuse. They are distorted rather in favor of micromanagement for the sake of civilian efficiency, as opposed to military effectiveness—a thing altogether different. The great irony is that the defense establishment is under constant pressure to maximize efficiency, and that its own leaders earnestly believe in that goal, when all along they ought to be striving to achieve military effectiveness, a condition usually associated with the deliberate acceptance of inefficiency.

Consider the divergence between efficiency and effectiveness in the employment of military manpower. Efficiency dictates that each individual should serve where his individual skills are most productive. Thus, for example, if we discover three gunners too many in one tank battalion and a shortage of the same kind of gunner in another battalion, we should promptly reassign the three men to the latter. Similarly, if we discover that one company is somewhat overstrength while another is short of men, we should immediately move the bodies around from one to the other to achieve efficiency. Then, too, one-soldier efficiency calls for the frequent removal of men from their units to attend skill-enhancing courses of all kinds. As for the reserves, efficiency prescribes that men be kept in reinforcement "pools" for individual assignment.

But an army's companies and battalions are not production units. Their goal is not to make the most efficient use of their equipment

---

[1] E.g., for Fiscal 1982 the House Appropriations Committee recommended inter alia that the Air Force not proceed with parts replacement for the J57 engine for the KC-135 tanker; instead it proposed that JT3D engines be purchased until GE/SNECMA CM56 engines become available.

but rather to fight—and men will not fight unless they are motivated in combat by the cohesion built up through the slow growth of comradeship and small-group solidarity. Military effectiveness therefore requires us to tolerate all manner of inefficiencies in order to keep the men together for as long as possible.

All who know anything at all about the essential nature of warfare will know that much; and indeed the vital necessity of achieving cohesion by forming fighting men into stable and intimate groups was already old hat by the time of the Romans—and was even given actual statistical proof more than a generation ago. But our "manpower managers" do not seem to know this, even though they are serving officers. Their pursuit of one-soldier efficiency (along with short volunteer enlistments and too many course assignments) has been keeping our forces in a crippling state of turbulence, which means that our soldiers are condemned to live among shifting bands of strangers—an environment that alienates, and which positively encourages violence and outright crime. Moreover, training becomes repetitive and boring for those few who do serve longer in a unit, since the same routines have to be practiced over and again every few months, to train the influx of new arrivals. In combat the price to be paid must be much higher.[2]

Quite recently, the Chief of Staff of the Army, General E. C. Meyer, reinvented this particular wheel, and has instituted daring new practices whose aim is to keep soldiers together longer, in units that would be more stable—not without encountering much resistance from those who decry the inefficiency that will inevitably result.

The conflict between civilian efficiency and military effectiveness is so pervasive that it even applies to defense production where, one would think, efficiency should indeed be the only true guide. But consider a common case. Two firms are competing for a weapon-production contract on the usual basis, that is, cost plus fee. One firm is highly efficient: its floor-space is just about the right size, and all its machine tools will be fully utilized by working three shifts

---

[2] *In Vietnam, a feckless military leadership was content to treat the fighting units as mere organizational aggregates filled by an endlessly rotating flow of individuals each serving his own twelve months—so that our soldiers were asked to fight and die among strangers. Considering this atrocious practice, what is amazing is that the troops fought at all, not that there were some desertions or acts of violent indiscipline. In the Iranian rescue attempt the fundamental error was willfully repeated. In that parody of a commando operation, men of four different services were involved (army, air force, navy, and marine corps)— when serious planners would have hesitated greatly before even mixing the men of two different companies from the same battalion.*

around the clock. The second firm is just as obviously inefficient: it is burdened by excessive capacity and it would work only one shift on the expensive machinery. Under present efficiency criteria, the first company will undoubtedly get the contract. But what happens if we actually *need* the equipment, that is to say, if we find ourselves at war? Then, surely, we would wish that we had given the contract to the second, "inefficient" producer, keeping it in business, for the latter would have an inherent industrial-mobilization potential in all that extra floor space and under-utilized machinery. As it is, the greatest weakness of our overefficient military-industrial complex is precisely that we lack the ability to expand production quickly enough to meet the needs of a war situation—and even in a very short war we would need to produce such things as torpedoes and tactical missiles, to reload all those expensive submarines, ships, and aircraft. At present our stocks are absurdly small,[3] and our industrial-mobilization potential is minimal.

• • •

But the crucial divergence between efficiency and effectiveness is most clearly manifest when we consider the central question of how the armed forces should be structured and equipped. Efficiency demands homogeneity and commonality, as opposed to what congressmen would decry as wasteful diversity and duplication. Thus in the pursuit of mythical economies of scale and irrelevant efficiencies, our air force and navy have repeatedly been pressed to accept a single standard fighter aircraft, even though the specific effectiveness of both the air force and navy fighters would thereby be lost. In this one case, narrow-minded bureaucratic impulses have served us well (the "common" fighter yet remains to be seen), but the pursuit of standardization in combat units and in equipment has otherwise done much harm, by restricting our combat repertoires (we have no mountain infantry and no arctic infantry, although each is needed), and by depriving us of the safety against technical countermeasures that only a diversity of equipment can provide.

Compare, for example, our antiaircraft forces with those of the Soviet Union. We equip all our ground forces with only one type of antiaircraft gun, one type of shoulder-fired antiaircraft missile, and just one type of full-size missile, which is supposed to intercept enemy aircraft in a wide band of altitudes, from the very low to the

[3] *In 1973 the Israelis seeking emergency resupply could not believe how little we had in hand. Since then, underestimated budgets have continued to be balanced during the fiscal year by cuts in the purchase of ordnance and ammunition, and our stocks of such "consumables" remain very small.*

medium-high. The Russians, by contrast, have a wide variety of antiaircraft guns and missiles, each specialized in some way or other, with the low-altitude SAM-7s, SAM-8s, SAM-9s and SAM-10s, the high-altitude SAM-2s and SAM-5s, and medium-altitude SAM-3s, SAM-4s, and SAM-6s. Our efficiency-oriented defense establishment, which has been spending vast sums for a decade to develop a truly optimal, all-purpose missile ("Patriot"), would recoil in horror before such wasteful diversity, and our congressional committees would never for a moment tolerate the gross inefficiency of all those different weapons and launchers, each of which requires its own expensive stock of spare parts and its own costly training and maintenance provisions.

But now consider not peacetime efficiency but rather effectiveness in combat. The Russian pilot who has to cope with our one missile may save himself if he has the right package of radar countermeasures, or else if he can fly too low for its specifications, or too high. But the American pilot is faced by a bewildering variety of weapons and has little chance indeed of evading them all. Even with the best of countermeasures he is not safe, since there are just too many different radar devices working against him, and some of the Russian missiles are guided by heat-seeking sensors, or even by plain visual guidance. And neither can the American pilot hope to fly high enough or low enough to evade the whole array of weapons, since with such diversity the Russians can have a missile specialized for very high altitudes, as well as shoulder-fired SAM-7s, various cannon, and a vast number of simple antiaircraft machine guns, which threaten even the pilot who dares to fly at treetop height.

Bookkeeping is one thing and strategy another—and we have too much of one and too little of the other. For example, "interservice rivalries" have given us three quite different aircraft for the close air-support role: the army's attack helicopter, the air force's A-10 (grossly overdesigned but still useful), and the marine's vertical takeoff Harrier. Instead of appreciating the value of this diversity for different terrains and different enemies, many in Congress are campaigning against the "wasteful duplication" of the three aircraft.

One could go on in this vein, but it should by now be obvious that the contradiction between civilian efficiency and military effectiveness is truly fundamental. The former belongs to the world of cooperative and constructive things, and is guided by the pursuit of optimality under benign assumptions (design a car that will work off the road, at extreme heights and in extreme weathers, and whatever else it may do it will not be fuel-efficient). The latter, by contrast, belongs to the world of conflict, where things must work under great stress (to go from A to B is easy enough, until one must do so under fire), and where above all there is an active will systematically seeking to undo all that one tries to achieve.

It is only when we fully recognize this central fact that the enormity of the defect built into our system of defense can be recognized. Under the pressure of a vast congregation of external agencies, of which Congress itself is only the most important; and under the internal pressure of civilian officials who know not war and think that it is reducible to economics, as well as of "demilitarized" military men who have lost sight of the essentials of their profession, our Defense Department and the armed forces themselves are not merely distracted from the large issues of strategy by the petty questions of micro-management, but they are in addition directed to pursue the wrong goal, namely, civilian efficiency. It is not surprising to find, therefore, that the best of our forces are precisely those which are most obdurately traditional and least "intellectual" (such as the marine corps in general and parts of the army). For they have been the least affected by those pressures, and by the advent of "systems analysis," which in effect institutionalizes the fatal displacement of war effectiveness by mere efficiency. In the meantime, while so much attention is given to the 5 percent or 10 percent that efficiency issues define (and that wrongly), the core questions that only strategy can answer continue to be neglected—and they of course determine the utility of our entire effort.

II

One need not at this late stage belabor the poverty of our strategy—which after all reflects our beneficial national emphasis on individualism and welfare. Nor can we repudiate our preference for one-thing-at-a-time pragmatism, which indeed works so well for us in most areas of life, with strategy being almost alone in requiring the contrary method. But even if our nation is too constructive to be greatly strategical, even if we are too happy and too safe to devote earnest attention to the uses of force in peace and in war, there is a minimum of strategic competence that we must attain, and unfortunately we have not achieved even that for a long time.

It is, for example, amazing to contemplate the fact that we have not managed to frame a naval strategy worthy of the name now that the Soviet Union is actively challenging our ability to use the oceans in the event of war. In the pronouncements of our naval leaders one finds, to be sure, the odd reference to Mahan's works and to his central theory—fittingly enough a theory long ago refuted. One finds also the frequent reiteration of the obvious: that sea transport remains indispensable for the United States since the American continent is bounded by wide oceans, while air transport can carry only small quantities (the entire 1973 airlift to Israel delivered less than one fair-sized ship could have done). But after that, what passes for "strategy" comes to an end, and there are only long lists of *desiderata* in the way of men and machines.

None of this can tell us what we urgently need to know: how can the United States recover that genuine naval supremacy which is one of the premises of our entire world policy? Since our chief antagonist on the planet happens to be lodged in the core of Eurasia, and does not strictly need to use the oceans while we must cross them to protect our vital interests, it is a true, outright supremacy that we need: anything less would mean defeat.

But we cannot hope to regain our naval power just by building ships. It is so much easier to deny the use of the sea than to assure safe passage that for each unit of resources the Soviet navy spends we might have to spend ten or more. It is only by strategy that the unfavorable exchange can be avoided—just as the British so successfully did. Since our naval personalities are fond of evoking the memory of Britain's once decisive naval supremacy, they might usefully begin to learn its real lessons. What Mahan celebrated in his well-wrought prose was not the true mechanism that made Britain supreme at sea but merely its visible result—a superioï fleet. Submarines aside, the superior force of battleships could indeed, by definition, keep the enemy's battleships impotent in port or sink them if they ventured out. Thus the enemy's cruisers could not challenge British cruisers for fear of the battleships. And the cruisers could in turn keep the enemy's destroyers from operating, so that finally a few British destroyers actually at sea would easily suffice to impose a stringent blockade on the enemy, even while Britain's own oceanic traffic would continue unmolested.

Until the advent of the submarine, the architecture of naval power that Mahan described was valid, and his work was useful insofar as it explained clearly why the handful of big battleships would actually make all the difference even if they remained in port, totally inactive throughout a conflict. But Mahan missed the fundamental point. How did Britain acquire its superior battle fleet in the first place? Certainly it was not by an economic superiority, for otherwise the era of British naval supremacy would have lasted a mere fraction of its long span, those few years when their early progress in the industrial revolution could actually have allowed the British to outbuild any European coalition ranged against them.

The true source of British naval supremacy, which Mahan missed, holds a lesson that is still valid for us. It was the statecraft that kept the major powers of Europe divided into hostile camps which made Britain supreme at sea, because the high cost of the Europeans' large armies precluded the building of powerful navies too. It was the ceaseless effort of diplomacy, the subsidies, the small but disruptive interventions, the bribes—and the willingness to change sides if their own allies became too powerful—that made the British so powerful at sea, and not the mere building of ships. (There was also a further and long-lived triumph of public relations in the successful advertisement of this policy as the "maintenance of the balance of power"—a phrase with benign connotations of parity and fairness which usefully disguised a policy that amounted to the stimulation of perpetual conflict.)

• • •

Needless to say, we cannot directly copy the British method, for neither our NATO allies nor the Chinese (let alone the Japanese) will seriously challenge the Russians on land and in the air to the point where they would have to restrict drastically their naval expenditures to pay for all else. But there is an alternative in our own domain, upon which a serious naval strategy might be soundly based.

Ever since 1945 the understandable Russian emphasis on the protection of the homeland from air attack has been manifest in the willingness to allocate huge resources for strategic air defenses. Our bomber forces of the 1940s, 50s, and 60s were not cheap for us, but it is safe to estimate that for every dollar of resources that went into those forces the Russians spent four or five times as much, for thousands of fighter-interceptors, elaborate radar networks spanning perimeters of thousands of miles, more than 12,000 anti-aircraft missiles, and countless guns. But from the mid-1960s our bomber force has continued to decline in numbers, and in 1972, through the ABM treaty, we ourselves precluded a most useful drain on Russian resources. In the futile attempt to build defenses against ballistic missiles, the Russians would undoubtedly have spent vast resources which have gone instead into forces much more threatening to us, and notably their navy. Acting in a fashion wholly unstrategical, we pursued for two decades the mirage of "strategic parity," losing in the process the very great reciprocal force-building advantage that the Russian propensity to defend their airspace was giving us.

Now that we are building a new bomber at long last, as well as developing the yet more advanced "stealth" aircraft, and also deploying large numbers of cruise missiles, we have an excellent opportunity to rekindle the Russian interest in strategic air defenses—although it is only the abrogation of the ABM treaty that would give us the more powerful benefit of diverting really huge Russian resources into ballistic-missile defenses.

Since even for a Soviet Union that has finally become a military empire there are limits on the proportion of total resources that can be allocated to the armed forces; since the Soviet economy no longer grows at all rapidly; and since strategic defense has the highest priority while the Soviet navy must have the lowest, there is every reason to believe that an energetic buildup in our own strategic-offensive forces would result in a sharp decline in the resources given over to the Soviet navy.

What this means for our naval strategy is obvious enough. The key to the restoration of our supremacy is not to outbuild the Russians but to force them to build less altogether, since we must now spend several dollars for every dollar-equivalent spent on the Soviet navy (whose role of sea denial is naturally much easier than our role of sea control), while, on the other hand, every dollar spent on bombers and strategic missiles is likely to take away several dollar-equivalents of resources from the Soviet navy.

Again, it is no accident that the appearance of substantially more ambitious and costly ships in the Soviet navy (such as the *Kiev* aircraft carriers, the *Kirov* nuclear-powered cruiser, and the huge *Oscar* cruise-missile submarine) followed, with the usual ten-year building lags, our own disastrous renunciation of the competition in strategic-nuclear weapons—the one area of armaments where we have an inherent comparative advantage. And if we now want to recover that naval supremacy which remains indispensable, we have no other way to follow than the British scheme in a modern guise. But that is not the strategy we are offered; there is instead a call for a "600-ship navy" on the ground that our present "460-ship" navy does not suffice. There is no doubt whatever that we need more ships, but to ask for numbers in so vapid a fashion only invites the still more vapid suggestion that we mass-produce large numbers of small ships. That would indeed be appropriate if our purpose were to defend our coasts or even shipping at sea. But it is not by small ships that our naval supremacy can be restored; it is only by forces so clearly dominant that they do not have to defend at all—and that is something that only a reciprocal strategy can achieve.

Those who know our navy and are familiar with its relentlessly institutional outlook may regard with amusement the implied prescription that our naval leaders should themselves proclaim a strategy under which bombers and strategic missiles would have first priority—if need be at the expense of their very own ships. One may likewise doubt that the admirals of the Royal Navy in its great days ever understood why the Crown's ministers were so generous in offering British gold to foreign kings or even Spanish peasants in revolt, while being so miserly in outfitting their own ships. But then the Way of Strategy is not given to all—and certainly not to those who would approach its truths from the perspective of a narrow-minded bureaucratic interest.

• • •

Now that the United States faces a strategic predicament of unprecedented difficulty, partly because of the pervasive effect of our loss of nuclear superiority, and partly because the Soviet Union has leapfrogged the boundaries of containment with its array of long-range intervention forces, and client troops, and with its outposts of aggression in Cuba, South Yemen, Vietnam, and Angola, the time has finally come when we can no longer get by unless we can devise truly strategical solutions, not only for our naval problem but for all our most pressing security problems. The simple, straightforward "logistic" approach followed since 1941, whereby all threats were to be defeated by mustering a sheer superiority in matériel and firepower, can only now guarantee defeat in the face of an opponent that can outgun us in all areas of the world adjacent to its territory.

In the Persian Gulf, for example, the full consequences of being greatly outnumbered are now upon us. By conservative estimates, the Soviet Union could employ twenty-five divisions in a move to the sea across Iran. Assuming ample warning,[4] we could respond with a maximum of four divisions. It will be understood, of course, that the reality of Soviet intentions, whatever that may be, is scarcely relevant. Our problem would remain even if it could somehow be shown that not one member of the Politburo has ever suggested any move against the Gulf. For unless we can credibly counter the potential threat, it can all too easily become actual. And should the So-

---

[4] Which would be forthcoming only if the Soviet army chose to recall reservists to fill the ranks of the divisions already deployed nearby, as opposed to leading the advance with full-strength divisions brought in from elsewhere.

viet Union reach the Gulf it would *ipso facto* obtain control over the flow of oil from Saudi Arabia, Kuwait, Qatar, and the rest. Those countries are not our allies but only our clients, and just as they look to us for protection now, they would promptly offer their clientship to the Russians, if Soviet power advanced to their doorstep across Iran uncontested by us. Since most nations in Western Europe, as well as Japan, Korea, and Taiwan, cannot do without the oil of Arabia, there would be little point in defending the security perimeters of Europe and East Asia if the Soviet Union were allowed to gain effective control over their oil supplies. In other words, the entire structure of Western security would be subverted by the extension of Soviet power to the Persian Gulf.

In such circumstances, it is essential that we ensure that the region is well protected, and we certainly cannot risk our great stake on the presumption that for some reason or other the Soviet Union will refrain from doing what it could now do so easily. To be sure, some insist that the Russians will do nothing in Iran because they already have their hands full in Afghanistan. But one statistic suffices to demolish that theory, with its implied comparison between our own ruinous war in Vietnam and the leisurely imperial pacification now unfolding in Afghanistan: the ground forces now in Afghanistan amount to 2 *percent* of the Soviet total.

In the event of a Soviet invasion of Iran, the obvious and necessary American response would be to establish coastal lodgments on the Iranian shore of the Gulf, with a forward shield in the long chain of Zagros mountains beyond the coast. But how can we make such a move with any confidence when our maximum of four divisions would have to face an offensive of twenty-five?

Characteristically, there is nothing new about this imbalance of forces. Given the geographic advantage of the Soviet Union and its long-standing possession of an army much larger than our own, the ratio of forces would have been just as adverse ten, twenty, or thirty years ago. The great difference, however, is that we cannot any longer seriously rely on nuclear deterrence—which in the past would alone have sufficed to make a Soviet invasion unthinkable. Moreover, we have lost the further advantages of an uncontested naval supremacy and of a crushing air superiority—which we would certainly have had ten, twenty, and thirty years ago.

True, our surface naval force could still clear the seas of any Soviet forces afloat (thanks to the much-criticized large aircraft carriers). But the navy's ability to help out on land by giving air support is now prejudiced by the threat of missile attacks launched from Soviet long-range aircraft, and even more by the Soviet sub-marine fleet—these twin threats making all combat deployment in the region hazardous, and prohibitively so within the Gulf itself. Similarly, our first-line air force fighters still retain a wide margin of advantage in air combat, and given adequate bases nearby they could keep Soviet fighter-bombers from harming our ground troops. But again our airpower could not provide prompt, positive help for the ground battle because of the great strength of the Soviet anti-aircraft units that would accompany each army formation. Our own ground forces have traditionally relied on powerful air support to make brute-force firepower tactics work, but in fighting the Soviet army little of it would be forthcoming—unless and until the Soviet air defenses were first suppressed in a preliminary campaign.

• • •

Some will argue that we need not worry any further about the im-balance of forces and the resulting strategic and tactical problems. Any combat with the Soviet army, some will say, would very quickly turn into a nuclear war, eventually intercontinental with weapons launched homeland-to-homeland until terminal destruction.

It is odd that those who dismiss the need to confront this and many other military problems by evoking the inevitability of a global nuclear war if any conflict occurs at all, still think of themselves as fervent advocates of peace and humanity. For in refusing to sanc-tion an adequate effort in conventional defense they are in effect ad-vocating our own immediate resort to nuclear weapons—which may indeed put us on the path to mass destruction.

Then there are those who believe—or affect to believe—that we need not prepare seriously for non-nuclear war with the Russians because they themselves would begin using nuclear weapons right away. It is certainly true that Soviet forces include nuclear weapons down to rather low echelons. But if it were their intention to fight us by tactical nuclear weapons from the very outset of a war, why do the Russians make the vast effort of updating and expanding their conventional forces?

The strategy that one may properly infer from the current pattern of Soviet force-building does not suggest an "all-nuclear" war scheme but precisely the opposite: the increasingly powerful intercontinen-tal nuclear weapons of the Soviet Union are meant primarily to in-hibit any use of our own. Similarly the greatly enhanced theater and tactical nuclear weapons are intended to deny us any resort to those weapons in protecting interests overseas. And finally, the Soviet Union's superior ground forces are to fight and win without having to rely on nuclear weapons themselves, while we for our part can no longer defeat them by air power or appeal to the "higher court" of nuclear weapons. Only this aim can explain the rapid (and very costly) upgrading of the Soviet conventional forces with much new equipment in a broad armament effort which has accompanied the equally impressive buildup in nuclear weaponry.[5]

These circumstances obviously call for a novel approach to the whole problem of defending Arabia and the Gulf. Since a conventional U.S.–style deployment of army and marine divisions would merely guarantee our eventual defeat by the sheer weight of numbers, we must either develop a novel theater-defense strategy based on drastically revised tactics, or else we must seek some indirect alternative, such as a naval offensive that would altogether remove the contest from a part of the world where the Soviet Union has the great advantage of a direct territorial contiguity.

Either solution calls for much concerted strategic thought and operational planning by senior civilian officials and military officers working in concert. For if one starts with the present tactical repertoire and takes it as the only possible set of tactics, it is impossible to construct a plausible strategy for a land defense. But on the other hand, the military hierarchy will not offer alternative tactics (such as, for example, a light-infantry mountain defense) unless a strategy is first formulated that demands those very tactics.

Conversely, for an indirect naval response (for which the desired tactical repertoire is already in place) it is the strategy of the option that must be fully explored in all ramifications, including for example the response of our allies. How would they react to a defense of their oil supplies, if it required us to launch a *worldwide* attack on Soviet naval power?

Perhaps such solutions are feasible and desirable and perhaps they are not. But we must find some solution, and that will not happen until we can go beyond the minutiae of micro-management to focus instead on the intricate dialogue between strategy and tactics. It so happens we do have some excellent tacticians in the army's Training and Doctrine command, but their novel ideas will not be

[5] *In the last ten years alone, we have seen the introduction of a whole new array of armored vehicles, the very expensive conversion of much Soviet artillery from classic towed pieces to self-propelled weapons, and the substantial (and especially costly) upgrading of anti-aircraft forces already very strong. In the air, the mass of cheap day fighters of the 1960s has been replaced by much more capable aircraft with considerable offensive potential.*

employed in our plans until that dialogue can uncover the new strategies which tactical innovation makes possible.

• • •

In theory we already have an institution dedicated entirely to such thinking and planning, the Joint Chiefs of Staff and their multiservice "joint" staff. But this organization embodies all the proclivities that one finds in an alliance of nations, whereby the severe choices that strategy imposes must always be compromised to accommodate a divergence of service interests. Officers detached for a tour in the joint staff from their parent service are under great pressure to take care of service interests in their work. After all, their career and promotion depend not on what they do for the Joint Chiefs, but what their own service thinks of them. Since every plan has some budgetary implications, since every force-decision and command arrangement will affect the bureaucratic interests of each service, obsessive attention is given to the allocation of fair shares for all. This is ruinous for our strategy. It precludes hard choices and all one-service solutions, even when these are most obviously needed.

Thus, for example, there is no reason why the Rapid Deployment Force should consist of units drawn from all four services under a multiservice command, with all the different layers of authority and all the complications thereby entailed—when in fact the marine corps alone could do the job, with other service elements attached if required, but under marine command. That would greatly simplify the conduct of war operations, but it would also of course deprive the army, air force, and navy of a high-visibility and budget-enhancing role (and of numerous billets for generals and admirals). The "joint" system could never sanction such a thing: regardless of the patriotism of its members, the *institutional* purpose is not to plan for victory but rather to reconcile interservice rivalries—at any price.

The natural consequence of doing things "jointly" is to degrade everything to the lowest common denominator, for a meeting ground of diverse and competing institutions is no place for subtle strategic discourse or operational originality or tactical innovation. Worse, the "joint" system leads to the outright perversion of military plans and operations to accommodate divergent service interests. In this respect, the Iranian rescue attempt was the very model of what we can expect from the "joint" way of doing things: service interests were very fully safeguarded (only the coast guard went unrepresented in the gathering at Desert One), with each being present for its share of eventual glory; there was a luxurious abundance of commanders and command echelons, all set to argue with one another as unplanned events called for decisions; there was plentiful variety in such things as communication procedures, so that the navy helicopters were under strict radio silence (some talk would have greatly helped in the sandstorm) while the air force crews chatted away; and finally the plan itself with its rare combination of unimaginative complexities could only have been formulated by the classic committee, its unique achievement being the violation of every single principle evolved in forty years of commando operations. The different services must of course be coordinated in some way; but there is a perfectly good alternative to the disastrous institution that civilians have built for our forces: it is called a General Staff,[6] and it works.

III

The poverty of our strategy is not, however, entirely unrelieved. Quite recently, the much-publicized decision on the MX intercontinental ballistic missile demonstrated how much can be gained when the relentless progression of bureaucratic decision is interrupted and reversed by solid strategic thinking.

In January 1981, when the new administration arrived on the scene, the engineering bureaucracy in the air force and their colleagues in the Defense Research and Engineering Undersecretariat and, of course, the senior air force commanders and the chairman of the Joint Chiefs (an air force general) were all set to start the so-called "race-track" deployment scheme. Under this scheme each of 200 MX missiles was supposed to be provided with its very own ring-road in the desert, each road having 23 shelters among which the one missile could hide. This was the famous MX/MPS scheme chosen by Jimmy Carter. With a new administration known to be strongly "pro-defense" and whose leaders were also reputed to be inexpert, the engineers and bureaucrats and the air force chiefs were quite confident that the MX/MPS would be approved in short order.

[6] *I.e., a body of officers who have risen high in their respective services to a given entry point; upon joining the General Staff, their future career is entirely within its own ranks and wholly independent of their services of origin. A sentimental affiliation will naturally remain, but soon enough the "non-service" General Staff would develop its own corporate spirit, and thus a substantial independence from service particularism.*

Naturally the rumor had reached the Pentagon that President Reagan and his Defense Secretary, Caspar Weinberger, were less than euphoric over the MX/MPS scheme, but it was assumed that those gentlemen would soon come around to the view that there really was no alternative. The scheme, to be sure, was rather expensive (estimates floated between $30 and $50 billion, both too low), and it did look rather absurd, with all those costly roads and shelters for only 200 actual missiles.[7]

But even if costly and very intrusive, the MX/MPS was *mechanically* sound. By moving about between the 22 shelters, each MX missile could be masked by 22 decoys at any one time, which meant that the Russians would need 4,600 accurate warheads on target to destroy the system—and indeed many more, to allow for malfunctioning warheads and those off course.

As far as the bureaucracy was concerned, there was no other way of preserving the American land-based ballistic missile force, with its special virtues of accuracy (as compared to submarine-launched missiles), promptness, and assured penetration (as compared to bombers), and ready controllability (submerged submarines are sometimes hard to reach, and their missiles cannot be retargeted as freely and reliably as in land-based forces). In sum, the bureaucratic process had offered up the MX/MPS and no other alternative was ready, so that an administration that proclaimed the urgency of closing the "window of vulnerability" would have only that one choice.

Actually the MX/MPS was the conjoint product of two great forces, each of which grew ever more powerful during the 1960s and 1970s, usurping the place of strategy itself. The first of these was the quest for arms control in the American style—that is, as an end in itself rather than as a tool of strategy. This great urge was propelled both by the internal pressure of the government's own arms-controllers (many of whom have dedicated their whole professional life to that pursuit) and even more by the external pressure of media and public opinion. Forever seduced by the alluring prospect of breaking the "mad momentum" of the "arms race"—as if it were some physical phenomenon and not the natural symptom of a competition between two systems of power and of values—the public remains insistent in its delusion, even while recognizing that

[7] *These missiles would have provided 2,000 separate warheads, in direct succession to the 2,100 warheads present on the 1,000 Minuteman missiles, now made vulnerable by the inexorable increase in the number of Soviet warheads, and their accuracy.*

there has been no "arms race" at all for many years, but only a one-sided Soviet military aggrandizement to which we have made a feeble and always belated response.

• • •

It was the imminent prospect of an arms-limitation treaty which would limit numbers that determined the size of the MX missile itself, making of it a large weapon with ten warheads, since only a "limited" number would be allowed. And similarly, it was the necessity for "verification" by satellite photography that shaped the specific features of the MPS deployment. In fact, that scheme was designed to cope with two separate Russians. The Good Russian, the sincere arms controller, had to be helped to identify each genuine MX missile, so that he could count them to ensure our compliance with the treaty. But then there was the Bad Russian, who would also want to identify each genuine MX missile, not to count them but rather to attack them with his own increasingly powerful missile warheads.

The MX missiles would thus have to be both visible and invisible, and the MPS scheme was an attempt to reconcile the irreconcilable: first, by allowing the missile to move between the shelters—but only within a closed-loop road, whose entrance would eventually be blocked by a great mound of earth once the system was assembled; second, by providing 23 shelters and decoy missiles for 22 of them— but then also having a sliding roof for each shelter, so that with prior notification all the roofs could be slid back in one ring-road at a time, thus allowing the Good Russian to "verify" that each 23-shelter site did indeed contain only one true missile.

The other great force that shaped the MX/MPS scheme was the unguided engineering ambition that luxuriates in the absence of sustained strategical discipline, or the serious pursuit of the operational art of war. An air force that has abandoned strategy to civilian experts, and which at the senior level has only a pro-forma interest in tactical and operational matters, has naturally become a science-and-engineering organization, devoted to the increase of technical performance for its own sake. As the only long-range ballistic missile in the Air Force's keeping, the MX became the vehicle for all the various innovations that were found to be technically exciting over the years, from carbon-carbon fiber structures to all the latest refinements in propulsion and guidance.

The weapon thus produced by the perverse intercourse of arms controllers and engineers is naturally a very large missile, much too large to be moved about on normal roads by normal vehicles. Although usually described as "mobile," it is merely movable, and then only by means of a huge transporter of special design.

This shortcoming of the MX is of crucial importance because in the presence of a Soviet missile force powerful enough to destroy thousands of targets even if both small and well-protected (and notably our missile "silos"), the simplest response would be precisely to build small and truly mobile missiles. Technically unexciting, but also cheap and reliable, a one-warhead missile (the MX has ten warheads, each separately targetable) could easily be made small enough to be moved about freely by truck, rail, helicopter, or by the common run of transport aircraft as well as by barge, large boats, all ships, or for that matter converted ice-cream vans. Thus the protection of the weapon by mobile concealment could be most easily and cheaply provided.

This path of development, however, was resolutely blocked by the arms controllers. Faithful to the pretense that the Russians would have to "verify" our missile force by satellite photography alone—as if they could not know just exactly how many missiles we were building by reading the *Congressional Record,* the technical or general press, or merely Pentagon news releases—the arms-control lobby insisted on having a large missile of classic form, which could *not* be hidden easily in the general flow of civilian traffic, or even moved about freely by ordinary military aircraft. And of course the engineering fraternity in the air force would have despised the notion of a missile that would be totally prosaic and entirely simple by the standards of such things (and also of course inefficient, since the ten warheads of the MX make it very "cost-effective"—until one faces the problem of deployment).

Finally, our senior military leaders also opposed the small missile. They recoiled before the public-relations problem of what they described as the "civilian interface," namely, the possibility of protests if nuclear missiles being moved about were involved in road accidents and so on. Since safety devices and arming restraints on our nuclear weapons are so highly reliable that the danger of a detonation is truly negligible, that should have been a manageable difficulty—given a willingness to confront the matter squarely and to educate the public (the very thing that we are now asking European leaders to do for the theater nuclear forces, which would also have to move about in civilian areas).

• • •

With the natural solution of small, truly mobile missiles thus long ago closed off, Caspar Weinberger and his advisers were offered the

MX/MPS as their only choice, a scheme mechanically sound and bureaucratically desirable but also strategically disastrous.

First, the cost of the 200 ring-roads, 4,600 shelters, and 4,400 decoys would have absorbed a great part of all the added money that the administration could hope to provide to restore our entire military strength across the board. Secondly, the cost-overruns and scandals that 200 separate major construction projects would unfailingly entail would have brought that much nearer the day of the inevitable reaction against higher defense spending.[8]

But the MX/MPS also had a third defect so fundamental that it alone should have sufficed to condemn the scheme. The very first rule of strategy is to evade the major and special strengths of an enemy (and then seek to attack his weaknesses). Yet the MX/MPS would have done precisely the opposite, by erecting an array to stand directly in the path of the greatest Soviet strategic strength. By building the 4,600 shelters, we would have provided the very targets that best suit Soviet land-based ballistic missiles, which are in turn the most powerful element in their strategic-nuclear array.

At present, to be sure, the Soviet missile forces could not yet destroy all the 4,600 separate aiming points of the MPS. But as we know full well, once the rigid industrial structure of the Soviet Union is finally geared up, it does produce very effectively indeed. By starting work on the MX/MPS, we would therefore have invited the Russians to do what they do best: mass-produce weapons of established design. Having thus stacked the deck against ourselves, we were then supposed to cope with the threat by negotiating arms-control limits that would have kept the number of Soviet silo-killing warheads under the danger line—and that, of course, was precisely the great virtue of the MX in the eyes of some. It is often said that the advent of nuclear weapons has invalidated all the old wisdoms of war, but in this case, the most elementary of tactical principles would have served us well. In the presence of massed, accurate firepower, wide dispersal and free mobility are called for (i.e., many small missiles), and not the aggregation of valuable forces into a system of fixed targets.

Finally, the MX/MPS had the well-advertised defect of requiring large amounts of land (or rather several thousand small plots across

---

[8] *We do have a clear record in such matters: the five-year surge of World War II, which was followed by a disastrously abrupt abandonment of effort; the three-year Korean-war upsurge, which might well have prevented that war had it come sooner; and the Kennedy build-up that was exhausted by 1964—more or less when the Russians began to build their strategic-nuclear forces in earnest.*

vast areas). And this land would have been needed in a part of the country where the national defense is held in high regard—but where the preservation of the wilderness is equally valued.

Had Caspar Weinberger walked the path that the defense bureaucracy had marked out for him, and then settled down into the usual routine of micro-management, to seek marginal cost savings in the building of roads and shelters and to ensure that no one would steal the odd bag of cement, the nation would have been provided with a solid if short-lived solution to the problem of Minuteman vulnerability. Our strength in land-based ballistic missiles would then have been reliably preserved, at least for several years— but only at ruinous cost. All our other military forces would have been deprived of funds greatly needed, and the loss would eventually have been compounded, since political support for defense in general would have been seriously eroded had the MX/MPS been built. The enormity of spending tens of billions of dollars for the housing of just 200 missiles, and the grotesquerie of all those roads and shelters (and sliding roofs) could not truly have been explained away by skillful public relations because the fundamental idea behind it all was itself strategically unsound. By adding strength in one narrow sector of capability while undermining our military strength across the board, the MX/MPS was in fact a sublime example of a weapon scheme that the engineer might find irresistible, but which the strategist must refuse.

In the circumstances the crucial move was to reject the MX/MPS, even if no fully satisfactory alternative could be found. The small missile certainly could not be available soon enough: it takes years to engineer such a weapon, even if based entirely on proven technology, while the time of danger is now upon us. As for the other genuine long-term solution, the provision of ballistic-missile defenses, it was ruled out by the 1972 ABM treaty—and even if that unwise agreement is to be repudiated, that could not be done abruptly and so early in the life of the new administration.

Hence the MX itself had to be built, for it was the only new land-based missile actually ready for production; but without the MPS, there was no fully plausible way of basing the new missile. Weinberger attracted much criticism and some ridicule by proposing a bundle of technically dubious solutions, from the super-hardening of missile silos, to the exploration of deep-hole basing, to the "big bird"—a long-endurance aircraft which could keep MX missiles safe from attack, on airborne alert.

None of these schemes was a known quantity, for none had been engineered and studied in detail. None was likely to be cheap, though of course any and all would have to be cheaper than the MPS. None perhaps was seriously meant, but in the meantime even if placed in vulnerable Minuteman silos, the MX would offer some residual strikeback capability. If fifty MX missiles were built, and no more than five would survive a Soviet attack, those five could still launch fifty warheads, and that alone would be a not insignificant force for retaliation.

Eventually, either the small missile or a silo-defense ABM will inevitably be accepted to preserve our land-based missile capability over the long term. But in the interim, Secretary Weinberger's makeshifts will do, just as in wartime the fight against German submarines was waged by converted fishing boats and improvised merchant-ship carriers, and not by the optimal antisubmarine vessels that the Navy might have desired, and which could not have been ready until long after the war.

• • •

Now that the predicament of weakness is upon us, now that we must finally pay the bill for the scientific mismanagement of the McNamara years, for all the bureaucratic follies of our armed forces in Vietnam, and for the carnival of self-hatred and elite irresponsibility that followed, we cannot assure our security by means of large defense budgets alone. Without them nothing can be done at all, but we also need a fundamental reappraisal of our strategy since our plans, our fossilized alliance arrangements, and the very structure of our armed forces are all based on outdated premises—and notably the implicit assumption of superiorities that we will not soon regain. New strategic solutions must therefore be found, and often they will be suggested only by new operational methods and new tactics—which only the active and persistent interest of our most senior officials can elicit.

But this great and urgent task cannot be accomplished unless the Congress in its wisdom drastically redirects its own attention, from the small issues to the large, from micro-management to strategy. The Constitution prescribes that Congress should manifest the will of the people in our defense policy as in all else, but surely the will of the people is more subverted than exercised when it is delegated to staff members who in turn seek to interfere in the most minute matters, upon which no body of electors could possibly hold any opinion at all. No great harm is done when a congressman intervenes to protect constituency interests, but once the military base back home is well secured, once the contract for the needy producer is duly obtained, let the remaining time be given over to the broad issues that truly count, and not to the petty matters that Congress now belabors, thus compelling the Pentagon to do likewise.

What this republic badly needs in its defense establishment is the wisdom of strategy and certainly not better "management" or yet more "efficiency." That is why we must reject the suspect prescriptions of James Fallows and his ilk, who would launch us on a quest for cheap solutions to problems that admit none, and for more things to cut from the budget (that being the purpose all along). And that is why we must firmly resist those politicians who refuse to fund our greatly overdue rearmament even while proclaiming their newfound enthusiasm for a "strong America," and who resolve the contradiction between true opinion and public stance by claiming that it is the "fat" they want to cut.

If the price of a wise strategy, of better operational methods, and of more ingenious tactics is indeed the neglect of micro-management, then so be it. We would then have good reason to welcome a little more "waste, fraud, & mismanagement" in the Pentagon.

6

DEUS EX MISSILES

*A*nti-aircraft missiles, anti-ship missiles, anti-tank missiles, anti-radar missiles, and even anti-missile missiles have been around for years now, but it is only quite recently that we have seen the emergence of the anti-defense missile, aimed primarily at the defense budget. We are hearing a great deal about the virtues of anti-tank missiles: they cost only a few thousand dollars apiece and have what the trade calls high-kill probability. This being so, why should we spend nearly $3 million apiece for the M-1 tanks that the army wants so badly, particularly as our opponents in combat have their own anti-tank missiles? The sinking of the HMS *Sheffield* in the Falklands war revived the naval version of this argument. Why build such expensive ships, costing hundreds of millions and even billions of dollars, when they can be sunk by "cheap" missiles costing only hundreds of thousands of dollars? In both versions the services are pictured as trying to foist upon us some sort of antiquated armored or maritime cavalry that will not only fail us in our hour of need but will squander our treasure as well.

It goes without saying that all institutions are conservative, that they will strive to perpetuate existing forms. And military institutions, with their rigid hierarchic structure, are even more conservative. Their tendency to reject the new should be taken for granted, especially when the old embodies the ethos of the institution, while the new makes its appearance in the guise of mere functionalism. The army defended its beautiful horses against the ugly and soulless tank—until the tank too developed its own ethos, which now in turn evokes powerful loyalties against the sterile functionalism of the missile.

Since military conservatism is an inherent tendency, since it can be costly and may also place us in great danger, we should indeed be ready to intervene and impose change when it is needed. But perhaps nowadays the greater danger is the opposite: the tendency, at least in our society, to impose the "modern" before it can really do the job, and sometimes when it will not work at all. In our culture especially the "tech-fix" illusion is deep and wide, and it affects our armed forces as much as any other American institution. In Vietnam, "tech-fix" delusions were ruthlessly imposed on a mediocre military leadership by Robert McNamara; systems analysis and statistical body-counts displaced strategy, "manpower management" displaced leadership, and the servicing of high-tech equipment (from multi-sensor barriers to "people sniffers") displaced tactics and the operational art of war. By such devices we compounded our defeat by costly and demoralizing absurdities.

A proper suspicion of military conservatism must therefore be balanced by a prudent attitude toward technological wizardry. In considering the true military worth of the anti-ship missile for example, the first thing to note is that this is the third apparition of that weapon. In September 1943, the German Luftwaffe sank the Italian battleship *Roma* and seriously damaged the *Italia* with the Fritz-X, the first effective air-launched anti-ship missile; since the Germans were about to deploy the even more effective HS-293 missile, the landings at Salerno, Anzio and in Normandy ought logically to have resulted in huge losses of Allied shipping to those precursors of the Exocet. But in fact the Fritz-X was out of business by the end of 1943 and the HS-293 was withdrawn a few months later. Powerful indeed against warships that were unprepared for them, both missiles were easily neutralized by simple countermeasures—devices as "cheap" as the missiles themselves. (The Fritz-X and the HS-293 were radio-guided, gliding missiles, and these two qualities proved their undoing. The gliding required that the missile be launched from a particular distance from the target; once that envelope had been identified, Allied fighters turned it into a death trap for German planes. The radio-guidance provided the opportunity of jamming; once the frequencies were located and devices installed, the missiles quietly glided down into the sea.) The second apparition was all the more dramatic since the background was uncrowded by the events of a large war: on October 21, 1967, at a time when a ceasefire was in effect, the Israeli destroyer *Elat* was sunk by Styx missiles launched by Egyptian missile boats. Articles and editorials very much like those being printed nowadays proclaimed the virtues of Styx missiles and the hopeless vulnerability of all warships. But in fact the Styx was soon thereafter neutralized by relatively simple countermeasures. Six years after the sinking of the *Elat*, more than fifty Styx missiles were launched at Israeli ships during the October War: only one suffered very slight damage from a near-miss, and none at all were sunk.

Now the Exocet has had its turn, we can anticipate two parallel developments: ample sales of that missile, and, concurrently, the swift development of countermeasures that will do to the Exocet what was done to the Fritz-X and the Styx. For there is one rule in strategy that is truly universal: nothing worthwhile comes cheaply. There are *no* cheap weapons that cannot be defeated by equally cheap countermeasures. The anti-ship missile is cheap because it is a single-purpose weapon; the warship is expensive because it has broad capabilities—and one way of using the space and weight, the sensors, power sources, and crew that a warship has to offer is to equip it with countermeasures against the anti-ship missile.

Naturally, the defender does not get off cheaply either: besides the direct cost of jamming devices, anti-missile weapons, and so on, there is a definite loss of offensive capability for every addition to a ship's defenses. Eventually the point will be reached when the procedure will no longer be worthwhile, when defenses against missiles and other weapons will take up so much of its capacity that the warship will become more trouble than it is worth. However, it will not be a "cheap" missile such as the Exocet which will put the surface warship out of business, but some more versatile and far more costly weapon—still, for now, a distant prospect. To be sure, American carrier task forces must already contend with a real Soviet missile threat. But that threat comes not from a few cheap missiles but from hundreds of rather costly weapons, launched from dozens of still more costly nuclear-powered submarines and naval bombers—and so far the balance is still favorable to the carrier forces, if properly equipped and trained (unless nuclear weapons are used against them, but then of course land bases would be even more vulnerable). The point is that at this interim stage in the evolution of naval weapons, it would be as foolish to abandon the large warship as to fail to provide it with proper defenses against anti-ship weapons, old and new.

The anti-tank argument is an old story, but it has recently acquired an entirely new and larger dimension because it has been invoked by the proponents of a "no-first-use" nuclear policy for NATO. The Soviet army consists largely of armored forces, organized, equipped, and trained to carry out deep penetrations at high speed, in a modern and more powerful version of the *Blitzkrieg.* NATO's declared readiness to use tactical nuclear weapons is meant to deter a Soviet armored offensive which could not reliably be defeated by the Alliance's non-nuclear forces, if only because the latter are widely distributed while the Soviet army could concentrate its divisions in a few powerful mailed fists to mount a surprise offensive. (And if a gradually escalating crisis provided enough warning for NATO to reinforce and deploy properly, that would be offset by the fact that the Soviet Union could mobilize many more divisions.)

That is the setting in which the humble anti-tank missile now enters, stage left, as a strategic solution to NATO's problem: it is no longer necessary to deter a (non-nuclear) Soviet offensive by tactical nuclear means, because with enough anti-tank missiles NATO forces could defeat a Soviet *Blitzkrieg.* There is no doubt whatever that today's anti-tank missiles can indeed destroy tanks. It is also true that the cost ratio between a modern tank and the best anti-tank missile system, the TOW, is roughly 100 : 1, and even the cheapest armored vehicle costs several times as much as the TOW. Thus, NATO could certainly deploy many anti-tank missiles, for each Soviet tank, especially if it gave up its own costly tanks. With hard facts like these on their side, it is not surprising that so many arms-control advocates, congressmen, and journalists have concluded that the tank in particular and armored forces in general are today's cavalry, perpetuated only by bureaucratic sentimentalism.

But strategy is more complicated than bookkeeping, because it has multiple dimensions. In a technical context, when the anti-tank missile is tested on the proving ground against a target of armor plate, the missile wins; but in a tactical context, where the missile crew must operate under enemy fire, or are unable to exploit the weapon's long range because of intervening obstacles or just smoke, the high-kill probabilities theoretically achievable are drastically reduced. In an operational context, where the total forces of both sides enter the picture, the anti-tank missile is finally reduced from a panacea to the more modest role of an adjunct to older anti-tank measures, including mines, terrain obstacles, anti-tank guns, and above all other tanks—the last having the huge advantage of being able to move about under fire to do their job. But it is the level of theater strategy that the delusion is finally exposed, for then we find that the cheap and abundant anti-tank missile will in fact be grossly outnumbered by the costly armored vehicle, for the latter can be concentrated in narrow-deep columns while the anti-tank missiles must be distributed all across the frontage established by the chosen NATO strategy, thus being immobile if dug in, or vulnerable to artillery if not. Of course, the anti-tank missile can also be made mobile, indeed much more mobile than any armored vehicle, by the simple expedient of providing a helicopter to carry the missiles and its firing crew—but then, of course, the weapon will no longer be cheap, and will in fact cost many times as much as the average armored vehicle. If we are more modest, and merely seek to equal the mobility of armored forces, in order to be able to match enemy concentrations with our own, we must provide a cross-country vehicle for our missile, and then armor to protect its crew. Next we would find that the missile-firing armored vehicle will usually be inferior to gun-armored vehicles: guns have a much higher rate of fire and, moreover, the new "Chobham" armor of the latest tanks is very effective in stopping the hollow-charge warheads of missiles, while tank guns rely primarily on high-velocity shots that destroy armor by plain kinetic energy—and the new armor is as vulnerable to them as the old. Having wrapped our anti-tank missile in armor and given it cross-country mobility, we would then find it advantageous to replace or supplement the missile launcher with a gun— and we would thus reinvent the tank. There is no free lunch in strategy.

III

THE WIDER
CONTEXT
OF STRATEGY

7

CHAPTER

THE EAST-WEST STRUGGLE

(BARRY M. BLECHMAN, CO-EDITOR)

OVERVIEW: 1983

The year 1983 was marked by economic travails and resulting political tensions in many countries, by the continuing deterioration of U.S.–Soviet relations, by the persistence of war between Iraq and Iran and in Lebanon, by lesser conflicts in Central America, Southern Africa and Southwest and Southeast Asia, all with East-West overtones, by significant foreign policy setbacks for the United States offset by one very large success, and by the greater problems and almost unrelieved failures of Soviet foreign policy. It was a very difficult year.

Until the destruction of KAL flight 007 in September, there were signs of improved U.S.–Soviet relations, including the re-opening of a substantive diplomatic dialogue, the conclusion of a five-year grain agreement, and lesser gestures suggesting a mutual desire to restore a more cooperative relationship. By August, there had even been talk of a possible summit in the spring. That in turn implied the prior achievement of at least some formal progress in the Geneva nuclear arms negotiations. The destruction of the Korean airliner, however, the American and indeed worldwide reaction to that act of savagery, and the even more disturbing pattern of Soviet conduct after the incident itself, all resulted in a very sharp increase in East-West tensions. So much so, in fact, as to stimulate anxieties that the world was drifting toward war.

The Reagan Administration made an attempt to stem this trend by again adopting a more conciliatory tone toward the Soviet Union, notably in the president's 26 September speech at the UN General Assembly. But the Soviet response was very prompt and totally negative. Within three days, General-Secretary Yuri Andropov had not only rejected President Reagan's proffered concessions but raised troubling questions about the overall content and directions of U.S.–Soviet relations. The USSR's suspension of talks on intermediate-range nuclear forces in November completed the sequence. At year's end, the two great powers remained at arm's length, their relations frozen in hostility and suspicion.

Within the industrialized world, at least, the United States fared substantially better than the Soviet Union during much of 1983. The Soviet quest for acceptance and respect suffered unprecedented setbacks within these regions of the world, a process symbolized by the mass expulsion from many countries of Soviet intelligence officers under diplomatic cover, and marked by bitter quarrels with countries as diverse as Sweden, Italy and Japan. Moreover, the Soviet attempt to break out of its perceived encirclement by improving relations with Beijing failed to yield any substantial result.

In Europe, the dimensions of the peace movement are evidence of the shadow of fear cast by Soviet military power, but Soviet attempts to aggravate tensions within the North Atlantic Alliance, and even to give electoral help to left-wing parties, certainly did not succeed and may even have backfired against Soviet interests. The overall failure of Soviet policy toward Europe was made tangible by the deployment, on schedule, of the first Pershing II intermediate-range ballistic missiles in Germany, and of the first Cruise missiles in Britain. In the wake of the "neutron bomb" debacle, these deployments represented a very significant success for the alliance, at least in this round of what promises to be a long and difficult struggle.

To be sure, the United States has had difficulties in the industrial regions as well, notably in relations with France; American policies in Central America particularly continue to be poorly received in Europe. American economic policies—which keep U.S. interest rates high by combining fiscal liberality with monetary restraint, thus attracting investment funds at the expense of the rest of the world and Europe especially—have also caused widespread resentment.

Moreover, the immediate failures of Moscow's policies toward Europe may mask longer-term gains in the case of Germany, where neutralist tendencies remain strong, and where more of the young are disaffected from the alliance than elsewhere in Europe. Generally unstated yearnings for a reunification of Germany and related desires for greater communications and movement between the two German states induce even conservative governments in Bonn to be more conciliatory toward the Soviet Union than Washington—or Paris or London for that matter—would like. To the extent that war fears have become more widely felt in recent years, both history and geography combine to make these fears more intense in Germany than elsewhere in Europe. This too has become a factor encouraging conciliatory policies toward the Soviet Union and it has made the German "peace" movement a distinctly stronger force than in most other European countries, though of course it still remains too weak to decide elections.

In East Asia, U.S. relations with Japan combined a substantial improvement in government-to-government relations with a continuing deterioration in society-to-society relations. The improved official atmosphere, evident during President Reagan's November visit, is associated largely with the advent of Prime Minister Nakasone and the more consensual view of security issues that he represents. How long it can persist in the absence of more tangible measures by the Japanese government to implement a more ambitious defense policy is a matter of conjecture. Improved official relations are further threatened by the two societies' increasing division on economic priorities and circumstances. These perceived, and also concrete, conflicts have a disturbing potential for economic conflict, which could have political and even strategic repercussions.

U.S. relations with China were marked by recurring disputes over minor incidents that always threaten to have broad consequences— at least on the Beijing side of the relationship. The "deepening" of U.S.–China relations, a process that has continued since 1971 in fits and starts, may be reaching the limits set by the profound incompatibilities between the authoritative political system of China and the pluralist American society. While there is still potential for more intense economic relations, the very narrow bounds that Chinese leaders set on anything hinting at security cooperation were perfectly evident during Secretary of Defense Weinberger's visit to China in September.

The Chinese also remained cool to the latest Soviet offers for a diplomatic accommodation; Deputy Foreign Minister Kapitsa's visits to Beijing seem to have produced little tangible progress, although the psychological atmosphere does seem more cordial. Soviet relations with Japan have deteriorated significantly, as the Nakasone government adopted a more openly declared anti-Soviet stance and at least suggested its intent to endow Japan with a more substantial military capacity.

Outside the industrialized world, the diplomatic contest between the United States and the USSR has been more evenly matched, and neither has fared very well.

In the Middle East, the Soviet Union is more established than ever as Syria's patron and Syria's success in asserting its interests over the Lebanon has repaired in some degree the damage inflicted on Soviet prestige by the Israeli defeat of Syria and the Palestine Liberation Organization in 1982. The United States, by contrast, not only failed to gain acceptance of President Reagan's comprehensive peace plan, but by permitting the stage to become successively dominated by, first, negotiations for the removal of foreign troops from the Lebanon and, second, negotiations among contending Lebanese factions, invested greater and greater resources and prestige for lesser and lesser objectives.

In Southwest Asia, Soviet relations with Iran deteriorated sharply, marked by the destruction of the Tudeh party in March, but this was offset to some extent by an improvement in relations with Iraq; the Soviet position there, threatened during 1982, was reaffirmed in 1983. The United States remained an almost entirely passive spectator in the Iran-Iraq War. While that conflict absorbs Iran's potentially disruptive energies, it could result at any time in a serious disruption of oil supplies, even by accident.

In South Asia, the Afghan war has had mixed consequences for the Soviet Union. The continuing fighting imposes some casualties and other penalties on the USSR, and has eroded the goodwill of some Third World nations for Moscow, but also has continued to remind all concerned of the Soviet Union's military capabilities and of its readiness to use them if it sees fit. The possibility of a negotiated settlement seemed to increase during the year, but this also raised the prospect that Pakistan would choose the path of accommodation with the USSR in order to assure its survival. This in turn reflects one of the benefits which Moscow obtains from its continuing alliance with India. The United States, by contrast, has failed to capitalize on the brutalities of the Soviet oppression of Afghanistan to evoke any intense protests by world opinion, and neither has the United States been very effective in increasing the military costs of the Soviet occupation by giving powerful help to the resistance. In both respects, therefore, Afghanistan is very far from being the Soviet Union's Vietnam.

In Southeast Asia, the Soviet Union remained firmly entrenched in Vietnam and, through that country, in Cambodia and Laos as well. This gives the USSR access to an important region, but the Soviet presence has in turn helped the United States to consolidate its relations with the countries which Vietnam's military preponderance continues to threaten: Thailand, Malaysia, Singapore, and Indonesia. Aside from the domestic turmoil that followed the assassination of opposition leader Aquino, which may threaten U.S. interests in the Philippines, American relations with the ASEAN countries continued to improve, while the Soviet Union failed to derive any benefit from regional fears of a future Chinese hegemony.

Except in Central America, the U.S.–Soviet competition remains almost insignificant in Latin America as a whole, where the scene is dominated by very serious economic difficulties and fundamental constitutional predicaments. American interests are threatened far more by the repercussions of these problems than by Soviet intrusions. The beginnings of global economic recovery scarcely alleviated the financial distress caused by the accumulation of external debt. And the deflationary measures imposed by the International Monetary Fund as prerequisites for the new loans and other financial concessions necessary to assure economic stability virtually guaranteed political unrest.

In Central America, on the other hand, the problems are political and military. The United States continued to support the government of El Salvador in its war against insurgents, continued to oppose the Sandinista regime of Nicaragua diplomatically and through continued assistance to insurgent groups and the government of Honduras, and began to explore the possibilities of a diplomatic accommodation without much success in any of these endeavors. The intensity of the American engagement—particularly the October invasion of Grenada—entailed worldwide political and diplomatic costs, but was not without benefit in the Caribbean itself.

In Africa, the American attempt to assist the government of Chad in conjunction with France began with some fanfare only to end inconclusively, partly because of a breakdown in Franco-American cooperation. The Libyan attempt to install a client regime failed, but so did the attempt to expel Libyan and Libyan-supported forces from the northern part of the country. In Southern Africa, the Soviet Union remained entrenched with its Cuban ally in Angola and Mozambique and the American attempt to combine a resolution of the Namibian question with the withdrawal of the Cubans achieved no progress during the year. In the meantime, American interests were ill-served by the spread of internal and external conflicts that now affect almost every country in Southern Africa.

The East-West Military Balance

Overall, the military balance between the United States and its allies and the Soviet bloc did not change substantially during the year. This in itself is of significance, because the United States and other NATO members, as well as Japan, are all committed to policies of rearmament to restore a tolerable balance and thus strengthen deterrence. The defense program of the Reagan Administration, as modified by the Congress, is funding future increases in the capabilities of strategic nuclear forces, the size of naval forces, much smaller numerical increases in tactical air power, and no increase at all in the ground forces. Qualitative improvements in American military forces have been more evenly distributed among the different types of forces. Whatever their effect on perceptions of the relative balance of military power, the concrete effects of these programs have not yet been large. Some of these weapons will not be in service for many years and others are being produced in numbers too small to achieve any rapid improvement.

In spite of hope and actual commitment, the overall military effort of the NATO allies and of Japan has remained too small to achieve any significant correction of the military balance. There has scarcely been any force expansion to reduce numerical imbalances, and equipment modernization has not been sufficiently rapid to restore the once wide qualitative advantage of Western armaments. On the Soviet side, despite recent signs of abatement, the large amount of resources allocated to military research and development during the past two decades, and to the still larger procurement effort, continued to result in the appearance of new weapons in considerable numbers.

Military power is supposed to yield diplomatic leverage, but the correlation was weak during 1983 for both the United States and the USSR. The causes of this weak relationship between military trends and the fortunes of Soviet and American diplomacy differed on each side—except that reciprocal neutralization remained of course the dominant factor.

In the case of the Soviet Union, it seems evident that the past successes of its quest for military preponderance in all adjacent regions have evoked, at least for now, an unfavorable reaction. Throughout the arc of the industrial democracies around the Soviet periphery, all the way from Norway and Sweden to Japan, and in many parts of the Third World also, there is a greater alertness in resisting Soviet encroachments, from KGB espionage and political action to actual military intrusions. While the actions taken during 1983 to contain Soviet aggressiveness are encouraging, unless they are also backed with concrete measures to strengthen defenses against Soviet military intimidation, they may not last long. Firm declaratory policies associated with weak military postures must be correspondingly fragile.

In the case of the United States, on the other hand, the greater diplomatic leverage and prestige that a vigorous rearmament program should yield are still offset by continuing doubts about the stability and consistency of American foreign policy, and about the political, strategic and operational competence of the United States in coping with armed conflict. The decisiveness of U.S. action in Grenada may have reduced these doubts, but the inconclusiveness of American policies in Lebanon and the Middle East more broadly can only have increased them.

OVERVIEW: 1984

The year 1984 was heralded by ominous portents not merely literary. As the year began, the Soviet Union, coiled in bitter isolation at the worldwide protests evoked by the destruction of KAL 007, was still threatening reprisals for the NATO missile deployments its earlier threats had failed to stop. The United States was seemingly entrapped in Lebanon and on the verge of a serious conflict with Syria, even as the seizure of Grenada suggested the likelihood of an armed intervention against Nicaragua as well. Western Europe was gripped in a recession so unrelieved as to induce the fear of a secular decline. Debt repudiation seemed imminent in Latin America, threatening a global banking collapse. And, finally, the Iran-Iraq war entered a new and broader dangerous phase that aroused fears for the world's oil supply as both sides began to attack tankers in the Persian Gulf.

Nevertheless, quite unexpectedly, 1984 turned out to be a year definitely anticlimactic—if by no means quiet. The crises with which the year began were at least alleviated, if not truly resolved, and no major crises in the making were added to an admittedly crowded agenda, except for India's so far circumscribed domestic travail and Africa's great famine. The much-awaited economic recovery began, with the locomotive of American demand pulling the entire train of the world economy with its imports—with the much-deplored U.S. trade deficit being merely the obverse of the much-praised recovery. And even those who still regard the state of Soviet-American diplomacy as the governing factor of world affairs (as opposed to the internal dynamics within each country) had grounds for some optimism by the end of the year as the two sides agreed to begin a comprehensive arms control dialogue.

U.S.–Soviet Relations: Back to Détente?

The transition from the low point of U.S.–Soviet relations at the year's beginning to the tentative improvement noted by its end was marked by sharply asymmetrical declaratory policies. On the American side, after the unusually sharp outbursts that attended the destruction of KAL 007 in the closing months of 1983, there was an evident desire to tone down the administration's language, a shift perhaps not entirely unconnected with the approach of the electoral season. On the Soviet side, by contrast, the normal drumbeat of accusations against the United States was supplemented by a series of exceptionally sharp attacks, not merely against American policy but against the president by name and Americans as a people. The implied message, evident enough, was that Americans are as dangerous as the Nazis once were, and that only the Soviet regime, with its defense and security apparatus, stands between the peoples of the USSR and the bloodthirsty Americans. Thus a regime whose performance has been less than brilliant in providing for the needs of the Soviet consumer could seek approval as a provider of security in a dangerous world, a role in which its claims are no doubt far more persuasive.

There was therefore an interesting contrast: in the United States the pressures of domestic politics clearly induced the Reagan administration to seek an amelioration in U.S.–Soviet relations; for the Kremlin, on the other hand, the poor state of those relations could be turned to advantage by the regime in its quest for legitimacy on the domestic scene.

War propaganda so sharply intensified is difficult to sustain for

long, short of the proclamation of a state of siege or the actual outbreak of war; the very fact that the anti-American campaign was so
exceptionally harsh presaged its eventual remission. And indeed the
Kremlin's campaign culminated in the announcement of May 8,
1984, that the Soviet Union would not send its athletes to the Los
Angeles Olympics (though its functionaries participated in full to
ensure their continued role in future games).

By the spring, the leaders of the Soviet Union had full cause to reflect on the high collateral costs of their withdrawal from arms negotiations and from their generic policy of noncommunication with
the United States. Very little of the Soviet Union's leverage in world
affairs derives from its importance as a trading partner, as a source
of capital and technology, as a societal model or cultural center. Indeed, in those transactional terms, the Soviet Union is at best a medium power, greater than Poland but far inferior to West Germany,
for example. It is, of course, the worldwide response to Soviet military power that generates the Kremlin's prestige and embodies its
real leverage in world affairs.

When Soviet-American relations are intensive, other countries,
and especially the allies of the United States, are under pressure
to emulate the United States or to compete with it in seeking to develop their own relations with the Soviet Union. As a result, the Soviet Union's role in world affairs rises far above its transactional
importance.

When, by contrast, Washington diminishes its own communications with Moscow, the Soviet role in world affairs tends to decline.
That is exactly what happened during the first term of the Reagan
presidency and especially after U.S.–Soviet relations further deteriorated in the closing months of 1983. Far from being able to isolate
the United States by intensifying relations with other countries and
especially America's own allies, the Soviet Union found itself relatively unattended and even disregarded.

The Kremlin, moreover, discovered that in the altered circumstances of their greater economic interdependence and renewed cultural connectivity with the West, most of the regimes of Eastern
Europe were seriously embarrassed by Moscow's stance. In the past,
East European regimes, themselves actively repressive, favored the
upkeep of bloc "vigilance" and a hard-line stance in general, obviously consistent with their own tone and policy; and of course the
value of Western trade, tourism, and capital loans was quite small
for their economies.

Nowadays, by contrast, only in Czechoslovakia are the old politics of repression still pursued with any enthusiasm. Elsewhere each regime seeks toleration, if not active approval, by offering varying combinations of economic amelioration, national and even nationalist affirmation, and a degree of political liberalization; each of these devices was hurt in some way by the deterioration of U.S.–Soviet and therefore East-West relations.

Only the Prague regime applauded and fully emulated Moscow's policy. Elsewhere, there was only the faintest applause and scant emulation, visibly under direct pressure as in the reluctant withdrawal of the East European teams from the Olympics. With others beginning to show some signs of independent judgment, if not quite action, Romania's declaratory policy preserved its distinctiveness by coming very close to a full-bore "third force" stance. Not only did Romania send its athletes to Los Angeles but it went so far as to offer its services as a mediator.

The Soviet Union was thus clearly the loser from the deteriorated state of U.S.–Soviet relations both in Eastern Europe and the world at large. This was reason enough for a change of policy, given that the undoubtedly advantageous domestic propaganda campaign could not have been kept up indefinitely.

As election day approached in the United States and the victory of Ronald Reagan became more and more certain, an attentive Kremlin must have been particularly sensitive to the disadvantages of remaining frozen in a stance of hostility to a leadership that would be in office for four more years. It is obvious that the Gromyko-Reagan meeting of September 28, 1984, greatly favored the incumbent president by vividly showing that he could also "talk with the Russians." The gain was scarcely diminished by Gromyko's very negative appraisal of the meeting itself or by the state of U.S.–Soviet relations in general. It is unlikely that the Kremlin would be so naive as to hope to obtain a postelection reward for its preelection favor. More likely, the Soviet Union was hoping to exploit the president's electoral vulnerability on the nuclear issue to reopen a dialogue, a step that, after the elections, might have been much more difficult to accomplish.

The Gromyko-Reagan meeting marked the beginning of a definite thaw, even if slow and tentative. The November announcement of a Shultz-Gromyko meeting scheduled early in January 1985 to discuss arms control was a further sign of improving relations, and the agreement at that meeting to reopen negotiations marked a clear return to a more normal relationship.

By the year's end, the triumphantly reelected president was faced with the politically related problems of deficit-reduction at home and the pursuit of some form of arms control with the Soviet Union. No positive interaction could be anticipated between the two. To achieve deficit reductions by savings on strategic arms obtained by successful arms control was quite unrealistic—strategic weapons account for only a small part of total military expenditures, and any obtainable savings would be long delayed.

The relationship between deficit-reduction and arms control actually went the other way. It was obvious that the new Congress would not cooperate in reducing the deficit unless defense expenditures were also reduced, but that would diminish the toleration of the president's core following for any arms control negotiations with the Soviet Union. Even in the peak years of détente, it will be recalled, arms-control agreements were accompanied by the start of new strategic weapons programs, in part to conciliate their opponents. Moreover, deficit-reduction competes directly for the president's time, energy, and political capital with all other policy goals, arms control included.

For all the undoubted sincerity of his declared intent, the president's decision to retain the secretaries of state and defense and also the national security adviser in their respective offices makes any truly substantive arms controls most unlikely—though it does not, of course, preclude negotiations as such. At a time when the prospect of restoring an American strategic advantage by the expeditious development of space defenses is attractive to many, it is fair to anticipate intense political and bureaucratic resistance to any limitations that would significantly impede or even prohibit this form of innovation. Such resistance is certainly not diminished by the obvious eagerness of the Soviet Union to negotiate limits that would nullify the U.S. lead in space weapons. At best, the natural state of the executive branch, or at least of the Pentagon, vis-à-vis arms control approximates a paralysis that can be overcome only by a persistent president, served by a highly dynamic and well-connected executor who fully shares his goals and who is able to reach out with his own associates to suppress opposition in all the relevant interagency committees.

No such attributes were in evidence in the leadership of the administration at year's end, and the appointment of a special arms control adviser, Paul Nitze, without a department of his own, did not seem to offer a persuasive remedy—nor did the new negotiators, two of whom lacked experience in the highly technical issues they would soon be confronting.

America Ascendant

During 1984, world politics continued to adjust to the phenomenon of a successful U.S. administration advancing toward a virtually certain reelection, a phenomenon not witnessed for many years. As always in politics, the intangibles of confidence and momentum counted for much more than the specific gains and losses of single ventures. While a troubled administration, adrift and pessimistic, may gain very little at home or abroad even from substantial foreign-policy achievements, one that retains the mark of success can absorb even an outright debacle, as the Reagan administration did over Lebanon.

The policy aim, to restore the sovereignty of Lebanon and the authority of its government, was flatly dismissed at the time by both friends and foes as utterly unrealistic, simply because of the absence of any unified political community upon which national sovereignty and a single lawful authority could be sustained. U.S. diplomacy, moreover, was a clumsy affair involving special envoys of varying qualifications whose chances of success were prejudiced from the start by the de facto alliance made with just one faction of one Lebanese community, among so many factions and communities. The conduct of the military operations that soon became necessary did nothing to enhance the prestige of the United States in a highly competitive arena. From the grotesquely unmilitary procedures that left so many servicemen highly vulnerable in a single building, to the ineffectual naval bombardments with huge but obsolete shells, to the indignity of a failed air strike in which the navy lost two aircraft where others lost none, it was a tale of complacent bungling by the higher chain of command. What happened could only inspire the contempt of a war-hardened region, especially when it was realized that the United States would not even try to punish the killers of the 243 marines and other servicemen in the Beirut attack of October 23, 1983. The legalistic excuse for inaction was that the exact identity of the culprits was unknown, as if there were any doubt of the Iranian or Syrian roles. The excuse was repeated even less persuasively to justify passivity when the U.S. Embassy Annex in East Beirut was attacked in September 1984.

Still, the positive dynamics of a successful presidency ensured that the political damage of the Lebanon tragedy was limited to the region itself—and with good reason. By seizing the opportunity offered by the call for help of its Caribbean neighbors to invade Grenada, rescue U.S. citizens in peril, and dislodge the murderous clique newly in power, the president demonstrated his ability to act decisively in difficult circumstances (the invasion took place a mere two days after the Beirut tragedy). Again, the military command structure revealed its inability to deviate from established bureaucratic priorities: although the administration's hostility to the Grenadian regime had long been advertised, no contingency preparations had been made, as shown by the fact that the troops had to go in without proper tactical maps. And the operational plan improvised on short notice was a notably clumsy affair, not at all the fast-moving *coup de main* that would have been appropriate. But in Grenada at least the feeble opposition ensured victory, and the very inadequacy of the higher command gave scope for some truly valiant combat by the troops, whose conduct justifiably evoked much public satisfaction.

Decisiveness over Grenada was matched by persistence in El Salvador. With both abandonment and direct combat intervention firmly ruled out, U.S. policy provided for a rising volume of military and economic assistance to the authorities while actively promoting their democratization. The results manifest during the year were clearly positive: the armed forces of El Salvador were both perceptibly strengthened and made more humane in their conduct, while in José Napoleón Duarte the country acquired a credible national leader and genuine reformer. As a consequence, U.S. policy in El Salvador became much less unpopular than it had been in Europe as well as at home, reducing the previously high political costs of the venture.

Elsewhere in Central America, the administration was much less successful. In Honduras, the apparent magnitude of rather small but grossly over-publicized U.S. military exercises evoked an entirely predictable nationalist reaction, especially after more than 7,000 acres were subtracted from the hemisphere's poorest agriculture to provide a training camp for Salvadoran as well as Honduran troops, making a highly visible "Regional Military Training Center" out of a venture that could have been quietly accommodated in any back-country farm. By the end of the year, the Hondurans were making impossibly large demands for aid in order to sanction continued military cooperation, partly to assuage popular resentment but more because of the need to balance the increased military power of El Salvador, with which Honduras has fought its only recent war, and with which border disputes remain unresolved.

In the case of Nicaragua, the failure—for now at least—of U.S. policy was more conspicuous and very clearly the result of divided counsels between Congress and the administration, and even within the latter. Both bilateral and multilateral diplomacy by way of the Contadora group was attempted by the administration but only halfheartedly, because of the deep conviction that the Sandinista leaders are entirely committed to the creation of a totalitarian state on the Soviet-Cuban model and would use any diplomatic agreement merely to buy time in pursuit of that goal. Not only to the Reagan administration but also to European Social-Democrats previously very sympathetic, the Nicaraguan leaders appeared far more interested in striking attitudes of revolutionary defiance than in occupying themselves with the humble tasks of economic amelioration.

Unable to accept the Sandinista regime, the administration was equally unable to arrest its further consolidation. Congress reacted to the CIA–sponsored mining of the Nicaraguan harbors by cutting off funds for the "Contras" just as they were attracting more volunteers and greater support from a Nicaraguan population increasingly discontented. Although obviously hurt by the cutoff, the Contras did not dissolve when their funding was ended and remained very much in the field. On the other hand, with the Sandinista military organization already highly developed, it is only by a guerrilla war most protracted that the Contras could possibly prevail—and that distant prospect of success depends entirely on the continued availability of sanctuaries in Honduras and Costa Rica. The Reagan administration undoubtedly applies its influence to that effect, but can do little more, having in effect lost at least for the moment its most promising indirect option. Rumors of invasions both preceded and followed the U.S. elections, but always without substance: Grenada is a precedent but also a warning of the very large scale of the effort that would be required given the current military procedures of the United States.

But the impasse of U.S. policy vis-à-vis Nicaragua was only of small import in the wider context characterized by the reaffirmation of American prestige. Nowhere was this more apparent than in relations between Washington and its NATO allies in Europe. The June summit meeting of the major industrial nations produced little of substance, but a highly positive atmosphere of intimate collaboration as European leaders muted their previously bitter protests against U.S. economic policies in admiration for the evident strength of the American recovery and its hoped-for effect on their own economies. The positive turn in the president's approach to the Soviet Union and arms control also helped to ease past tensions within the alliance, as did a more constructive U.S. approach to military planning within NATO's various organs. The December meeting of defense ministers, for example, was apparently particularly productive, as agreement was reached on a new program to strengthen NATO's conventional capabilities. Some progress also was reported during the year on collaborative efforts to develop the "emerging conventional technologies," even though considerable disagreement remains about the potential of these programs.

NATO's underlying problems remained unresolved to be sure, and differences between Washington and the European capitals—with Paris over Mitterrand's conciliatory approach to Libya, with Brussels over the unyielding U.S. position on missile deployments, for example—surfaced repeatedly during the year. In general, however, the allies were swept along with the tide of U.S. economic recovery, and specifically, President Reagan's political success, making clear as early as the summer—demonstrating their confidence in the predictive value of U.S. opinion polls even sooner than the Russians—that they had no reservations in looking forward to working with a second Reagan administration.

Many factors contributed to the relative success of U.S. policy in 1984. But most of all, it was that intangible sense that the nation was again on the move—the re-emergence of American confidence and, accordingly, prestige. However damaging to U.S. industry, the high quotation of the dollar reflected worldwide perceptions of an American resurgence, in which technological success, social stability, and an economy growing rapidly for much of the year loomed larger than the twin deficits of national finance and foreign trade. In addition, the restoration of the physical constituents of U.S. military power was seen as more important than the operational deficiencies that clearly persisted. It was, however, the sharp contrast with a Soviet Union visibly faltering that perhaps did more than anything else to create the image of a successful America.

The Soviet Impasse

The Soviet scene was dominated during the year by the evident sclerosis of the inner party leadership, which left the Soviet Union without a plausible leader endowed with a presumptive longevity sufficient to consolidate a new leadership capable of long-delayed reforms. With half its available investment resources absorbed by only two sectors—energy extraction, which produces declining supplies of energy, and agriculture, of persistently low and unstable productivity—and with very heavy military expenditures precluding increases in total investment, the Soviet economy is now in relative decline. Most experts project very low, or even zero, economic growth for the USSR through the 1980s. The Stalinist formula, which yielded high growth in exchange for large injections of industrial investment, has been compromised by the high investment in agriculture (almost five times the U.S. proportion) even as the Stalinist formula of allocation is of diminishing effectiveness when planners must choose among a myriad of chemical and electronic intermediate goods in lieu of the steel, electricity, timber, and cement of yesteryear. But no new formula for growth has been devised and no substitute has been found for the central planning that once worked so powerfully when only a few command decisions had to be made. Much-advertised administrative reforms that leave farm collectivization and central planning intact come and go without positive results, as the Soviet leadership continues to prefer the political safety of continued centralization over the economic attractions of liberalization.

The net effect of economic stagnation and political paralysis on Soviet external conduct is to reduce its dynamism and flexibility. Resources continue to flow to the established accounts, whether it is the upkeep of the present array of armed forces or the subsidization of Cuba, but there is neither the growth nor the dynamic reallocation needed to start new accounts, whether for the development of space weapons or the subsidization of potentially rewarding new clients, such as Angola and Mozambique, both of which have been left to seek other remedies. The perceptible loss of dynamism of Soviet foreign policy thus has a concrete material basis.

During 1984, the Soviet Union had a less varied conflictual experience but one of far greater dimensions in its Afghan war. More and more clearly, the nature of Soviet military action was revealed as a campaign of imperial pacification of the most purely classical kind, whose aim is de facto annexation and whose tempo is deliberately slow. With not much more than 100,000 troops in a very large country, the aim of Soviet military action is certainly not to control the territory but rather to transform the human geography by killing and extruding those Afghans who persist in resisting the new order, by herding nomads into settled areas, and by depopulating the countryside in areas of especially intense resistance. With perhaps 5 million of Afghanistan's pre-invasion population of 14 million already driven out of the country to fill refugee camps in Iran and Pakistan, and with at least 1 million more already forced out of their ancestral lands into zones more easily controlled, and with the steady killing of the more combative among the more warlike ethnic groups, the long-term Soviet strategy is not seriously impeded by the many brave tactical successes of the resistance.

Because no military supplies reach the resistance directly by air, all weapons and ammunition not captured in the field must pass twin hurdles: first, being limited in quality as well as quantity by changing Pakistani estimates of what level of supply the Soviet Union will tolerate; and then being filtered into the country, often across vast distances, by scarce and vulnerable trucks or more usually by caravans of pack animals.

As a result, the resistance is well provided only in small arms; even the simplest anti-tank weapons are in short supply, and there are hardly any antiaircraft weapons with which to fight Soviet helicopters. The Afghan resistance receives the applause of many all over the world, but not much tangible effective aid.

India After Indira

The murder of Indira Gandhi in October and the mob attacks that followed against Sikh property-owners, lone travelers, and even Sikh neighborhoods promptly induced speculation of greater troubles to come, mainly in the Punjab, where Sikhs account for roughly half the population. Once again, as so often before, the survival of a united India was brought into question by many observers of varying expertise. The centripetal tendencies inherent in a multi-ethnic society, further divided on linguistic-regional lines, are part of India's reality, but so is the determination and ability of the inherently centralizing political and bureaucratic elite, which has the loyalty of a first-class army. India's unity is much less fragile than its friends fear or its foes hope, a fact that became clear with the prompt reestablishment of order, the orderly succession, and the well-run electoral campaign and successful election in December.

The Iran-Iraq Conflict

There were other conflicts during the year in many parts of the world but the war between Iran and Iraq continued to be by far the most important.

A new pattern was established in the war without however bringing a resolution any nearer. Iraq tried to force Iran to suspend the war by interrupting its oil revenues by means of air attacks against the tanker traffic to and from the Kharg Island loading terminal and against that facility itself. Though amply dramatic, as huge vessels laden with oil were repeatedly set on fire by air-launched missiles that France continued to supply, Iraqi attacks were not, however, sufficiently intensive to achieve their purpose. Insurance rates did increase but not beyond the level that Iranian discounts could off-set, while owners had no difficulty in finding crews willing to accept the risk for modest amounts of danger money. Thus Iran's oil income was only marginally reduced and its imports of both food and military supplies continued at a level scarcely diminished, without any great decline in the country's hard currency holdings.

Iranian attempts to force a cessation of Iraqi attacks by attacking in turn the tanker traffic serving Iraq's chief allies and providers, Kuwait and Saudi Arabia, eventually evoked a firm response that was not merely verbal; in July, an Iranian F-4 fighter-bomber was successfully intercepted by Saudi-piloted F-15s vectored on to their target by a U.S.-manned AWACS airborne-radar aircraft. All three parties chose to minimize the importance of the incident but the message was evidently persuasive; Iran abandoned its indirect strategy even though Iraq continued its own sporadic air attacks.

In the primary warfare fought on land, Iran remained on the offensive throughout the year in the theoretical sense that the Iraqis did not even threaten any large offensive of their own; but Iran's forces were themselves unable to stage any large-scale attack that could promise decisive results. With Iraq's potentially most vulnerable Basrah frontage secured by increasingly elaborate minefields, artificial barriers, and fortified lines held by much armor and covered by a great mass of artillery, Iran's two-step method of war, whereby advancing foot infantry is to seize ground under the cover of artillery barrages, was effectively neutralized.

Only powerful armored forces could have crossed the wide interdiction zones covered by Iraq's artillery, but the swampy terrain and Iraqi antitank barriers would have impeded any large armored advance, even if Iran had the requisite armor, which was not the case. Iran has been able to maintain large numbers of infantrymen at the front (some 400,000 army troops and volunteer Revolutionary Guards), successfully replacing vast losses, and it has also managed to keep a large inventory of artillery serviceable and supplied. But Iran has not been able to rebuild the shah's once magnificently equipped armored forces, so that even the most successful infantry attacks could not be exploited to achieve real results by penetrations in depth. Iran's relative disadvantage in air power was acute but not of great consequence, for the Iraqi air force seemed unable to make much use of its impressive inventory. During 1984 there were a number of lesser Iranian attacks on peripheral sectors of the front, but the long-prepared offensive against the Basrah sector failed to materialize.

With Iraq still able to pay for its war by residual oil exports and foreign subsidies, and with Iran likewise able to fight on if not to great effect, the war seems likely to continue, at least as long as the Ayatollah Khomeini lives; the latter is said to be 85 years old, but his remaining span may outlast the century judging by his father, who reportedly died at 103, and his brother, who is said to be 97 years old.

Given that both the United States and the Soviet Union have long favored a peaceful resolution of the Iran-Iraq war, its persistence is proof enough of the diminished leverage of both the leading powers over world events. Specifically, neither has been able to persuade its allies and clients to suspend arms sales to the belligerents (Soviet supplies to Iraq were only resumed once it became clear that Iran would continue the war), and neither has been able to muster the diplomatic leverage necessary to impose a termination of the war.

In Conclusion: The Decay of the Bipolar Order

With a Soviet Union less dynamic than ever before in memory and a United States averse to all but the most trivial conflictual engagements, there is now much more scope for third-party action in the entire realm of international security. In the 1960s it required a leader of the caliber of De Gaulle and a country with all the attainments of France to struggle for a modicum of strategic independence in a world dominated by two highly dynamic superpowers eager to project their influence into every corner of the world. Nowadays, De Gaulle's achievement is far more easily replicated, whether in tentative and eminently constructive forms, as in the late stirrings of the Western European Union, or in unilaterally activist forms as in the case of Syria and South Africa now successfully acting as regional powers, or even in forms chaotically aggressive, as with Qaddafi's Libya, the very model of a piratical state, whose unpunished outrages amply demonstrate the inability of the greater powers to impose a modicum of order in world affairs.

8

THE ECONOMIC
INSTRUMENT
IN STATECRAFT

INTRODUCTION

Nations may fail in an infinity of ways in the realm of national strategy but have only one path to success. It is only when the diverse instruments of state power and notably the economic as well as the military are harmoniously exploited under the discipline of a coherent external policy that the full power-potential of the state can be realized, through the medium of diplomacy. While not in itself an instrument of state power, diplomacy realizes the potential of all the instruments, precisely to the extent that the latter are placed in its service, by being first subordinated to a coherent external policy. Thus, for example, by evoking the capacity for military mobilization that the state is perceived as having, diplomacy can throw into the balance of world politics the military power that could be, perhaps to add greatly to the military power that is. Similarly, by evoking the prospect of economic facilitations or economic restrictions, diplomacy can influence the conduct of interested foreign powers, in the degree that such claims are deemed credible, and the resulting transactions are deemed valuable.

Without the subordination of the diverse instruments of power to a coherent external policy, even high achievement in some instrumentality or other need not bring success. Conversely, even a mere adequacy in the single instruments can bring great results if the harmony of a coherent policy is achieved in the exploitation of them all.

Obviously there is no economic advantage that is sufficiently great to generate even an iota of state power, if it is plain that the diplomacy of the state can neither give nor deny its benefits.

There is therefore no automatic correlation between the productive capacity of a state, its converse ability to offer rich markets for the production of others, its creativity in developing desirable technologies and its talents in providing valuable intangible services on the one hand, and the diplomatic leverage of that state. A skillful diplomacy will still no doubt find ways of weaving such economic advantages into a backdrop of generic prestige, to yield authority which other states may choose to concede but that is all, if the diplomacy of the state has no real control over the economic transactions with foreign powers.

When we survey in retrospect the best-known examples of successful national strategy in the most diverse of circumstances, what we find is precisely the concerted exploitation of economic and other instruments in a coherent external policy. In the best-known case of them all, it is a commonplace of historiography that the last century of Roman imperial control in the West was redeemed by a diplomacy based on the economic instrument at a time when the might of the legions was no more than a memory. Thus the Visigoths could still be adequately controlled till the first decade of the fifth century by the opportune granting and withholding of the privilege of buying grain. And so it was for the Vandals, the Alani, and the Burgundians, who erupted into imperial territory only to find themselves becoming manipulated agents, whose own exertions would then provide what was left of Roman power. Four centuries before, the Empire in its fullest strength smoothly controlled the German tribes across the Rhine by the comfortable device of opening and closing the well-regulated channels of trade, as well as by the timely extension of small subsidies. And in all the years in between, the same array of economic measures most usefully complemented the power of Roman arms while it was still great.

In striking testimony to the universality of the phenomenon, we may recognize a clear parallel in the policy of the Ch'ing in their successful domination of Altishahr, Zungharia and Ulghuristan. A world away from the centers of Manchu power, vast lands inhabited by the most turbulent of peoples were successfully secured by the combination of very small garrisons of Banner troops and a most comprehensive policy of trade control. The same Ch'ing practices which Westerners encountered in outmoded form along the South China coast, and which there brought only humiliation and defeat for the Ch'ing, had been very successful indeed in controlling the peoples of central Asia—for the latter were of course in the organically dependent situation of the economically more backward.

Access to the markets of Kashgar, Yarkand, Kulja old and new, Urumchi, Khitai and the rest was reserved as a carefully regulated privilege, granted only to those who would take good care to cooperate with the Ch'ing. And that sufficed to ensure that during the eighteenth century and into the nineteenth the Manchu power was manifest throughout Central Asia, in a great arc from Kashmir to Ferghana and northeast to the Altai. At no time during this period could the authorities in faraway Peking hope to control the vast expanse of Central Asia by outright force; the scattered 2,000–3,000-man garrisons of Banner troops could, however, suffice but only in conjunction with the relentless pressure of the foreign merchants, who dissuaded hostility towards the Ch'ing power in the internal politics of the statelets and tribes round about.

What the Visigoths that Rome had to contain and the Khirgiz and Kazakhs that the Ch'ing controlled had in common was their inherent vulnerability to economic manipulation, the inevitable result of technical and economic inferiority. Today's Soviet Union is as dependent on external grain supplies as the Visigoths ever were, and as dependent on skilled manufactures as the Khirgiz and Kazakhs, who imported their cloth and metal artifacts from Turfan, Hami and points east. And yet far from being the object of the successful economically-based diplomacy of others, the Soviet Union obtains, on balance, a net increment of power from its scant economic capacity—simply because it pursues a coherent external policy, in a world where others are content with a day-to-day diplomacy frequently contradictory, and almost always shortsighted.

THE SOVIET UNION

The Soviet Union must trade, and it does; the Soviet Union must even sometimes make political concessions in order to obtain what it wants. But in spite of its persistent need for modern industrial technologies, for products of refined manufacture, and for grains—all of which can be obtained only from a rather small number of countries that are all ostensibly hostile to its purposes—in spite of thus being in a fundamentally weak situation that offers, in theory, ample opportunities for external manipulation, it is rather the Soviet Union that does the manipulating, instead of the other way around.

Thus we see Soviet oil being sold at a great variety of prices to different customers, with the oil being priced not by its inherent quality but rather by the qualities of the recipients. And of course the Soviet Union has most skillfully succeeded in extracting great political leverage by manipulating the foreigners that want to supply its market, poor though it is. The Russians have indeed managed to bring into existence what *Pravda* would call an "objectively" pro-Soviet party among the grain farmers of the United States, the steel-pipe makers of Germany, and a whole variety of other Western industrial interests.

The refinement of Soviet policy is manifest in the carefully graded treatment given to different Western traders, which has created among them a sharply defined hierarchy of favorites. Those who stand at the very top of that hierarchy have been made into household names in their respective countries, so that figures already influential in some degree could have yet more influence. Thus we know of Mr. Kendall, whom the Russians have endowed with an eminence that wholly transcends his natural status as the head of a soft-drink company, and we are called upon to celebrate the majesty of Armand Hammer, who would otherwise have remained in a greatly deserved obscurity, except among his fellows in the oil business. Similarly there are certain Germans and Frenchmen, Italians and Belgians who can be relied upon to endorse Russian *desiderata*, and who serve as willing dragomans at the gates of the Kremlin, always ready to convey opportune messages aimed at Western public opinion.

SOVIET TRADE AND TECHNOLOGY DEPENDENCE

In 1980 the gross national product amounted to some 462 billion in 1970 rubles at a factor cost,[1] or 1,280 billion in 1980 dollars.[2] In the same year, imports from the developed countries of the West amounted to only 24 billion dollars.[3]

[1] H. Block in Soviet Grand Strategy, C & L Associates (1982).
[2] H. Block, The Planetary Product, U.S. Department of State (1981).
[3] Handbook of Economic Statistics 1981, National Foreign Assessment Center, NF HES 81-001 (November 1981), Table 58.

Thus trade with the West amounts to a very small percentage of all the transactions that make up the Soviet economy. And yet that trade, small though it is, is very important indeed for the Soviet economy. By now we know enough about the intimate workings of the Soviet economy to recognize the reasons for the paradox. First, the peculiar weakness of the Soviet economy is its slow rate of innovation, itself the entirely natural result of the lack of incentives for risk-taking (and there is no innovation without risk). (The pervasive restrictions imposed on the flow of information within the Soviet system must also be judged as a contributing cause.) The second reason is that supplies readily available from abundantly supplied Western markets can compensate in a timely fashion for the unplanned shortages that chronically arise in a centrally planned economy whenever the plan fails to correspond—as it often does—with the pattern of supplies of intermediate and consumer goods. And then, of course, there is the chronic underproduction of Soviet agriculture, and even more its exceptional vulnerability to weather-induced fluctuations.

As one surveys these deficiencies, which are the source and origin of the Soviet need for economic access to the West (for of course the Soviet regime would much prefer total self-sufficiency), it is obvious that they are in each case deliberately accepted by the regime. The practices and structures that cause the deficiencies are in fact manifestations of the political system itself. That the central-planning mechanism must function more and more poorly in an economy further and further removed from the severities of the rudimentary "war economy *sui generis*" of the 1930s, must by now be a commonplace to every member of the Soviet Politburo. And indeed we have seen a wide variety of abortive reforms of the system, reforms officially proposed and just as officially abandoned. It seems that the central-planning system is no longer capable of major reform, simply because it is the broadest source of power in the Soviet policy. A Communist party that can no longer have a satisfactory ideological role, has become in effect a logistic organization, whose leaders great and small have found predominantly economic roles for themselves. Party leaders will only rarely be skilled managers and must certainly lack the attributes of the entrepreneur. They can still operate with sufficient success in the centrally planned system, which requires only administrative skills from them; but obviously party leaders in the roles of economic management could not survive if the central-planning mechanism were abandoned, thus forcing them to make decisions which they are mostly unqualified to make, and to take risks which they are certainly unwilling to accept.

In agriculture this same phenomenon is fully manifest but, in addition, there is an organic obstacle to efficiency which the Soviet system has never been able to transcend whether by terror or by incentives, whether by compulsion or investment: agriculture deals in the heterogenous, with each field, each crop and each season having its own particularities. This heterogeneity makes it extremely difficult to compel performance from the unwilling by instruction, supervision and sanctions. It is not by accident that slave agriculture was only truly successful in one-crop plantations, where overseers could effectively ensure compliance with minimum standards by means of rare incentives and the frequent use of the whip. (Where slave agriculturalists nevertheless performed in a satisfactory manner outside the plantation setting, we find that in each case this was so because performance was successfully induced by a quasi-competitive reward.) Those who work in Soviet agriculture are not juridically slaves, but many of them seem to have assimilated the working habits and attitude of that status. The full measure of the failure of the Soviet agricultural system is that its ability to motivate productivity is not distinctly superior to that of a slave agriculture.

TRADE AND REGIME MAINTENANCE

If the Soviet Union did not have access to timely infusions of Western technology to offset its scant ability to innovate, the regime would be forced to choose between the acceptance of a cumulative and generic industrial obsolescence—which would eventually be manifest in the military industries also—or some drastic surgery upon the central-planning system, which would of course endanger the political basis of the regime. Similarly, if the Soviet Union did not have access to frequent and large external supplies of grain, it would be forced into alternative policies, each exceedingly undesirable from the viewpoint of the regime:

1. *An incremental-investment solution,* whereby the attempt would be made to force more grain output from the system as it now is, by disproportionate investments and/or incentives. Soviet agriculture was notoriously starved of investment capital throughout the Stalin era. Since then, it has absorbed notoriously large infusions of capital investment to yield returns notoriously low.

Clearly the exchange rate between increments in investment and subsequent increments in output is very low, and moreover the rate is subject to sharp climatic fluctuations. This, however, is the one option that does not require political devolution or political risks, and therefore it is the most likely to be exercised.

2. A *structural solution*, whereby the land would be turned over to private farming (as was done in Poland and Hungary to a large extent) by de-collectivization and the dissolution of the "state farms," or by a very *large* reallocation of land, within the current structures, from collective and "state" to private plots. The radical variant of this solution would of course amount to nothing less than a disestablishment of the rural branches of the CPSU; or, in Soviet terms, to a retreat of the state power from the countryside. The partial variant of this solution would mask and soften the political consequence at a great cost in overall production, since the natural tendency of the collective farmers and "state" farm-workers is to devote their labor and care to the private plots first and last; and also to misappropriate collective and "state" tools, fertilizer, etc., for their own private farming. It is reasonable to assume that if, say, a 50/50 allocation were instituted, the result would be efficient farming on *half* of the available land with the rest being farmed even less efficiently than now.

3. *An austerity solution.* The Soviet consumer is not well provided by Western standards, but he is far better supplied nowadays than he was, say, thirty years ago. The Soviet regime could therefore in theory respond to the denial of grain from the West by restricting consumption. But thirty years ago the political circumstances of Soviet society were very different:

a. the Stalinist police terror powerfully dissuaded the manifestation of popular resistance to austerity;

b. exhortation based on deferred-consumption arguments could still be effective;

c. political propaganda could be based on an ideology that could still inspire many; and, most important perhaps,

d. the ravages of the newly won war provided a very good excuse for the regime; the final victory was a source of tremendous pride for the Russians especially; and moreover, wartime conditions defined standards of consumption so minimal that even the stringent postwar austerity could still be deemed relatively comfortable.

None of these conditions obtain at present. The system of police control is still very much in place, but it has lost its capacity to terrorize the population into silence. A reversion to midnight arrests, summary shootings and mass deportations could quickly restore an atmosphere of terror, but it is most unlikely that such actions would be compatible with the present politics of the Politburo, or the temper of its current members. There is no doubt a large supply of Stalinists in the CPSU who would be well content to restore the terror, but that would imply a radical change in the composition of the leadership—which the latter is most unlikely to engineer of its own volition.

Secondly, Stalin's future of promised prosperity is today's distinctly unprosperous present; the regime could not again rely on exhortation to induce acceptance of a diminished supply of food, since promises of prosperity deferred, once more, could not be plausible. Thirdly, the appeal of the official ideology has waned very greatly and thus the effect of political propaganda to justify austerity must be greatly diminished also. Fourthly, the Second World War is now thirty years removed and it would be bizarre if it could still serve as an *alibi* and as a standard of what is acceptable; pride in the victory of 1945 there must still be, if only attenuated, but it would be strange if it could still be an emotional substitute for meat on the table. Finally, demographic change, cultural evolution and the relaxation of police terror have set the stage for the rise of non-Russian (and indeed anti-Russian) nationalisms within the Soviet Union's own "Third World" in Central Asia and the Caucasus, as well as for an intensification of nationalist feelings in areas of long-standing national consciousness.

For these reasons, the austerity solution would be highly dangerous for regime stability, and would indeed entail serious danger even if it were merely one element in a combined response to the denial of grain supplies from abroad.

In summary, therefore, it is evident that the consequences of effective restrictions on the availability of Western industrial technologies, skilled manufactures and grain supplies would wholly transcend in their dimensions the rather small monetary value of those transactions in the Soviet GNP. In each case, the Soviet leadership would have to make highly undesirable trade-offs between political costs and risks as well as a choice between the latter and long-term growth prospects (in the case of technology transfers).

Finally, it is important to recognize that the Soviet vulnerability to access restrictions has greatly *increased* even as the Soviet economy has grown in size and sophistication. In the case of technology and skilled manufactures, the innovation differential has increased in significance simply because the generic (world-standard) rate of innovation has tended to accelerate in certain crucial sectors (and notably micro-electronics: to be "ten years" behind in vacuum-tube days could mean little; nowadays it would be catastrophic). In the case of grain supplies, the transformation of the Soviet diet (which political conditions have imposed) has obviously created a dependence on large supplies of feed grains that was wholly absent in the meatless days of Stalin's regime.

EVIDENCE FROM THE RECENT PAST
AND ITS IMPLICATIONS

The state of the Soviet economy and the nexus between its systemic deficiencies and the structure of the regime appear to offer an exceptional potential for the use of economic controls in dealing with the Soviet Union.

And yet it is the prevalent opinion of scholars and practitioners alike that (i) "economic sanctions" are ineffective in general and (ii) that they are particularly ineffective in regard to the Soviet Union.

This skepticism is solidly grounded on very definite empirical evidence, and yet at the same time it reflects a misunderstanding of the *full* implications of the evidence:

The *myth*, still curiously prevalent, is that the sanctions imposed on Mussolini's Italy and Tojo's Japan were ineffective in themselves, i.e., as economic measures. In fact, as we now know, even the feeble League of Nations' sanctions imposed on Italy (to punish its invasion of Ethiopia) caused very serious economic difficulties, while in the case of Japan the impact of the final US–imposed trade limitations was little short of catastrophic.

The *fact* is that the sanctions imposed on Italy and Japan did not merely fail to achieve positive change in the *conduct* of the two countries, but were actually counterproductive, causing Italy to draw closer to Hitler's Germany (at a time when the Austrian question was dividing the two countries), and actually inducing Japan to go to war against the United States, the British Empire and the Dutch East Indies—instead of suspending undeclared war against China.

The correct lesson to be drawn, fully valid as an analogy for our present dealings with the Soviet Union, is that *ad hoc* economic controls designed to force *changes of conduct* are likely to be ineffectual if not actually counterproductive. This is so for economic and political reasons so fundamental that they are likely to be almost universally valid:

1. *Ad hoc* controls on supplies of commodities cannot have an immediate *and* compelling effect because (a) stocks can absorb the initial impact of denial in most cases; (b) leakages can attenuate the impact thereafter; and (c) structural reorientation can, over time, reduce dependence on the denied commodities. Oil is the one exception in some degree, but the very example of Japan reminds us that a raw material that mines itself and is found in a variety of weak countries scattered throughout the globe can be seized at source if not voluntarily sold.

2. *Ad hoc* controls on access to markets (the most powerful sanction used against Italy) cannot have a compelling effect because (a) the general resources and reserves of the economy will attenuate the effect of lost foreign-currency earnings; (b) leakages will allow the continuation of some part at least of the export flow (e.g., Rhodesian chrome); and (c) structural reorientation can in some degree reduce the need for exports, by investment in import-substitution capacity and/or in redirected export capacity for commodities or services that are inherently more difficult to boycott, or which are aimed at different markets.

3. *Ad hoc* controls on technology transfers can have no immediate and compelling impact because by their very nature they affect the *long-term* efficiency of the recipient's and can have little or no effect in the interim.

4. Finally, the political reason is of dominating importance and may suffice in itself to nullify or pervert the intent of the sanctions. *Ad hoc* economic controls designed to punish specific actions and (usually) obtain their reversal are obviously very intrusive without being compelling in a literal, physical sense, as effective military action might be. The intrusion can normally be represented by the leadership to its people as an insulting *diktat;* this will normally evoke a supportive response from the population, which will at least mitigate the political costs and risks of defiance; indeed, that response will often make defiance to the supposed *diktat* actually advantageous for the leadership (not infrequently, an unpopular leadership is redeemed by for-

eign intrusions that arouse a nationalist action). And it may happen that economic threats or reprisals will evoke a popular response which actually forces the leadership to strike poses of defiance regardless of its own inclinations.

These are the well-founded reasons for the widespread notion that the economic controls are weak or actually counterproductive as tools of policy, but it is here that the misunderstanding of the evidence intervenes: What the evidence shows is that *ad hoc* measures designed to achieve *changes of conduct* are ineffectual or even counterproductive. This does not, however, mean that the economic instrument is ineffectual, for there is an "effect" which can indeed be achieved, and whose long-term strategic value may be far greater than any change of conduct: the *long-term* denial of commodities and technology can evoke structural responses, which then in turn substantially reduce the external-action capacity of the affected state.

In the specific case of the Soviet Union, the most powerful measure would be the long-term denial of external grain supplies. Owing to the considerations discussed above, the successful denial of grain imports into the Soviet economy or their substantial reduction would reduce the overall magnitude of Soviet military power either in the medium term (if added investment in agriculture is taken from military spending) or in the long term (if the investment is reallocated from non-agricultural purposes).

To be sure, long-term grain denial could not be accomplished by casual diplomacy—let alone after the event (as in the case of the 1979 post-Afghanistan partial grain denial). It would require, rather, a costly long-term *restructuring* of the world grain market within an agreed diplomatic framework involving at least the classic exporters (Canada, Australia, Argentina, and the EEC as well as the United States). Agreed reductions in subsidization (US, EEC), increased controlled-destination concessionary deliveries to poor countries, US-subsidized "conservation" programs, other non-agricultural incentives, and yet more innovative actions would all be required; annual costs amounting to, say, 5 percent of the US defense budget might begin to define the costs involved.

On the other hand, the added investment that the Soviet Union would have to allocate to the agricultural sector and the cognate industries would be substantially larger than $12.5 billion. Under the current Five-Year Plan, *no* increase in the flow of overall capital investment is anticipated. For the first time since 1945, other demands on resources preclude growth in investment. Therefore increases in agricultural investment can be provided only by (1) reducing consumption; (2) and/or reducing all other investment; (3) and/or reducing military outlays. The former would entail the same risks as the food-austerity option reviewed above; the second choice would mean that an economy already close to a *zero growth* situation would actually regress (since with a declining labor input, capital input must rise simply to maintain the *status quo*). Finally, a reduction in military expenditures would of course achieve the objective directly (instead of indirectly, as would be the case if it is industrial investment that is reduced).

Similarly, a serious commitment of policy attention, *and resources*, would be required to restrict further the transfer of technology to the Soviet Union. To move beyond the formalistic categorization of "strategic" and non-strategic technologies, to extend restrictions as widely as possible in order to intensify the innovation dilemma, the United States would have to offer appropriate inducements of one sort or another to several of its allies in a bilateral or multi-lateral framework. Since it must now be assumed that the Soviet leadership will *not* embark on reforms to promote innovation (i.e., a dismantlement of the central-planning system), to the extent and degree that technology flows are successfully restricted, the Soviet Union must either (1) accept an intensification of the relative obsolescence of Soviet industry; or (2) reallocate R&D manpower and resources from military to industrial purposes. In either case the United States would derive a long-term benefit.

To affect the demand side of the food and technology inflow, by reducing the Soviet capacity to earn foreign currency, must be even more difficult than to deny external grain supplies or to widen technology transfer restrictions to cover the full spectrum of technologies, military and not. For one thing, the major Soviet exports are, at present, anonymous commodities for which there is a fluid and uncontrollable market (oil, gold); other exports are primarily directed at countries which would not have the slightest interest in cooperating with a US–organized boycott (notably the Soviet arms sales to paying clients, e.g., Syria, Iraq or Libya); and then there are export flows that the United States itself would not want to curtail. Nevertheless, there is some scope for action. The Yamal pipeline is an exemplary case of a (potential) source of Soviet foreign-currency earnings that it would be most worthwhile to deny. Once again, however, it is quite futile to try to achieve such denial by an *ad hoc*, last-minute diplomacy. What is needed, rather, is the provision of energy-supply alternatives of at least comparable value to the affected parties; diplomacy can only facilitate (and gain time) for *substantive* action. In the case of the Yamal gas-supply scheme for example, only the development of a Norwegian and/or Algerian alternative, as well as guaranteed deliveries of US coal at guaranteed prices could create a genuine possibility of stopping the scheme.

CONCLUSIONS

In the contemporary world, their inherently delayed effect and essential indirectness greatly restrict the utility of economic controls as short-term instruments of statecraft. In fact such measures cannot be effective in obtaining favorable changes of conduct except in exceptional circumstances. Only long-term methods can be effective to an important degree, and then only if these have a substantive economic character, whereby the external environment is restructured around the target economy. And then finally the effect will *not* be manifest in the conduct of the affected party but would rather take the form of reduced capacity for external action.

To be sure, neither the Romans nor the Ch'ing relied on such structural effects in their successful use of economic controls, but they, of course, were dealing with much simpler economic entities than, say, the contemporary Soviet Union: there were no stocks in the Visigothic food economy; neither would the merchants of Kokand be influenced by long-term growth calculations. The methods of Rome and the Ch'ing are indeed still usable in the contemporary world to obtain changes of conduct, but only in dealing with countries with small and fragile economies.

At this writing, the conjunction of an activist American administration and a Soviet Union both very powerful militarily and on the verge of economic decline should logically result in a very determined American effort to make maximum use of the economic instrument of statecraft. That is of course far from being the case at present, but then of course strategy always demands far more than mere talk from those who would practice its arts.

9

CHAPTER

A GEOPOLITICAL PERSPECTIVE ON THE US-SOVIET COMPETITION

(BARRY M. BLECHMAN, CO-EDITOR)

*I*t is only natural that the relationship between the United States and the Soviet Union should be described in phrases inherited from the great power confrontations of the past. Thus memories of the Anglo-German, Franco-Prussian and even older Anglo-French rivalries linger in our minds to affect our understanding of the present competition between the United States and the Soviet Union.

But this inheritance misleads.

First, the Soviet Union and the United States are physically remote from one another, except in their virtually uninhabited extreme peripheries. Thus the territorial frictions and threatening proximities of the great power confrontations of the past are entirely absent.

Second, as a converse, successive American and Soviet leaders have little or no personal familiarity with each other's countries. To round off Oxford with Heidelberg was a fashionable accomplishment for young Englishmen of political ambition—especially after the advent of Anglo-German rivalry; young Germans went to both

British and French universities with equal ease; foreign study remained unusual for the French but lengthy student tours in Britain and Germany were mere routine. And it was outrightly eccentric for the British and the Germans not to visit Paris for ample vacations. Americans and Soviet officials do not frequent each other's universities in their youth, and in their maturity Americans do not take the waters at Soviet spas, any more than Soviet officials bring their families to American resorts. When the railways first arrived to accelerate the rhythms of conflict, they also served to convey British, French and German high officials to Paris, Berlin and London on many a private visit, but very few senior American officials have been to Moscow, and of their Soviet counterparts still fewer have been to Washington.

Given this veil of ignorance, it is not surprising that the two sides forever disappoint those who would impose highly responsive "action-reaction" models on Soviet-American dealings, whether in the accumulation of armaments or in the conduct of diplomacy. The unfriendly intimates who once conducted the great rivalries of Europe could act and react in close reciprocity as in a game of cards; the remote rivals of today are not even playing the same game.

The introduction of major armaments by one side does tend to evoke some sort of offsetting or competitive response by the other, characteristically after a fairly long delay. But a good many Soviet and American armament initiatives owe more to one-sided strategic goals, traditional preferences and bureaucratic priorities than to any prior initiative by the other side. Certainly, the commonplace image of an "arms race" purely propelled by reciprocal reactions does not correspond to the evidence.

One aspect of American-Soviet relations, too obviously novel to be forced into ill-fitting antique patterns, is very inadequately described by the phrase "ideological rivalry."

To be sure, during the first years of the Cold War, there was indeed a symmetrical and overt ideological struggle, in which each side employed all possible media of propaganda to discredit the rival's ideology and promote its own, above all in Western Europe and chiefly in France and Italy where large Communist parties were made yet more powerful by their control of the major trade unions. In those years, the broadcasting, publications, fellow-travelers and other outlets used to promote the ideological campaigns of the Soviet Union were answered most effectively by an equally broad American effort, whose instruments ranged from subsidized journals for intellectuals to board games which explained the Marshall plan to children, as well as numerous ad hoc devices, such as the letter-writing campaign in which Italo-Americans asked their relatives still in Italy to vote against the Communist party in the 1948 elections.

But on the American side the effort was not sustained, not so much because of congressional opposition, which did not emerge until the 1970s, but rather because it never acquired an organized institutional base, nor a professional constituency. The officials who took over the conduct of public diplomacy from the fervent ex-Communists and anti-Communist socialists so prominent in the early years of the Cold War had neither the background, training, nor disposition to engage in ideological debate; nor does such a struggle fit well with the fundamental character and values of American society. It is only most recently that the Reagan administration has tried, with scant success so far, to revert to an active ideological confrontation.

On the Soviet side, of course, the propaganda machinery is a core institution of the regime and has steadily expanded its scope. Propaganda by radio, both overt and not, in dozens of languages, has attained industrial dimensions, and so has the printed variety (even the *Soviet Military Review* appears in several languages), with overt publications being supplemented by supposedly independent journals and even daily newspapers published outside the Bloc.

The resources of Soviet propaganda are more impressive than its results, however. Once seen by many as the very embodiment of a modern humanism, or at least as the greatest promoter of social and economic justice, and of course as *the* state of the proletarians, the Soviet Union has now acquired a new identity in the eyes of many of its former supporters as a rigid bureaucratic despotism inherently repressive at home, and imperialist in Eastern Europe and beyond. The decline of Soviet ideological influence upon Western intellectuals began as far back as the Hungarian revolution of 1956 but during the 1970s it perceptibly accelerated. The drastic change that has taken place in the attitude of French intellectuals has been especially important because of their widespread influence throughout southern Europe and South America. The reasoned and radical opposition to the Soviet Union's conduct at home and abroad which is now prevalent in French intellectual circles is already beginning to have its influence in Rome and Madrid, and will in due course reach Buenos Aires and Athens. The Soviet Union's once large following among trade-union leaders in all the industrialized countries except the United States and Canada has also diminished very greatly, although there are still some isolated groups which remain loyal to Moscow. Certainly the most successful of the Western Communist parties are the ones which have most clearly declared their differences with Moscow. It is only among the most radical elements in the most troubled parts of the Third World that the Soviet Union has been able to claim new converts, but the guerrillas and terrorists who now profess loyalty to Moscow seem mostly attracted by the appeal of Soviet arms and diplomatic support, not Soviet ideology.

Far more important than overt propagandistic manifestations of the ideological competition as such is the natural political incompatibility between American pluralism and Soviet centralism. Soviet ideology—regardless of its transient tactical trappings—has been, is now, and almost surely always will be fundamentally hostile to the core values, objectives and very essence of Western democratic liberalism. While not denying the possibility of US–Soviet cooperation for specific purposes of common interest—for example, avoiding nuclear war—this basic fact does place very definite limitations on plausible ameliorations of the East–West struggle. It is precisely when Washington and Moscow are actively trying to cooperate, as in 1972–74, that this natural incompatibility makes itself manifest. While the leaders of the Soviet Union have the prerogative of making such ideological compromises as they deem necessary, in the United States the Executive cannot defy congressional interventions designed to impose American values, or merely domestic preferences, on the conduct of relations with the Soviet Union.

A limit is thereby set on the scope of diplomatic accommodation: a conciliatory Executive naturally inspires confrontationist moves in Congress, simply because there are so many aspects of Soviet governance that are repugnant to some sector or another of American public opinion. This countervailing mechanism does not preclude the successful negotiations of agreements covering all sorts of subjects, including the control of armaments. But it does preclude any permanent or widespread amity which would in any case be most ill-fitting to both sides. Certainly there is no sign of that process of "convergence" that was anticipated by some observers during the 1970s.

Intermittent ideological rivalry and the substantial incompatibility of the American and Soviet political systems are superimposed upon a worldwide diplomatic competition for access and influence, and a set of much more focused geo-strategic confrontations in Western Europe, the Levant and Persian Gulf regions, North-East Asia and of late in Central America. Developments during the past year in several of these regions are described later in this chapter. So too is the central manifestation of the direct confrontation between the great powers—the nuclear balance. Let us consider first, though, certain underlying factors.

In both competition and confrontation, there are fundamental asymmetries between the strengths and weaknesses of the Soviet Union and the United States and this too serves to complicate their relations, since even the achievement of parities of one sort or another need not bring a true equilibrium any closer. Thus, for example, a parity in intercontinental ballistic missile forces would weaken the Soviet Union given the American preponderance in manned bombers; and, more broadly, a nuclear parity overall results in a heightened military disequilibrium since there is no longer an offset for Western inferiority in conventional forces; and more broadly still, an overall military parity would leave the Soviets greatly inferior, given the Western superiority in most instruments of statecraft for the military. These fundamental asymmetries make difficult the successful negotiation of arms limitation measures confined to single categories of weapons—precisely the kind of negotiations which present the fewest technical obstacles.

Russia's gross national product was roughly 50 percent of the American in 1913. By present estimates, the Soviet gross national product does not amount to more than 60 percent of the American, notwithstanding the intense sacrifice exacted from the peoples of the Soviet Union precisely for the sake of economic growth. The per capita Soviet GNP is roughly 40 percent of the American, but with both investment and military purposes claiming much more of the Soviet national product than of the American, the Soviet standard of living is certainly not as high as 40 percent of the American. On a *relative* basis, as compared with all other industrialized countries, the Soviet standard of living has in fact declined during the last two decades, and is now beginning to be matched by the more successful among the developing countries. Naturally, what is more embarrassing for the Soviet government is the poverty of the Soviet consumer as compared to his counterparts in Eastern Europe. Aside from the ease of comparison that proximity allows, the Soviet Union's far greater wealth in natural resources and its much longer enjoyment of all the supposed benefits of communism both sharpen the contrast.

The large degree to which the Soviet economy remains autarchic has obvious advantages for internal control and the independence of its statecraft, but it means that the Soviet Union's ability to provide both markets and capital to developing countries is very much smaller than that of the United States. This should be reflected in the diplomatic competition between the two, but in fact the Soviet Union's inferiority as an economic partner is partially offset by its ability to make available internal security assistance and large quantities of weapons at moderate cost and, just as important, at short notice. To be sure, American weapons enjoy a reputation for higher quality and their "after sale service" is even better regarded as compared to the notorious Soviet record in such support, but these US advantages are more important in peaceful times than in crises or war.

As against all these disadvantages, the very system of centralized control that hinders Soviet production allows much more of total Soviet output to be allocated for the purposes of external power, chiefly to augment the quantity and quality of Soviet military forces. The material aspect of the Soviet-American military balance is of course conditioned by the accumulated investment of each side in deployed weapons, maturing research and development, bases and other facilities, ammunition stocks, and whatever else is neither consumed nor obsolete. At this particular time, the American-Soviet military balance is conditioned by the large excess of Soviet over American military investment which accumulated from the later 1960s to the mid-1970s, by which the Soviet Union has enhanced its prior advantage in land forces as a whole, diminished the American lead in naval forces, and eliminated the former American advantage in strategic nuclear forces.

This result is all the more remarkable in the light of the continued American advantage in advanced technologies of military relevance. During this period, the American lead in invention and development was in fact outstripped by the much larger scale of Soviet production which allowed the replacement of old weapons with new ones at a much faster rate. American prototypes continued to be far more effective than their Soviet counterparts but in the operational forces as a whole the Soviet technological lag diminished steadily. In the average quality of air and naval armaments the United States remains superior. In the realm of air-to-air combat, for example, this quality advantage should prevail over Soviet numerical superiority. This is not so in the case of ground-combat weapons where the American lead was narrow to begin with, and where residual technological advantages do not have great tactical value. Certainly the great Soviet numerical superiority in ground forces is not offset by the rather slow introduction of the latest American tanks, combat carriers, and so on.

Obviously, the altered military balance has influenced the worldwide diplomatic competition, offsetting to some extent the decreasing appeal of Soviet ideology and the growing ill-repute of the Soviet Union as a model and promoter of economic development. It is of course in the more focused geo-strategic confrontations that the material balance of military forces has the greatest impact, and this is especially true of Western Europe.

Following the Axis defeat in 1945, the comparative advantage of the Soviet Union in ground forces and that of the United States in naval and air forces, as well as geographic factors, favored the emergence of a Soviet hegemony over the entirety of the European continent, paralleled by an American hegemony over the territories of the former Japanese empire, including as much of China as the Nationalist government could keep.

Given the very great and indeed unchallengeable comparative advantage of the Soviet Union in ground forces, and the similar advantage of the United States in naval power, each could have remained comfortably secure in its own domain even with the rather small military effort that could be expected from a Soviet Union ravaged by war, and a United States most eager to demobilize.

What thwarted this outcome was the unexpected persistence of the United States after VE-Day. Having arrived on the scene as the co-liberators of Western Europe from the Germans, the Americans were universally expected to go home. In fact, the United States did demobilize its armed forces so quickly and so fully that they were virtually dissolved as fighting organizations by 1947. Nevertheless, in a series of reactions to Soviet policy, the United States rapidly emerged as the chief protector of much more of Europe than the Anglo-American forces had ever liberated. Some of the European lands thus shielded from Soviet power would otherwise have become client-states more constrained to obedience; others would have retained a much greater autonomy but not of course a full independence, except for the United Kingdom. That the Soviet Union was in 1945 devastated by war, that it had only just begun to absorb its new conquests and suzerainties of Eastern Europe are quite irrelevant. Except for the presence of the United States, Soviet hegemony would have followed automatically. To preserve the peace, appropriate governments with or without Communist participation would duly have been formed in one country after another, to conciliate the Soviet Union in one way or another. It was this unhappy expectation that induced the American leaders of the day to accept long-term responsibility for the security and independence of Western Europe; the prospect of a Europe entirely subjected to a Soviet hegemony was unacceptable in itself, and moreover many believed that the Soviet Union would not for long remain content in Europe, but would rather strive to harness its newly acquired European resources to pursue further expansion.

The unexpected emergence of America as the protector of Western Europe, and the successful expansion of that role to embrace alliance boundaries extending from the North Cape to Eastern Anatolia, required a great deal more than the evident desire of a vast majority of Europeans for such protection. It required the steady support of the Congress and thus of American public opinion for the most entangling alliance that could be imagined; the formation of a purposeful consensus among the opinion leaders and other individuals active in foreign affairs; new diplomatic expertise for coalition-building in the very complicated setting of post-war Europe; large amounts of economic aid to help restore the great damage and greater dislocations caused by the war; and, finally, it required all the arts of political action, overt and not, to oppose the widespread subversive efforts of the Soviet Union and its supporters.

Each requirement was met. The ideological threat of communism at home was small but vivid and served to secure public and congressional support for the open-ended costs and risks of opposing communism abroad; bitter memories of the failure of 1919 served to provide a foundation for a consensus among elite groups at least, which opposed all forms of neo-isolationism; and the war-created intelligence and propaganda agencies, and the war-expanded diplomatic corps supplied the expertise which the United States had never needed before.

Nevertheless, all these achievements would have been of no avail on their own for the United States still lacked a strong army, the one essential attribute of a great European power. In fact, after demobilization was completed in 1947, the United States scarcely had an army at all. But there was an offsetting strength and it sufficed: the very large superiority of the United States in long-range aviation and its monopoly over the atomic bomb. Regardless of the modest role of atomic weapons in contemporary military planning, notwithstanding the skepticism of most officials about the actual usability of atomic weapons in countering a Soviet invasion, the nuclear monopoly was the most important counterweight to the Soviet army.

By 1948 the Soviet Union too had moved beyond the boundaries of its comparative advantage as a European-centered land power by actively supporting the Communists in China, and possibly also by encouraging North Korean preparations for the invasion that was to take place in June 1950. It can be argued persuasively that Soviet support for the Chinese Communists was reluctant and indeed imposed by circumstances; and that in Korea it was not the Soviet Union that took the initiative. The fact remains that for a Soviet Union whose salient form of military power then, as now, consists of rail-deployed, tank-heavy divisions, the projection of power into remote East Asia—including Soviet East Asia—imposes disproportionate costs.

A much greater departure from the Soviet Union's comparative advantage was presaged by Stalin's naval program underway by 1948 (and terminated at his death), whose goal was to build a "blue water" navy, complete with aircraft carriers. Here too the motive remains equivocal. Since land-based aviation would dominate the Baltic and the Black Sea in any conflict, the aircraft carriers, battleships and cruisers could be intended only for oceanic use, but that could be congruent with no wider purpose than the interdiction of American deployments into Europe.

Had the Soviet Union pursued Stalin's naval program to its logical conclusion (US–Soviet naval parity by the 1960s), a balance of comparative disadvantages would have obtained between a United States permanently under strain in its ill-suited role as a continental land power and a Soviet Union similarly going against its comparative advantage in attempting to become an oceanic power. In reality, only the United States remained under strain, as it remains still in its assumed role as a great European power that lacks a commensurate army.

As soon as the American A-bomb monopoly was lost in 1949 the strategic non-sequitur between the assumption of security responsibilities in Europe and the lack of an army of commensurate size became a chronic problem in need of a solution. During the last generation several remedies have been tried; each was valid for a while, each has left a residue still in place, but none could provide a lasting solution to the strategic non-sequitur.

A symmetrical solution was seriously attempted only once. The American and British reaction to the outbreak of the Korean War in June 1950 was to initiate general rearmament; it was widely feared at the time that the North Korean attack was merely a diversionary prelude to a Soviet invasion of Western Europe. The natural West European counterpart to the American rearmament was the large-scale deployment of ground forces, to be achieved by the serious implementation of conscription in Belgium, Denmark, the Netherlands and Norway, by the greatly expanded supply of US–made weapons to the already very large but grossly ill-equipped French, Greek, Italian and Turkish armies, and finally by the rearmament of West Germany. All these measures were in fact agreed to by the NATO allies in the 1952 Lisbon program; had it been fully implemented, a symmetrical military balance would have been achieved in Europe, on the strength of some 90 NATO divisions, with commensurate air power.

But of course the Lisbon solution was thwarted by the repudiation of the force level promises on all sides. Its present residues include the rearmament of West Germany, the acceptance of the German demand for a preclusive strategy designed to avoid any losses of territory ("Forward Defense"), and the large divisional count in the armies of Greece, Italy and Turkey, although these divisions never were in fact equipped in the manner required to defend against the Soviet army.

Following the failure of the Lisbon program, there was a reversion to an asymmetrical solution, based on a restored qualitative advantage in strategic nuclear form, achieved by production of the H-bomb and the subsequent adoption of a "strategic first-use" policy ("Massive Retaliation"). This was thwarted within the decade by the Soviet Union's acquisition of the same weapon of long-range bombers of intercontinental range, as well as the first ballistic missiles of medium range. The American response to the advent of the Soviet H-bomb in 1952 could not emulate the reaction to the Soviet A-bomb test of 1949. The Soviet detonation of a fission device had been followed by the outbreak of the Korean War and the fears of a worldwide conflict which it inspired; in that climate, a broad effort of conventional rearmament obtained much political support in both the United States and Western Europe. But the Soviet H-bomb test was followed by Stalin's death in 1953 and a sharp relaxation of tensions; in the atmosphere of the first postwar détente (1953–58) there was no question of a greater military effort, and indeed it was during those years that the Lisbon program was repudiated. With a conventional rearmament ruled out, and with the nuclear offset to Soviet superiority on the ground now lost, a remedy was found in the introduction of "tactical" nuclear weapons, that is, nuclear artillery shells, bombardment rockets, short- and medium-range missiles, atomic demolition mines, and nuclear bombs for tactical aircraft. The bureaucratic interests of the Army and of the tactical air exponents gave an important impulse to this development, because Eisenhower's "New Look" strategy strongly emphasized nuclear weapons, and till then only the Strategic Air Command had possession of them. Nonetheless, the new category of "tactical" nuclear weapons provided the means for the so-called "trip-wire" strategy whereby NATO would deploy only modest conventional forces to guard the front and test an attack, while relying on tactical nuclear attacks against an all-out invasion. Naturally this meant that NATO would have to adopt a "first use" firing policy, under which the members of the alliance declared their readiness to use nuclear weapons, even against a conventional invasion. The very great attraction of the new strategy was of course its cheapness. Instead of having to provide large and well-equipped conventional forces at great cost, the United States and its allies needed little more than a border guard to provide the "trip-wire." By the same token, of course, the "first-use" policy in conjunction with the lack of serious conventional defenses would guarantee an escalation to nuclear war in the event of any large-scale Soviet attack.

During the late 1950s there was mounting dissatisfaction with the "trip-wire" strategy, especially among expert American observers. By its almost exclusive reliance on nuclear capabilities, the strategy offered a most economical solution, but one which entailed the danger of an almost automatic escalation in the event of a Soviet invasion of NATO territory. A strategy so dangerous was also of dubious effectiveness. What if the Soviet Union would invade West Germany only to a depth of ten miles or so. Would a tactical nuclear response still be warranted? Obviously not, and yet "trip-wire" forces could scarcely be expected to counterattack successfully, so that in the absence of a nuclear response the Soviet Union would simply remain in control of its conquest, gaining not merely some territory but the probable disintegration of the Alliance. And what would happen if the Soviet Union did stage an invasion, but only against northern Norway or eastern Turkey rather than Germany? Again, the strategy did not provide adequate conventional strength, while a tactical nuclear response could seem disproportionate to the point of being incredible. The critics of the new strategy deplored the military policies that were derived from the "trip-wire" assumptions (fighter-bombers were being designed for one-way delivery, with no self-sealing fuel tanks; Army stock-levels would sustain combat for only a few days) and challenged the new strategy's "credibility," a coinage of those days.

With the advent of the Kennedy administration the European NATO allies came under increasing pressure to deploy larger and more capable conventional forces in a partial reversion to symmetry and defense, as opposed to asymmetrical deterrence. The rapid increase in strategic nuclear capabilities achieved by the United States naturally made the European allies more willing to cooperate, and the integration of conventional and nuclear forces in a "Flexible Response" strategy was formally adopted by the Alliance in 1967. Under the new strategy, greatly strengthened US and NATO forces would defend against invasion for as long as possible by non-nuclear means, while being ready to use nuclear weapons if absolutely necessary; this readiness to escalate, also needed to deter Soviet escalation, would extend to the threat of nuclear attacks against the Soviet homeland.

The new strategy logically required a progressive improvement in the non-nuclear balance to diminish pro rata NATO's reliance on escalation. In fact, the European NATO allies never agreed to provide non-nuclear forces on the required scale. It was the French withdrawal from the military command structure of NATO that had made the adoption of the new strategy possible. But although only the French had explicitly opposed the policy, the remaining allies proved no more willing than France had been when it came to the actual implementation of the decision. In Washington, it was believed that with time European cooperation would be forthcoming, but as it turned out time had already run out. The deepening American engagement in Southeast Asia, the subsequent decline of US military strength, and the earlier Soviet decision to increase the rate of accumulation of virtually all forms of military power, all resulted in an adverse change in the European military balance which the European NATO allies did not see fit to counteract. By the end of the 1970s, the relative non-nuclear strength of NATO was excessive (and needlessly costly) for a "trip-wire" strategy but greatly insufficient for a "Flexible Response" strategy as officially defined, which called for a successful resistance to invasion over a period of weeks.

One reason why such a fundamentally unsatisfactory security situation has been tolerated by the member-governments of NATO is that the danger of war has not seemed truly imminent for more than thirty years; but another is certainly the fact that technological delusions have repeatedly intervened to offer the prospect of cheap and yet powerful defenses. A decade ago, it was the anti-tank missile that was to provide a cheap answer to the armies of the Warsaw Pact. Following the apparent success of Soviet anti-tank missiles in Egyptian hands during the 1973 war, much was heard about the newly revealed weakness of the tank-based Soviet army. In the years since, of course, it was discovered that the technically superior anti-tank missile is tactically outmatched by the concentration of armored forces against its thinly distributed linear deployments (and to out-concentrate tanks by helicopter-borne missiles converts a cheap solution into a very expensive one).

At the time of writing, great hopes are being placed in the development of "deep-attack" systems which are to identify, locate, and destroy groups of enemy vehicles in the deep rear.

Strategically, such systems could provide a solution for the long-standing problem of coping with the so-called "second echelon" of a Soviet offensive. With luck, the frontline forces of the Alliance might cope with an initial Soviet surprise attack launched by the forces already in place across the border. But within a few days of that initial clash, and before being substantially reinforced, the NATO front would be attacked by the next wave of forces coming from the Soviet Union itself. Hence the peculiar value of deep-attack capabilities that would diminish NATO's short-term reinforcement disadvantage by destroying and delaying Soviet follow-up forces. It has been pointed out, however, that it is unrewarding to attack follow-on forces if NATO's front could withstand the forward-deployed forces of the Soviet "first echelon." In this regard, it has been noted that the Soviet army is now experimenting with all "first echelon" invasion schemes, associated with the "operational maneuver group" concept, whereby NATO command and control centers, airfields and missile bases would all be engaged at the start of hostilities by commando-type forces as well as air attacks, while the first wave itself would be greatly reinforced.

Operationally, the proposed new capabilities would differ from the long-standing interdiction capabilities of NATO air forces because they are supposed to be able to find and destroy moving targets far more reliably, and because they should be much less vulnerable to the array of Warsaw Pact air defenses. It should be noted that there is a fundamental difference between the interdiction of fixed targets (as notably in NATO's counter-air mission) and the envisaged attack on Soviet forces in transit; the ability to direct weapons accurately at long ranges is now far greater than the ability to find elusive targets.

Technically, the proposed "deep-attack" systems would exploit Western, and especially American, technological advantages by combining accurate sensors, computer-assisted battle management centers, aircraft attack pods and carrier missiles to finally launch precision-guided sub-missiles at the individual targets. There is no doubt that if deployed on a serious scale, these new systems would add to the strength of the alliance, by providing new capabilities of value or at least by forcing the diversion of Soviet resources into counter-measures. It has been argued, however that NATO should proceed with caution before investing major resources to develop and field the new systems. It has been noted specifically, that the proposed "deep-attack" capabilities must be less robust than front-line forces of conventional form because of their entire dependence on sensors inherently vulnerable to technical counter-measures. Needless to say, there is no absolute choice to be made but rather a series of trade-offs; the only proposition generally valid is that the Soviet Union's broad and costly invasion capabilities obtained by the mass deployment of mechanized forces cannot be reliably countered by narrow and cheap capabilities even if they contain the most advanced technology.

The defense policy of the Reagan administration emphasizes naval as well as strategic nuclear capabilities while providing no increase in the size of the ground forces and only a fractional increase in the tactical air forces.

The centerpiece of the naval program is the construction of two more nuclear-powered aircraft carriers of the *Nimitz* class with associated escorts, including Aegis air-defense cruisers—the most costly surface warships ever built. (The priority accorded to the latter suggests that it is the Soviet naval bombers that now present the salient threat to the carriers.) The freely deployable tactical airpower of the Navy's aircraft carrier task forces is the key ingredient in making the long-range expeditionary capabilities of the United States superior to those of the Soviet Union. In fact, it is because of the carriers that the United States retains its clear superiority in surface naval forces—the only major category of military power in which the United States remains distinctly superior to the Soviet Union. In addition, carrier task forces have been much used as the tools of "naval suasion" in a variety of roles, from ritual show-the-flag visitations to outright coercion. The formidable presence of the carriers has attended almost every crisis in which the United States has been involved in recent years.

Nevertheless, the very large investment now being made in the additional carriers, their especially costly aircraft and the associated escorts, is being questioned more and more insistently by a widening circle of critics. First, critics stress the fundamental geographical facts which diminish the value of carrier-based airpower in the contemporary strategic setting. The Soviet Union is clearly much less vulnerable to attack from the sea, or attacks on its seaborne assets, than Japan was during the Second World War, or even Germany. And of course carrier-based airpower could not contribute significantly large capabilities for the defense of the European central front. In fact, it is only in the event of very protracted non-nuclear warfare that the carrier task forces could have more than a marginal role in a full-scale East-West conflict. To be sure, carrier-based air power would certainly be very important and could possibly be decisive in the "sideshows" of an East-West conflict (north Norway, eastern Turkey), or in the event of a localized East-West conflict (for example in Southwest Asia), and of course in lesser conflicts fought with third parties in regions remote from main US bases. In other words, the relative value of aircraft carrier forces increases as the intensity of the conflict declines. Critics challenge the fundamental logic of allocating vast resources to a category of military power which becomes less useful as the envisaged contingency becomes more serious.

With regard to the use of the carriers in crisis situations, the critics point out that the tendency to send carrier task forces to crisis areas does not in itself prove that any useful purpose is thereby served. To the extent that crisis deployments are gestures meant perhaps more for domestic consumption, which in fact have no discernible impact on crisis outcomes (for example, Iran 1979–80), the length and variety of these deployments does not prove the utility of aircraft carriers.

Finally, critics note that the inherent vulnerability of the carriers is steadily increasing because target-finding and precision-guidance missile capabilities are becoming available at increasing stand-off ranges. As this trend continues, the ability of US Navy carrier-based fighters to reach and destroy Soviet naval bombers from their patrol stations before the bombers can launch their missiles is declining, as is the corresponding ability of the anti-submarine defenses to destroy Soviet submarines before they can launch their cruise missiles; in addition, the threat of even more remote attacks by ballistic missiles is looming. The critics fully recognize that carrier task forces can cope with the rising level of the threat if more and more layers of defenses are added, including specifically anti-missile defenses. They point out, however, that in the process a greater and greater part of the overall capacity of the task forces is absorbed for self-defense. The carriers may thus remain well protected to the end, but will finally reach a point when their "positive" capability will decline to insignificance. It is not any defect of the aircraft carriers that leads to that outcome but rather their very great value, which justifies the concentration of enemy efforts against them. Nor, finally, can the carriers exact a reciprocal effort greater than their own cost: Soviet naval bomber and submarine forces can be surged as needed, while the carriers must be constantly operated at high levels of readiness.

Reverting to NATO, it has been noted that the Reagan administration is not funding any significant quantitative increase in the ground or tactical air forces; and the European allies are not doing so either. As for the qualitative improvements now underway or projected both for the US forces and in NATO at large, these can do no more than regain the qualitative advantages lost during the last decade as far as the ground forces are concerned. In the case of tactical air power on the other hand, the US forces at least are retaining their sharp qualitative lead. But the qualitative advantage in airpower is much smaller for NATO as a whole, and may not suffice to offset the numerical inferiority of Western air forces.

In any case, the central predicament of ground-force insufficiency for a credible, sustained "Forward Defense" of the NATO central front remains acute. More precisely, the Warsaw Pact countries can begin a war on the central front with a significant numerical advantage in ground forces; they can then reinforce more rapidly than NATO during the first thirty days of a war, widening their advantage still further during the next thirty days, and it is only thereafter that NATO can outpace Warsaw Pact reinforcements—assuming that US reserve forces can in fact reach the scene by sea lift.

It is above all NATO's reinforcement disadvantage that compels reliance on the present strategy of flexible response, including the threatened "first use" of nuclear weapons if necessary, that is, if conventional defenses are about to be overwhelmed. Always questioned by some on the American side for its ultimate escalation risks, this strategy has now come under increasingly weighty attack in Europe as well. The argument for the present strategy is that "first use" is especially appropriate for deterrence on the part of a strictly defensive alliance whose stance precludes pre-emptive attack—thus placing the entire onus of a war-starting decision upon the Soviet Union. The argument against it is not the long-standing Soviet possession of tactical-nuclear weapons as such. It is rather that the credibility of "first-use" deterrence has declined now that NATO can no longer advantageously escalate to either theater-nuclear or strategic-nuclear levels. NATO's "first use" was fully compatible with tactical-nuclear parity so long as the United States retained a complex of strategic-nuclear superiorities which deterred a Soviet tactical-nuclear response; now that there is parity at best in the higher balances, the tactical-nuclear balance is more consequential. But this of course does not invalidate the fundamental advantage of the "first-use" threat to NATO as a defensive alliance.

NATO's fundamentally unsound security system compels a fresh re-examination of the options, old and new:

1. The restoration of a qualitative advantage in strategic-nuclear form through the deployment of advanced strategic defenses for the United States, thus rehabilitating the credibility of US nuclear guarantees and their extension to the deterrence of non-nuclear aggression (that is, a return to "Massive Retaliation"). This option is implicit in the current strategic defense initiatives now being explored by the Reagan administration. A variety of ballistic missiles defense concepts are now under study even though it is the most futuristic of these concepts which have received the widest notice.

The defects of this option—apart from its technical feasibility, which remains to be demonstrated at this time—include the very long period of gestation (ten years is the lowest estimate), the costs, which conceivably could preclude deployment, and the possibility that anti-satellite forces could be inherently cheaper and more rapidly producible than the envisaged satellite-based forces, thereby foreclosing that avenue of military development. (If the tanks of 1915 had to face truly effective anti-tank weapons already deployed, one may be certain that no tank forces would have come into existence.)

2. The reversion to a symmetrical solution through the deployment of many more ground formations. Any major increase in *active* forces remains politically infeasible. Nor is it militarily indispensable. Two-thirds of the total Soviet ground forces to be countered consists of reserve divisions, and these could be matched by organizing the outflow of trained conscripts from the NATO

armies into reserve divisions on the Israeli model, that is, fully equipped, refresher-trained organized fighting formations available for combat on short notice. NATO's divisional count on the "central front" could be doubled in a few years and tripled within a decade with only a marginal increase in defense spending.

The defect of this solution is of a fundamental character. Any symmetrical solution implies a readiness to engage in protracted non-nuclear war. So far European governments, particularly the West German, have preferred the very low risks, if very high cost of failure, of deterrence with a minimum of sustained conventional defense. Of course, if the NATO "first-use" policy were repudiated, the logical necessity for greatly strengthened conventional defenses might be recognized by public opinion. If so, the reserve-division solution might then become feasible politically, although it must be recognized that delusions of conventional adequacy are easily sustained by the sheer cost of realistic deployments.

3. A "defensive primacy" solution for an asymmetrical non-nuclear defense, through the organization of large territorial militia forces manning prepared fortifications and barrier systems, to complement the present NATO corps. Though numerically inadequate on their own for a maneuver defense, the NATO corps are already well-structured (and numerically adequate) to serve as the counter-attack "sword" in a "sword-and-shield" defense, where territorial militias and extensive terrain enhancements would provide the "shield."

In practice, this solution would entail the conversion of a frontal area of 50 kilometers or so into a densely fortified combat zone featuring fixed and expedient minefields, prepared demolitions, extensive road and river-crossing obstacles, linear anti-vehicle barriers across all trafficable approaches, and some tens of thousands of weapon positions including many built in concrete, as well as the induction of the entire military-age population into the new territorial militia. The defects of this solution are twofold. In addition to the German (and not only German) reluctance to plan explicitly for sustained conventional war, there is the specifically German objection to frontier fortifications that would be intrusive to people living in the area, and which would also reaffirm symbolically the division of Germany. If the necessity for greatly strengthened conventional defenses were to be accepted, the "reserve-division" solution (option 2) is likely to be judged less intrusive and more equitable. For this option—"defensive primacy"—

would of course be based on German territory and a German militia.

There are other possible solutions, including relaxation of the "Forward Defense" obligation, but the three above seem to define the more realistic options. If only because of the mechanics of NATO decision-making, some mixed solution is always more likely to find acceptance than any pure solution. What is certain, however, is that the NATO allies will not on their own resolve the predicament of the United States, which continues to seek to negate the Soviet Union's coercive potential upon non-Communist Europe while lacking an army large enough to compensate for the wide disparity between the Soviet army and the combined strength of the Allied armies. In geopolitical terms, the fundamental character of the US–Soviet competition is unlikely to change.

THE NUCLEAR BALANCE

Strategic nuclear forces constitute a key element in the US–Soviet military relationship; the nuclear balance is the one aspect of their relationship in which the great powers compete directly in an abstract context, rather than along with allies in concrete regional situations.[1]

Both the United States and the Soviet Union think of strategic nuclear forces as the bedrock of their national security policies. In the hands of the opponent, the enormous devastation of which these weapons are capable poses the greatest threat to each nation's security; in their own hands, these same weapons are believed to pose the ultimate deterrent against attack. As a result, strategic nuclear capabilities—specifically, changes in relative strategic capabilities—are interpreted by officials in both the United States and the USSR (and in third nations as well) as indicators of the two great powers' standing with important political consequences. It is their strategic nuclear forces, after all, along with their great conventional military capabilities, which most distinguish the United States and the

[1] As used here, strategic nuclear forces include both the central nuclear forces of the two sides—those of inter-continental range intended primarily for use against the other's homeland—and their intermediate-range nuclear weapon systems, which are thought of primarily in the context of theater-level conflicts, but which would still be used for strategic purposes. There are of course large numbers of shorter-range nuclear weapons on the two sides, but these are intended for tactical use on the battlefield and are discussed in the regional sections of this report.

USSR from other nations, setting them apart with global responsibilities—and global ambitions. This is perhaps truer of the USSR as, unlike the United States, without its military strength, the Soviet Union's economy and political system would certainly not place it in the forefront of world leadership.

Comparisons of the two sides' strategic capabilities are made difficult, among other reasons, by the well-known asymmetries in their respective force postures and by the variety of uncertain factors—timing, tactics, the actual performance of these complicated systems in unprecedented battle situations—which would influence the outcome of any exchange. Such static measures of offensive capabilities as the number of warheads or the amount of equivalent megatonnage in a force ignore these uncertainties, but provide some indication of trends in one side's capabilities over time and of relative capabilities. These static indicators of offensive potential are used most often in public discussions of the nuclear balance. We have attempted to broaden the analysis in this report, however, by including a dynamic assessment of the likely outcome of an exchange between the two forces. The section also includes a discussion of developments in the other types of military systems, such as command and control systems, which influence the nuclear balance, as well as the potential consequences of arms control negotiations for the two force postures, and developments in the nuclear forces of third nations.

In general, 1983 was a year of preparation and anticipation as concerns strategic nuclear forces. The United States moved forward in its wide-ranging strategic modernization program, securing domestic support for most of it, and progressing substantially in key development programs. The deployment of intermediate-range missiles in Europe, and C-4 Trident I missiles and air-launched cruise missiles with its central strategic forces, permitted the United States to begin to reverse what had been a several year trend toward a relatively stronger Soviet position in the strategic competition. More significantly, perhaps, the ongoing developmental program suggests major increases in US strategic capabilities in the future. Disappointments for US strategic planners during 1983 included the failure to resolve decisively the controversy over proposed deployments of new inter-continental ballistic missiles (ICBMs) and Congressional cutbacks in funds requested to improve defensive forces.

The Soviet Union seems to be at a different phase in its strategic deployment program. Deployments in 1983 suggested the USSR is nearing the end of a generation of strategic weapons; with the exception of *Typhoon*-class strategic submarines, the next generation of Soviet weapons—believed to include two types of ICBMs, the first Soviet heavy bomber to appear in 25 years, and a variety of modern cruise missiles—seems still a few years away. Many observers believe that Soviet planners are at crucial decision points in their weapons acquisition process, decisions which could be affected by both developments in US forces and progress, or the lack thereof, in strategic arms negotiations.

Despite huge political pressures for agreement, progress in either the talks on intermediate-range nuclear forces (INF) or central strategic forces eluded US and Soviet negotiators. At the end of the year, the INF talks had been suspended by the USSR and agreement on central forces seemed far away. Continuing questions about Soviet compliance with existing treaties further clouded the prospects for negotiated reductions in nuclear capabilities.

UNITED STATES OFFENSIVE FORCES

There seemed to be a greater convergence of opinion in the United States during 1983 on the basis of planning for strategic forces. Following the Congress' rejection of the proposed "Dense-Pack" basing mode for the new MX missile in late 1982, President Reagan appointed a Commission on Strategic Forces chaired by former national security advisor General Brent Scowcroft. The commission's report, issued in April, was widely praised as presenting a sensible and pragmatic approach to nuclear planning. While dismissing previously popular, if mechanistic, views of the consequences of maintaining components of the strategic force which were vulnerable to an enemy's first strike, the report stressed the importance over the long-term of building survivable forces. The commission suggested developing a small, mobile ICBM toward this end, and deploying it in sufficient numbers in the 1990s so that in the event of a crisis, the USSR would not be presented with incentives to launch a first strike. The commission also stressed the positive role which arms negotiations could play in assuring survivable, and therefore stable, strategic force postures. These suggestions, along with the commission's endorsement of submarine and bomber modernization programs, were widely accepted in the Congress and endorsed by the administration. More controversial was the commission's recommendation that up to 100 MX ICBMs with multiple warheads be deployed in existing silos as an interim measure. This proposal was also endorsed by the administration and, eventually, funds for procurement of the missile were approved by the Congress. The margin of support was so small, however, and the debate so rancorous, as to suggest continuing controversy during 1984.

The administration's approach to nuclear planning changed in other ways during 1983 as well. Public pronouncements in 1981 and 1982, particularly by President Reagan and Secretary of Defense Caspar W. Weinberger, had given the impression to many observers that the administration took the possibility of a nuclear conflict somewhat lightly. Moreover, the administration seemed to stress the goal of winning a nuclear war, even at the expense of preventing such a conflict. This impression was reinforced by the disclosure in mid-1982 of a Department of Defense planning document ("Defense Guidance") which discussed the goal of "prevailing" in a protracted nuclear conflict. The ensuing public uproar in both the United States and Europe caused great difficulties for the administration. As a result, public pronouncements in 1983 were much more cautious. The Annual Report for Fiscal Year 1984, for example, issued by Secretary of Defense Weinberger in February 1983, insisted that the administration's policy was not fundamentally different from the policies of past presidents. The document also stated that while neither superpower could win a nuclear war, the United States must continue modernizing its forces to deter the Soviet Union from beginning such a conflict. Likewise, the new internal "Defense Guidance," completed on March 1, omitted mention of protracted nuclear war.

While the administration has moved to tone down its public statements on nuclear strategy, it is still reported to be revising plans for the targeting of US nuclear weapons. In a significant departure from previous administrations, the new revisions may provide for a closer integration of theater (that is, intermediate-range) nuclear systems deployed in Europe into overall nuclear targeting plans. In the past, theater weapons were included in targeting plans but were aimed only at targets which had direct military relevance for a theater-level conflict; for example, railroad marshaling yards in Eastern Europe. Under the new plan, intermediate-range systems, particularly cruise missiles and Pershing II ballistic missiles based in Europe, may be aimed at strategic targets in the Soviet Union itself. ICBM command and control installations would be one example of such a target. The administration may also be revising targeting plans to include additional "limited nuclear options"; that is, less than all-out attacks on the Soviet Union largely focused on military targets. If true, this would continue a trend which began during the Nixon and Ford Administrations and continued under President Carter, the goal being to capitalize on the increasing accuracy and flexibility of the nuclear weapon systems entering the US inventory, to strengthen deterrence by expanding the range of options available to US decision-makers in crises.

It also was made clear in 1983 that the administration contemplates a fundamental change in nuclear strategy over the long-term of potentially far-reaching significance. The President's March "Star Wars" speech posited the long-term goal of moving away from a deterrent strategy based on the threat of instant and overwhelming nuclear retaliation and toward the construction of active strategic defenses capable of shielding the United States (and perhaps its allies) from incoming missiles. A scientific panel chaired by former NASA director James Fletcher evaluated a broad array of alternative missile defense systems during the summer. Its recommendations were endorsed by the administration in the fall. The most frequently discussed concept of such a defense would be based on directed energy weapons (lasers or particle beams) deployed on satellites orbiting the earth.

There is considerable controversy over the proposal. Some eminent experts, such as nuclear physicist Edward Teller, maintain that an effective space-based missile defense system could be deployed in the 1990s at a reasonable price. Others, such as former under secretary of defense for research and engineering William Perry, are skeptical that it would ever be possible to build an effective system at an affordable price. The Defense Department officials who actually manage relevant research programs seem on the whole to be reserving judgement, arguing that the technologies must be developed further before an informed decision can be reached on the possibility of deploying the system in the next century. In the late summer, it was revealed that US–directed energy programs were being rechanneled from the short-range chemical lasers that they had previously concentrated on to a new emphasis on ultra-violet lasers which could be used to attack nuclear warheads in space.

The president's speech in March stimulated considerable public debate and internal government study of the fundamental premises of US nuclear strategy, and of the feasibility and ramifications of a shift from nuclear deterrence to active nuclear defenses. The speech could mark a watershed in the evolution of US defense policy with important implications for relations between the United States and

USSR, as well as between the United States and its allies. It will be years, however, before the extent of such implications, if any, become evident.

In the meantime, the United States continued to modernize its strategic offensive forces across the board. 1983 marked the initial appearance of several of the new generation of nuclear weapons now being fielded by the US; others remained in development with deployments projected over the next several years. Changes in US offensive nuclear capabilities are summarized in Table 1 and described in the following paragraphs.

Intermediate-range nuclear forces. Pershing II ballistic missiles and Tomahawk ground-launched cruise missiles (GLCMs) began to be deployed in Western Europe at the end of 1983. By 1988, it is expected that there will be 160 GLCMs in the United Kingdom, 36 GLCMs and 108 Pershing IIs in the Federal Republic of Germany, 112 GLCMs in Italy, 48 GLCMs in Belgium and 48 GLCMs in the Netherlands.[2] The Pershing deployment was particularly controversial, largely because of Soviet contentions that the missile posed a first-strike "decapitation" threat which would necessitate a response on their part, but also because of the missile's mixed developmental test record (see Table 2). This record led some critics to charge that the missile's schedule was being accelerated for political reasons. A test planned for August was delayed until September because of concerns about the impact of movement on the missile's engine. When that test proved successful, however, the overall deployment schedule was maintained.

While deficiencies at the time of deployment in the data necessary for the Pershing's guidance system restricted the missile's effectiveness, both the Pershings and the cruise missiles represent significant improvements over NATO's previous theater nuclear systems, particularly in accuracy and range. They are intended to be more survivable, as well, although their ability to withstand a major Warsaw Pact attack has been questioned. Perhaps more important than their military impact, NATO's ability to weather the storm of controversy which accompanied preparations for the deployments provides important evidence of the alliance's basic political cohesion and determination. Successful initiation of these deployments is an important step to assure the continued viability of the alliance.

[2] *The final Dutch approval of GLCM deployments had not yet been given at the end of the year.*

TABLE 1   Deployed US Nuclear Delivery Systems

Type	1 Jan. 83	1 Jan. 84
Intermediate-range missiles		
Pershing II	0	9
Ground-launched cruise missiles	0	32
Bombers		
B-52 D	31	0
B-52 G/H	241	188
B-52 G equipped with cruise missiles	16	49
FB-111	62	62
Submarine-launched ballistic missiles		
Poseidon C-3	304	304
Trident 1 C-4	250	264
Intercontinental ballistic missiles		
Minuteman III (Mk 12A)	300	300
Minuteman III (Mk 12)	250	250
Minuteman II	450	450
Titan II	49	38
US tactical aircraft capable of being armed with nuclear weapons		
F-111	318	274
F-4	1323	1323
F-16	490	610
A-6	144	144
A-7	288	288
F-18	0	0
Allied aircraft capable of being armed with nuclear weapons		
F-104 (several nations)	290	261
F-4 (several nations)	172	142
F-16 (Netherlands)	65	108
F-16 (Belgium)	50	90
Tornado (FRG)	45	130
Tornado (Italy)	10	65

Bombers. Conversion of B-52G bombers to carry 12 air-launched cruise missiles (ALCMs) per aircraft continued in 1983. One squadron of 16 aircraft at Griffiss Air Force Base in New York State had been equipped with ALCMs in 1982. Conversion of the squadron at Wurtsmith Air Force Base in Michigan began in April and was completed in October. That same month, work began on outfitting a

TABLE 2   Pershing II Tests

Date	Result	Comments
(1) 22 July 1982	Failure	Problems with propulsion forced termination of test in 17 seconds.
(2) 19 November 1982	Partial success	Guidance system failed in first operational test.
(3) 21 January 1983	Success	First test conducted at Cape Canaveral. Program accelerated to achieve initial operational capability in Dec. 1983.
(4) 9 February 1983	Success	Range of test increased to 800–900 miles.
(5) 26 February 1983	Success	First apparently successful test of guidance system.
(6) 13 March 1983	Success	
(7) 25 March 1983	Success	Flew 853 miles downrange but guidance system could not be tested because flight was conducted over water.
(8) 10 April 1983	Success	Repeat of seventh test.
(9) 22 April 1983	Success	Terminal guidance fully tested in 75-mile downrange flight.
(10) 6 May 1983	Success	Guidance tested in 88-mile flight.
(11) 27 May 1983	Success	Flight of 980 miles, longest range yet flown.
(12) 2 June 1983	Success	
(13) 19 June 1983	Failure	Accuracy failure probably caused by an electrical short.
(14) 28 June 1983	Success	Reported to have landed in the target area with desired accuracy.
(15) 16 July 1983	Failure	Accuracy test failed; caused by test equipment malfunction.
(16) 27 July 1983	Failure	Missile broke apart after 70 seconds.
(17) 7 September 1983	Success	First test carried out by troops; the missile flew 980 miles in a test of long-range performance.
(18) 17 September 1983	Success	Final accuracy test.

B-52 squadron at Grand Forks Air Force Base in North Dakota. All 17 aircraft in the squadron were completed by the end of 1983, bringing the overall total of B-52Gs equipped to carry cruise missiles (along with short-range attack missiles and gravity bombs) to 49.

All B-52G and H models gradually are being outfitted with the avionics (such as new radars) necessary to accommodate cruise missiles. Other improvements will help B-52s to deliver weapons more effectively and make the aircraft more reliable and easier to maintain. Some B-52s are also being outfitted with better electronic equipment to improve their ability to survive the effects of the electromagnetic pulse caused by nuclear explosions.

B-52D bombers, the oldest model in the US inventory, were placed in storage as ALCMs were deployed. All remaining aircraft had been phased out by the end of the year.

Strategic submarines. The USS *Michigan,* delivered to the US Navy in September 1982, became operational in May. The second *Ohio*-class ballistic missile submarine to join the Navy, the *Michigan* will carry 24 Trident I missiles, each armed with eight 100-kiloton warheads. *Ohio*-class submarines can travel faster, run more quietly, and stay at sea longer than older types of missile-carrying submarines. The third *Ohio*-class submarine, the USS *Florida,* was delivered in June 1983, but will not become operational until early 1984.

Land-based intercontinental ballistic missiles. Retirement of Titan II missiles, begun in December 1982, continued throughout the year. These missiles are being deactivated at a rate of one every six weeks, beginning with the 390th Strategic Missile Wing at Davis-Monthan Air Force Base in Arkansas. All Titan IIs will be retired by the end of 1987, the result of financial stringencies, to say nothing of concern about the safety of these more than twenty-year-old weapon systems.

The US continued to improve the existing force of Minuteman II and Minuteman III ICBMs, concentrating on upgrading the computer software for these missiles. These changes are designed to improve Minuteman's accuracy modestly, as well as its reliability. The provision of a better independent power source at the same time will improve each missile's endurance.

SOVIET OFFENSIVE FORCES

Official Soviet views on strategic doctrine are difficult to discern from public statements, and Western experts disagree on many fac-

ets of Soviet strategic policy. There have been indications that Soviet nuclear doctrine may have begun to change, beginning in the
late 1970s. For example, the previous conviction of Soviet spokesmen that victory was possible in a protracted nuclear war seems to
have eroded; nowadays, Soviet officials and military writers empha-
size that victory is not possible. Likewise, there is some evidence to
suggest that the Soviets are addressing such Western concepts as
crisis stability and strategic stability, ideas which have never seemed
to interest them in the past.

Aside from these potentially positive developments, other aspects
of Soviet policy may be moving in an undesirable direction. In 1983,
a number of spokesmen raised the specter of adopting a "launch on
warning" policy, namely the launching of nuclear weapons immediately upon receipt of radar warnings of an enemy attack. These
statements were linked explicitly to the NATO deployments of intermediate-range weapons, particularly the Pershing II, which is
able to reach targets in the Soviet Union within a few minutes.
While such public Soviet statements clearly were intended to influence Western opinion, they may also have reflected a genuine
concern about the implications of the new weapons for Soviet strategic forces. It is not clear from publicly available sources to what
extent Soviet nuclear forces may already be in a launch-on-warning
posture, a necessary prerequisite for determining whether or not
there is such a response to the Pershing deployments.

The Soviet Union seems to be approaching the end of the deployment of its current generation of strategic weapons. The major
changes during the year reflected a shift to newer models of the
basic types already deployed. This is summarized in Table 3 and described in the following paragraphs.

Intermediate-range nuclear forces. Modernization of Soviet intermediate-range nuclear forces seems to have continued in 1983, with
the phasing out of the few remaining, obsolescent liquid-fueled
SS-5s and the deployment of additional SS-20s at four sites in Asia.[3]
As each SS-20 carries three warheads, the Soviet weapon count has
risen quite sharply. The number of SS-20s which the USSR intends
to deploy eventually is unclear and will hinge, to some extent, on
the Geneva negotiations on intermediate-range nuclear forces. Ap-
proximately two-thirds of the SS-20s are based in Europe, the remainder in Asia. Recent SS-20 deployments in Europe have been
limited to missile sites already under construction at the time of the

[3] *Technically, the SS-4 is classified as a medium-range missile.*

TABLE 3   Deployed Soviet Nuclear Delivery Systems

Type	1 Jan. 83	1 Jan. 84
Intermediate-range missiles		
SS-20	333	369
SS-5	16	0
SS-4	232	220
Bombers*		
Bear	100	100
Bison	45	45
Backfire	100	115
Badger	325	325
Blinder	150	150
Submarine-launched ballistic missiles		
SS-N-5	57	48
SS-N-6	384	384
SS-N-8	292	292
SS-N-17	12	12
SS-N-18	224	224
SS-N-20	20	20
Intercontinental ballistic missiles		
SS-11	550	520
SS-13	60	60
SS-17		
MOD 1	30	0
MOD 2	10	0
MOD 3	110	150
SS-18		
MOD 1 3	16	12
MOD 2	92	0
MOD 4	200	296
SS-19		
MOD 1	80	0
MOD 2	10	0
MOD 3	240	360
Tactical aircraft capable of being armed with nuclear weapons		
Fencer (SU-24)	600	650
Flogger (MiG-23/27)	2000	2400
Fitter (SU-17)	900	800
Fitter (SU-7)	200	200

* Excludes bombers assigned to Soviet Naval Aviation.

late Chairman Brezhnev's March 1982 announcement of a moratorium on such missiles in the European part of Russia. Additional SS-20 deployments have taken place in Soviet Asia. It seemed unlikely at the end of the year, however, in view of NATO's deployment of Pershings and GLCMs, that the moratorium will continue to hold.

The SS-20's advantages over its predecessors include: (1) faster response times because of its solid fuel propulsion; (2) greater accuracy and range; and (3) somewhat greater survivability because of the weapon's mobility, although the missile must still be deployed within a certain distance of its fixed depot.

Bombers. The number of TU-26 Backfire bombers in the Soviet inventory continued to grow, while the inventory of older bombers remained constant. Modernization of nuclear-capable tactical strike aircraft also has continued with an emphasis on models capable of flying under all weather conditions and striking deep behind enemy lines. Third generation aircraft, the SU-24 Fencer and MiG-27 Flogger, first deployed in the mid-1970s, continued to enter Soviet operational inventories as older models were phased out. These aircraft have greater range, carry larger payloads, and are equipped with more capable avionics. Soviet inventories of nuclear-capable tactical aircraft have risen about 40 percent between 1973 and 1983.

Strategic submarines. Launched in 1980, the first *Typhoon*-class ballistic missile submarine entered active service in 1983 after extended sea trials. A second *Typhoon*-class boat, launched at Archangel on the White Sea, began sea trials during the year. The *Typhoons* will be stationed at a new Russian naval base at Yokanda on the Kola Peninsula. The new submarines carry twenty SS-N-20 missiles, each armed with six to nine warheads. Because of their special hull design, it has been suggested that *Typhoon*-class submarines are designed to operate under the arctic ice-cap, thereby improving their ability to survive an attack.

Production of *Delta* III-class submarines continued to wind down. Sixteen boats were built between 1979 and 1983, 14 of which are now operational. One submarine was launched in 1982 and none in 1983; the last 2 can be expected in 1984. Each *Delta* III carries sixteen SS-N-18s, the first Soviet submarine-launched ballistic missile with multiple warheads. Three versions are operational, one with one warhead, one with three warheads, and one with seven warheads.

Land-based intercontinental ballistic missiles. While launcher levels remained constant in 1983, the USSR continued to improve its ICBM force. Older versions of SS-18s, SS-19s and SS-11s, fitted with single warheads, are being replaced with newer models of SS-18s and SS-19s carrying ten and six warheads, respectively. The new missiles are also more accurate than their predecessors. A more accurate version of the smaller SS-17, first introduced in 1982, is also being deployed. In conjunction with this latter program, the USSR continues to harden existing missile silos to enhance their resistance to nuclear blasts.

US AND SOVIET OFFENSIVE CAPABILITIES

Table 4 contains data indicating the relative offensive capabilities of US and Soviet strategic nuclear forces at the beginning of 1983 and the start of 1984. The table is divided into two panels, one presenting data on the static capabilities of the two sides; the second measuring those forces which would survive an attack. The first panel includes indices for all strategic forces, central forces only, and intermediate-range forces in Europe alone. Indices of surviving capability are presented only for central forces.[4]

Both sides have large strategic forces which increased in size and capabilities during the year. The United States added 650 weapons to its inventory; the USSR also added more than 1,000 weapons.

The Soviet Union has a small lead in the overall number of weapons with which their forces could be equipped, derived largely from their major advantage in intermediate-range forces deployed in, or designated for use in, Europe. This lead increased very slightly during the year. When central strategic forces are considered alone, the United States has a near 15 percent advantage in weapons, which decreased very slightly during the year. Given the current status of the two sides' weapon programs, the next several years will likely see a relative increase in the size of the US force, unless the Soviet Union accelerates the now apparent deployment schedules for MIRVed submarine-launched ballistic missiles and Blackjack bombers with cruise missiles.

---

[4] *Indices of global and intermediate-range capabilities are exaggerated in the table because of the need to account for nuclear-capable tactical aircraft. In the preparation of these figures, the weapons load of all such aircraft were included in each index. In reality, all these aircraft are capable of both nuclear and conventional missions and a majority would probably be reserved for attacks with conventional ordnance.*

TABLE 4   The Nuclear Balance*

Indicator	US 1983	US 1984	USSR 1983	USSR 1984
Number of weapons[a]				
Total	13 470	14 120	15 180	16 200
Central forces only[b]	9 540	9 900	8 140	8 590
World-wide theater forces	3 930	4 220	7 040	7 610
Equivalent megatonnage[c] (EMT)				
Total	4 510	4 530	9 070	9 250
Central forces only	3 660	3 620	6 120	6 100
World-wide theater forces	850	910	2 950	3 150
Counter-military potential[d] (CMP)				
Total	47 400	50 000	52 870	57 020
Central forces only	31 680	33 120	25 910	27 770
World-wide theater forces	15 720	16 880	26 960	29 250
Dynamic indicators (central forces only)[e]				
Surviving weapons	6 470	7 780	4 930	5 110
Surviving EMT	2 200	2 310	3 750	3 790
Surviving CMP	20 690	24 650	13 080	13 840

* These calculations were made by Michael Zagurek, Jr., on a DEC VAX-11/780 computer.
[a] = Bombs and warheads.
[b] = Includes all theater nuclear systems with ranges of nearly 1000 kilometers or more excluding all French nuclear systems and British Polaris submarines.
[c] = EMT takes account of the number and explosive yield of weapons to measure the capability of a force to destroy large areas.
[d] = CMP is the ability of a force to destroy point targets.
[e] = Attacks are executed assuming that US and Soviet forces are on full alert.

The much greater size and number of Soviet intercontinental ballistic missiles more than compensates for whatever US advantage there may be in central forces; however, when equivalent megatonnage—an indicator of the potential of a force to destroy large areas—is examined, the Soviets have a more than two-to-one advantage overall, and a more than 60 percent lead in central forces alone. Deployments during the year resulted in virtually no change in either side's equivalent megatonnage reflecting the fact that new weapons on both sides are smaller than those they are replacing. The prospect in the future is for small reductions in the Soviet advantage: new US missiles are larger than their counterparts, while the two ICBMs being tested by the USSR would decrease the size of their force.

Counter-military potential is an indicator of each force's ability to destroy such point targets as missile silos and command complexes. These weapons could be used against specific civilian facilities in addition. The figures in Table 4 are calculated on the basis of a formula used by the Strategic Air Command. The large Soviet lead in theater forces results mainly from its SS-20s. The narrower US advantage in central forces is derived largely from its much more capable force of heavy bombers. Both sides' counter-military potential increased substantially during the year, a trend likely to accelerate in the future. It should be noted that another index freque atly referenced in discussions of strategic forces refers to each si le's ability to destroy hardened targets promptly, meaning with ballistic missiles; the Soviet Union has a clear advantage in that index.

The calculations of surviving capabilities postulate a first strike by one side against the central forces of the other, and then assess the number and characteristics of surviving missiles, submarines and bombers. It takes no account of the possible degradation of surviving capabilities through the destruction of command and control systems and similar phenomena.

Despite the much greater vulnerability of US ICBMs, the much more capable American bomber and submarine forces combine to assure a roughly 25 percent US lead in surviving weapons and a nearly 40 percent US advantage in surviving counter-military potential. These US advantages increased measurably during 1983 as a result of the deployment of cruise missiles and Trident SLBMs. The US gains are not sufficient to offset the huge Soviet advantage in equivalent megatonnage, however; the USSR would retain a 70 percent lead in this index, even when calculated after a hypothetical attack; this margin declined slightly during the year.

OTHER FACTORS INFLUENCING THE NUCLEAR BALANCE

A nation's nuclear strength depends on far more than its offensive forces. As these additional types of military systems do not lend themselves to quantitative assessment, however, they tend to be overlooked in discussions of the nuclear balance. They might be decisive, though, should the relative strengths of the superpowers ever come to the test.

Of particular importance, perhaps, is the command, control, communications, and intelligence systems which would make it possible to employ nuclear forces in an appropriate and flexible manner, so as to obtain their necessary military utility while minimizing the scope and intensity of any conflict. The Soviets have long been known to stress survivable command and control systems, in all probability the mirror-image of the emphasis in their offensive doctrine on disrupting the enemy's command and control system. In recent years, the United States has paid renewed attention to these systems, particularly to the ability of its command and control system to withstand a Soviet attack and execute a retaliatory attack. Without such a survivable command and control system, US retaliatory threats would become less credible and thus its ability to deter an attack less certain. In 1983, these efforts to improve the US command and control system began to produce results.

The US administration was less successful in 1983 in efforts to build more capable strategic defenses as the Congress cut back sharply on proposals to rejuvenate US air defenses, a cost-saving move reflecting the feeling that to invest heavily to protect the United States from the small Soviet bomber force made little sense in the face of US vulnerability to the far greater Soviet missile force. A sizeable cut was also made in the administration's proposals for ballistic missile defense research and development, reflecting concern about the program's lack of appropriate focus. Facing a far more significant bomber threat, the USSR has in the past and continued in 1983 to invest heavily in air defenses. It also pursued vigorously the development of missile defenses.

A final important development concerned anti-satellite capabilities. Here, the USSR—with an existing anti-satellite system of limited capability—staged no tests of such systems and proposed a mutual prohibition on weapons in space. The United States resisted congressional pressures to enter anti-satellite negotiations; a planned first test was postponed, however. Not visible to the public, moreover, were whatever efforts both sides may be making to develop anti-satellite systems utilizing ground-based, directed energy weapons.

Command, control, communications and intelligence. In late 1981, President Reagan stated in National Security Decision Directive 12 that command, control, communications and intelligence programs should enjoy a resource allocation priority at least equal to that of "high visibility" weapon systems. The administration plans to spend $23 billion over five years on these programs; funding in 1983 amounted to about $2.9 billion. Program objectives are to: (1) assure reliable performance in peacetime; (2) have a capability to execute nuclear war plans both during and after a nuclear attack; and (3) be able to support continued operations during a conflict that lasted beyond an initial exchange. Major initiatives are designed to modernize and improve capabilities in five functional areas: communications, command posts, indicators and warnings, navigation and position fixing, and satellite mission control.

A number of new systems became operational in 1983 (see Table 5), all of which would improve command and control during the initial phases of a nuclear conflict. Their utility during a protracted nuclear war would be questionable, however. Still other programs are underway, but will not become operational until later in this decade.

In conjunction with the deployment of Pershing IIs and cruise missiles in Europe, command and control in that theater, based largely on four systems (see Table 6), also is being improved. The current European network is reported to be vulnerable to direct attack as well as to nuclear effects. In early 1983, the first ground station linking the SATCOM communications satellite with NATO's integrated communications system became operational. In 1984, operational testing of a mobile satellite ground terminal will begin, of which 200 will eventually be deployed. The new system would provide a secondary transmission route for emergency messages to fire nuclear weapons. It is planned that by the end of 1988, a network of transportable, high frequency radios, resistant to jamming and hardened against nuclear effects, also will be operational.

While the Soviet command and control system remains highly centralized, some efforts are underway to delegate more authority to continental and regional commanders. Higher echelon "theaters of military operations" (TVD), both oceanic and intercontinental, have been created to achieve specific military objectives derived from central directives. Details of Soviet hardware initiatives are sketchy, but recent programs seem to include both the proliferation of hardened command and control facilities above and below ground and the addition of bunkered and buried antennas. These programs seem to be related to current deployments of fourth generation ICBMs and may end when the missile deployments are completed. In addition, according to Western sources, the Soviet Union has begun to expand its satellite command and communications system in a program likely to continue over the decade.

TABLE 5   *Selected US Programs to Modernize Command, Control and Communications Systems*

Program	Purpose	Wartime Utility	Developments in 1983
Air Force Satellite Communications System (AFSATCOM)	Primary Air Force program for command and control of strategic forces, providing two-way communications between command authorities and nuclear-capable forces.	Early phase	AFSATCOM became fully operational; funding provided to improve the ability of ultra-high frequency terminals to withstand jamming.
Defense Satellite Communications System III	Primary national communications system.	Early phase	
Defense Satellite Program	Early warning of the launch of enemy missiles.	Early phase	To improve survivability, the Air Force has developed a truck-mounted, mobile ground terminal; the 4th, 5th, and 6th terminals were procured in 1983 along with jam-resistant secure communications vans; two additional satellites were procured in 1983.
Looking Glass (EC-135) Upgrade	"Looking Glass" is an aircraft that serves as a mobile command center for the Strategic Air Command.	Early phase	Existing aircraft were hardened against nuclear effects, particularly electromagnetic pulses.
Take Charge and Move Out Aircraft (TACAMO)	TACAMO are the primary, survivable means of communicating with ballistic missile submarines.	Early phase	The procurement of a fleet of 18 aircraft was completed, providing continuous coverage of the Pacific Ocean for the first time. An ongoing program to harden these aircraft against nuclear effects continued.

Airborne Command Center (E-4B)	Improve existing airborne command centers by: (1) hardening for nuclear effects; (2) adding super high frequency satellite communications; and (4) adding high powered anti-jam, very low frequency communications equipment.	Pre-attack and early phase	The first of 3 E-4A aircraft modified to the advanced E-4B was delivered to the Air Force in July 1983; the second was delivered at the end of the year.
Ground Wave Emergency Network	A low frequency overlay on the existing commercial communications networks, the system will consist of many nodes spread across the continental US. They will be hardened for nuclear effects and are planned to survive a nuclear attack long enough to disseminate warning information, launch orders, and emergency actions messages.	Pre-attack and early phase	A thin system of 9 to 10 stations became operational in 1983. (By the end of 1984, 45 stations will be operational and by the end of the decade, 300 sites.)

TABLE 6   Main NATO Nuclear Command, Control and
Communications Systems

Name	Purpose
Cemetary Net	The primary means for transmitting emergency action messages to nuclear weapon storage sites, based on a ultra-high frequency radio network.
European command and control console system	A teletype/radio system for the control of nuclear weapons during peacetime.
Regency Net	A high frequency radio/telephone system intended to replace Cemetary Net with more secure and jam resistant channels in 1988.
NATO integrated communications system	Designed to integrate communications about nuclear weapons with other NATO channels.

Air defenses. The Soviet Union continued to invest heavily in air defenses in 1983, attempting to improve its capabilities at all altitudes, but especially at the very low altitude bands at which B-1B bombers and cruise missiles would try to penetrate Soviet air space. A new airborne warning and control system, code-named "Mainstay" by NATO, is expected to be deployed late in 1984. By late-decade, as many as 50 of these aircraft could be operational. Other important Soviet air defense programs included: (1) installation of an improved radar on existing Soviet airborne warning and control aircraft; (2) deployment of a new hypersonic surface-to-air missile system, the SA-10, which is able to attack more than one aircraft at a time, and possibly cruise missiles as well; and (3) deployment of a modified MiG-25 Foxhound interceptor with an ability to detect and fire at targets flying below it.

The Korean air liner incident in September revealed once again that despite its massive investments in air defenses the USSR continues to face serious problems in air defense operations. Such a conclusion was also implied by the very successful Israeli operations against Syrian-manned but Soviet-built air defense systems during the 1982 war in Lebanon, and also by reports from Soviet defectors and the examination of captured Soviet equipment. The September incident reinforced these suspicions.

In the Korean air liner incident, Soviet radars appear to have tracked flight 007 for some time before it entered Soviet air space, but Soviet interceptors were relatively slow to respond and to locate the aircraft once it entered Soviet territory. The aircraft spent 31 minutes over sensitive Soviet military installations in Kamchatka without being intercepted. It took Soviet interceptors another 30 minutes to find the air liner the second time it entered Soviet airspace as well. These delays occurred, of course, when the target was a civilian aircraft flying a non-evasive course at fairly high altitudes; a military aircraft flying low, employing electronic warfare and other devices and deliberately attempting to evade defenses, presumably would be more difficult to find.

The behavior of Soviet pilots and ground controllers during the incident, according to US Air Force Chief of Staff Charles A. Gabriel, demonstrated the Soviet system to be very inflexible. General Gabriel also stated that the performance of Soviet defenses "gives us a little more confidence" in the ability of the United States to overcome those defenses.

The Administration plans to modernize the US air defense system, but the program has run into problems in the Congress. The North American Air Defense Master Plan, completed in 1982, focuses primarily on closing gaps in the current surveillance system at low altitudes by:

1. Replacing F-106 aircraft with F-15s: one squadron at Langley Air Force Base in Virginia was converted in 1982 and a second at McCord Air Force Base in Washington State was completed this past year; Congress deleted funds for conversion of a third squadron in fiscal year 1984.
2. Constructing eight regional control centers to process and display data on aircraft in US airspace; the first two centers at Tyndall Air Force Base in Florida and Griffiss Air Force Base in New York State began operations in 1983.
3. Random patrols by Airborne Warning and Control System (AWACS) aircraft along US coasts, which began in 1982, increased in 1983; an additional twelve AWACS aircraft were planned to be procured during the next five years, but funds have been denied by the Congress.
4. Upgrading "Distant Early Warning Line" radars to fill gaps in low-level coverage across northern Canada.
5. Developing over-the-horizon radars on the east and west coasts

to become operational in 1986 and 1987, respectively; this program has encountered continuing technical difficulties and its capabilities are uncertain.

Ballistic missile defenses. Both the United States and the Soviet Union maintain vigorous research and development programs to hedge against abrogation or amendment of the 1972 Anti-Ballistic Missile Treaty. (The agreement prohibits deployment of more than 100 anti-ballistic missile launchers at any one site, limits the number, type and location of radars which can be deployed, and restricts the development of certain kinds of systems at the flight-testing stage.)

The Soviet ballistic missile defense program apparently continued in 1983 to concentrate on improving the current 32-launcher system deployed around Moscow by: (1) building new silos for launchers at the Moscow site; (2) stockpiling the ABM-X-3, a new interceptor missile; (3) constructing several large, phased-array radars. The location of one of these phased-array radars, however, as well as other possible treaty violations, has raised serious concerns about the Soviet Union's compliance with the 1972 Treaty and its future intentions regarding ballistic missile defenses.

The treaty restricts each side to two large, phased-array radars within the one permitted ABM site. It also permits an unlimited number of early warning radars, but to ensure that the latter are not used for other functions—particularly the management of battles between interceptors and attacking missiles—it specifies that early warning radars may not be constructed, "except at locations along the periphery of its national territory and oriented outwards" (Article VI b). In the summer of 1983, US intelligence systems detected a large, phased-array radar under construction north of Mongolia. Rather than facing in a southeasterly direction toward China, which might have been interpreted to be consistent with the treaty's terms, the Soviet radar seems to be facing northeasterly toward Alaska which, if true, would be a violation of the Treaty. The fact that the radar is proximate to existing ICBM sites is said to suggest a battle-management role.

The discovery of this radar prompted the United States to call for a special meeting of the Special Consultative Commission (SCC), the bilateral forum set up by the treaty to deal with such compliance questions. The USSR denied the request, pointing to the already planned regular meeting in September to discuss the matter. According to published reports, the USSR maintains that the radar in question is intended for tracking objects in space, which would exempt it—like comparable US radars—from the treaty's restrictions. The issue remained unresolved at the time this report went to press, but Soviet responses in the SCC were said to be unsatisfactory.

The United States does not have an operational ballistic missile defense system but does maintain an active research and development program. This program has been restructured under the Reagan administration and now concentrates on the development of systems to defend missiles in fixed silos. A significant program to develop techniques to intercept incoming missiles after they have entered the atmosphere, without using nuclear warheads on the interceptor missiles, was started at the end of 1983. Previous US interceptors, like current Soviet interceptors, were armed with small nuclear warheads, which raise obvious political and military problems. Flight testing of the new interceptor is expected by 1985. If successfully developed, this weapon would be coupled with the results of studies of non-nuclear interception outside the atmosphere, which also continued in 1983, into a two layered defensive system. The first test of an exo-atmospheric interceptor was conducted in February, and was followed by three additional tests during the year.

It is hard to predict the future of US BMD programs. The administration had planned to spend more than $8 billion on ballistic missile defense research through 1988, but the Congress reduced the requested appropriation for 1984 by more than 25 percent. On the other hand, both questions of Soviet compliance with the ABM Treaty and the president's goal of developing a space-based defensive system would imply a renewed commitment to research in this field. As we went to press, unofficial sources indicated the president would announce a new program to develop space-based defenses by the next century; Congress's view is more difficult to predict.

Anti-satellite systems. The United States is developing a miniature homing vehicle which would be launched within the vicinity of its target satellite by a two-stage, short-range attack missile and the "Altair 3" booster deployed on F-15 interceptor aircraft. This system is expected to be effective primarily against satellites orbiting the earth at low altitudes. Testing of the system's components began in late 1982. The planned first test in September was postponed because of congressional concerns and technical problems. Deployment is planned for 1987, however, when two F-15 squadrons equipped with the system will be assigned to the North American

Aerospace Command; additional systems would be available for rapid deployment with F-15 squadrons deployed abroad. The system could also be deployed on missiles (Trident is under consideration) to intercept satellites at higher altitudes.

The Soviet Union already has an operational anti-satellite system deployed on SS-9 missiles. The booster places the killer satellite in the same orbit as its target and then fires a non-nuclear charge consisting of small pellets at the target. A variant consists of a killer system which is placed initially at a lower altitude and then pops up to destroy the target. The Soviet system, which has had a poor test record over a 15-year period, theoretically could be used against satellites in low orbits, such as reconnaissance, older navigational and meteorological satellites. At present, the Soviet system could not be used against communications and early warning satellites, which are maintained in higher geosynchronous orbits, although expanding the system's capabilities would not be infeasible.

FUTURE DIRECTIONS IN US NUCLEAR FORCES

1983 was the third year of the major US effort to modernize and expand the capabilities of its intermediate-range and central strategic nuclear forces. While much of the program has gained the substantial public and congressional support necessary to assure deployment—particularly efforts to improve command and control systems, to deploy intermediate-range missiles in Europe, and to modernize the bomber and sea-based central forces—the ICBM program remained on a weak footing, and efforts to rebuild air defenses seem to have fallen victim to budgetary stringencies, at least for the time being. Nonetheless, the programs already approved will be likely to lead to a significant expansion in US nuclear capabilities before the end of the decade.

Land-based missiles. As previously noted, initial deployments of Pershing II ballistic missiles and Tomahawk cruise missiles began in Britain, Germany and Italy at the end of 1983. Unless the now suspended US–Soviet negotiations on intermediate-range nuclear forces result in an agreement specifying a reduction in current plans, 572 of these weapons will be deployed in five West European nations within the next five years.

Not so clear, however, is the future of intercontinental range missiles based in the United States. Following the recommendations of the President's Commission on Strategic Forces, chaired by General

Brent Scowcroft, the administration proposed in April 1983 to deploy 100 MX ICBMs, each carrying 10 very accurate warheads with yields up to 500 kilotons, in existing—but possibly strengthened—Minuteman III silos at bases in Wyoming and Nebraska. The Congress, which had rejected the administration's two previous proposals for MX basing modes, read the Scowcroft Commission's conclusions more comprehensively. It insisted that such a deployment should only be part of a more comprehensive policy, incorporating two additional elements: (1) major changes in the administration's position at the US–Soviet Strategic Arms Reduction Talks (START) to facilitate more rapid progress in the negotiations; and (2) development of a smaller ICBM that would be equipped with only one warhead, so as to be in a position in the 1990s to shift to a less vulnerable force of land-based missiles, thus providing lesser incentive for a Soviet first-strike in a crisis.

There ensued throughout the summer and much of the fall a protracted negotiation between the administration and several groups of legislators. Agreement was soon reached on development of the small ICBM, which became known as "Midgetman," but there was considerably less comity on the issue of what would constitute a sufficient change in the administration's START position. A promise of greater flexibility was adequate to give the administration narrow victories in key votes in June and July, thus assuring continued funding for the development of the MX and authorizing appropriations for its procurement. The first flight-test took place in June. The package seemed on the verge of coming apart in the late summer, however, when the Soviet attack on the Korean air liner combined with the administration's acceptance of congressional demand that a "build-down" proposal (i.e., agreement to retire two weapons for every new one deployed) be added to the START position, enabled the initial appropriations for procurement to squeeze through the Congress. The issue will be joined again in 1984, and the polarizing effect of the US electoral campaign would suggest that chances for its resolution are not great.

Sea-based missiles. In part because of this continuing controversy over ICBMs, the overall importance of sea-based strategic forces is likely to increase during this decade. Current plans envision a fleet of 20 Ohio-class submarines as the mainstay of this force. By 1990, ten of these boats will have been deployed, each to be armed eventually with 24 D-5 (Trident II) missiles (see Table 7). The new missile, which is substantially more accurate and powerful than the

TABLE 7   Delivery Schedule for Ohio-Class Submarines

Submarine	Authorized	Expected Delivery Date
	Fiscal Year	
SSBN 726 (Ohio)	1974	October 1981
SSBN 727 (Michigan)	1975	September 1982
SSBN 728 (Florida)	1975	June 1983
SSBN 729 (Georgia)	1976	February 1984
SSBN 730 (Henry Jackson)	1977	October 1984
SSBN 731 (Alabama)	1978	June 1985
SSBN 732 (Alaska)	1978	February 1986
SSBN 733 (Nevada)	1980	October 1986
SSBN 734	1981	December 1988
SSBN 735	1983	August 1989
SSBN 736	1984	April 1990
SSBN 737*	1985	December 1990
SSBN 738*	1986	December 1991
SSBN 739*	1987	December 1992

* Not yet authorized.

existing C-4 (Trident I) missile, is expected to join in the fleet beginning with the ninth Ohio-class in late 1988, but eventually will be deployed on all Ohio-class submarines. This D-5 missile can carry up to nine 475-kiloton warheads, sufficiently accurate to destroy even the hardest Soviet targets.

Prospects for the overall program are good. Although the Ohio-class had experienced substantial cost overruns and delays, the program now seems to be on schedule. Full-scale development of the D-5 missile will begin in 1984; initial funds for procurement will be included in the fiscal year 1985 budget. While the total cost of Ohio-class submarines and Trident missiles will be nearly $50 billion, submarine-launched ballistic missiles are the least controversial of all strategic programs and have had little difficulty in gaining congressional approval.

Initial deployments of the sea-launched cruise missile (SLCM), scheduled to begin in June 1984, were delayed during 1983. The nuclear-armed SLCM, along with conventionally armed variants designed to attack ships and targets on land, were planned to be deployed on attack submarines as well as on several types of surface vessels. Designated platforms would be modified to carry a new vertical launch system capable of carrying twelve cruise missiles.

While initial plans reportedly called for the deployment of large numbers of SLCMs on many ships and submarines, technical problems and consideration of the effects of such deployments on other naval capabilities are causing a re-evaluation. Moreover, deployment may slip to a later date, as technical problems have been reported for both the anti-ship and conventional attack versions of the SLCM. Responding to these problems, the Congress has deferred the surface ship program until the Navy submits a plan specifying how the weapon would be employed operationally.

Bombers. Development of both the B-1B and advanced technology "Stealth" bombers continued in 1983. The B-1B, with its reduced radar signature, high penetration speed and new electronic counter-measures, is expected to be able to penetrate improved Soviet air defenses well into the 1990s. In this context, a new nuclear bomb, the B-83, will enter the inventory in 1985 and will be deployed primarily on the B-1B. Capable of more accurate delivery than previous strategic bombs, the B-83 is designed especially to destroy hardened targets. When not armed with gravity bombs, the B-1B is capable of carrying up to 20 cruise missiles, but will almost certainly not be equipped with this maximum load, which would severely reduce its ability to penetrate Soviet defenses. One hundred B-1B aircraft are scheduled to be deployed from late 1985 to 1988, the first at Dyess Air Force Base in Texas. Flight testing may begin as early as October 1984, five months ahead of the originally planned date. The "Stealth" bomber is expected to enter production in the late 1980s and become operational in the early 1990s. Full-scale development is scheduled to begin in 1985.

Significant changes are planned in the US air-launched cruise missile (ALCM) program. The current program to procure ALCM-B models will be discontinued in 1984 after 1739 missiles have been purchased, about one-third of the number originally planned to be acquired. Conversions of B-52 G and H bombers to carry cruise missiles will continue, however, and be completed by 1988, while the Air Force develops an advanced cruise missile model. The improved model, expected to be operational in the mid-1990s, will incorporate: (1) advanced propulsion systems for greater range and payload; (2) more accurate guidance and targeting systems; and, most importantly, (3) "Stealth" features to decrease detectability. The change seems to have been motivated both by faster than anticipated advances in Soviet air defenses, especially the deployment of "look down, shoot down" radars and new surface-to-air missiles, and important gains in US research and development programs. Reports indicate that about 1300–1500 of the new missiles will be built.

FUTURE DIRECTIONS IN SOVIET NUCLEAR FORCES

Since initiation of the US modernization program in 1981, Soviet military and civilian leaders have stated frequently that they intend to keep pace and perhaps even outdo the United States in building nuclear weapons. On 6 December 1982, for example, Marshal Dimitri Ustinov, Minister of Defense, warned that "the United States Administration should not hypnotize itself with the possibility of achieving military superiority. If the US deploys the MX, the Soviet Union will deploy in response a new ICBM of the same class." These comments were echoed by the then new Soviet leader, Yuri Andropov, on 21 December when he emphasized "we will be compelled to counter the challenge of the American side by deploying corresponding weapon systems of our own."

This Soviet emphasis on at least maintaining parity with the United States in weapons technology, while seeking superiority in numbers of weapons, is reflected in their acquisition programs and, by the mid- to late-1980s, Soviet strategic forces consequently will be likely to begin to receive a broad range of new weapon systems. Particularly noteworthy is the Soviet Union's first generation of long-range cruise missiles designed to attack targets on land. The Soviets consider cruise missiles an important technological innovation and appear to be making a vigorous effort to whittle down the American lead in these weapons. The anticipated appearance of the first Soviet intercontinental bomber in over twenty years, code-named Blackjack by NATO, is also a noteworthy new development. Aside from these departures, the Soviets are continuing to develop new inter-continental ballistic missiles and a new submarine-launched ballistic missile, while completing deployment of the current fourth generation of missiles.

Land-based missiles. A fifth generation of Soviet ICBMs could become operational by the mid-1980s, with apparently two models being tested. The first, the SS-X-24, a silo-based missile similar to the MX, was first tested in late 1982, but the program has encountered significant problems: four out of five tests have failed. The second, a smaller, probably solid-fueled, mobile missile, the SS-X-25, began a more successful test program in early 1983 (see Table

TABLE 8   Reported Soviet Missile Tests

Date	Type	Outcome
26 October 1982	SS-X-24	Failure
December 1982	SS-X-24	Success
8 February 1983	SS-X-25	Success
March 1983	SS-X-24	Failure
April 1983	SS-X-24	Failure
4 May 1983	SS-X-25	Success
30 May 1983	SS-X-25	Success
3 September 1983	SS-X-24	Failure

8). Controversy continued throughout the year over the SS-X-25s. The unratified but informally observed SALT II treaty limits the United States and Soviet Union to testing and deploying one new ICBM. While some Americans have claimed that the SS-X-25 is a second new missile, the Soviets contend it is merely a permissible version of an older ICBM, the SS-13.

Sea-based missiles. Deployment of *Typhoon*-class ballistic submarines carrying SS-N-20 missiles seems certain to continue. The final number to be deployed is unclear and may depend on any future strategic arms control agreement. A new submarine-launched ballistic missile, possibly intended to replace the SS-N-18, is expected to be tested soon. Future Soviet missiles are likely to embody improved guidance systems and solid-fuel propulsion.

Bombers. Code-named Blackjack, the new Soviet bomber is expected to be used primarily for strategic missions, but some may also be assigned to the Soviet navy for warfare at sea. A swing wing aircraft somewhat larger than the B-1, Blackjack is designed to carry cruise missiles as well as nuclear and conventional bombs. Flight testing has begun; deliveries of operational aircraft are expected to commence in 1987. By 1990, 50 to 75 aircraft could be operational. The Soviets are also reported to have begun to test a variant of the Bear bomber designed to carry modern cruise missiles.

Concerted Soviet efforts to build modern cruise missiles began toward the end of the 1970s; testing of a new air-launched cruise missile was started in late 1978. After a pause, the program has accelerated over the past few years, concentrating on the testing of a sea-launched version. The air-launched version, with a range of 1500 nautical miles, will probably be carried on the new Blackjack bomber. The sea-launched version, the SS-NX-21, has a similar range and is expected to be deployed on former *Yankee*-class ballistic missile submarines. Since the SS-NX-21 can also be fired out of torpedo tubes, it may also be deployed on other modern Soviet submarines. A ground-launched cruise missile is also being developed. All three Soviet cruise missiles could be operational by the mid-1980s.

KEY UNCERTAINTIES

Projecting potential US and Soviet nuclear capabilities is a fairly straightforward task. Nuclear weapon systems are complicated and costly pieces of equipment requiring long periods of time to develop, build, test and deploy. Most such weapons are designed and manufactured in specialized facilities by well-known organizations. Moreover, they must be tested extensively before deployment and, particularly, flight-tested repeatedly over observable ranges. As a result, it is possible to project the potential capabilities of the two sides several years in advance.

What is more difficult to predict is the degree to which each side will in fact exploit its full production potential. Here the vicissitudes of politics and economics in the two nations, as well as the changing relationship between the two powers, come into play. In the United States, for example, experience suggests that both practical difficulties in development programs and swings in public moods will lead to actual deployment schedules very different from those which might be projected on the basis of an analysis of the plans proposed by the administration and approved by the Congress in any one year. The continuing saga of the MX land-based missile is a vivid demonstration of this point, but other illustrations also could be mentioned. Projecting actual Soviet capabilities is even more difficult, of course, since we are given only rare glimpses into Soviet force planning and what "data" are made known can be noted only as statements which Soviet officials have made for unknown reasons. US government agencies do of course closely observe Soviet weapon development programs, particularly as they reach the testing stage, and a considerable amount of this information is made known to the public, either officially or unofficially. Even so, the Soviet Union typically develops several competing systems for each mission and then deploys some number of one or more of the competitors based on their evaluation of the candidates' capabilities and other factors. Forecasting such decisions is at best guesswork; and even official

US government projections of Soviet forces some five or ten years in the future not too infrequently prove to be inaccurate. Projecting the US–Soviet nuclear balance is particularly hazardous at present, given the large uncertainty about future directions in the overall relationship between the two powers, and the sharp debate in the United States and other Western nations about the roles and risks of nuclear weapons, the degree to which negotiated agreements can or cannot contribute to security, and the proper Western posture to contain Soviet expansionism.

Over the past decade, Western opinion has swung between the hopes raised at the height of detente in 1972 that East-West cooperation for mutual benefit was possible, even probable, and the tough-minded confrontational stance which seemed essential only seven years later, when the Soviets invaded Afghanistan. In fact, however, the consensus supporting either approach has never been very stable.

Many Americans are suspicious of the USSR, and hostile to its apparent values, but the policies required by a purely confrontational posture tend not to remain popular for very long. The use of coercive economic instruments present obvious difficulties and, as demonstrated during the first year of the present administration, even a tough politico-military stance—involving frigid political relations, a strong defense build-up, and an unyielding position on arms negotiations—can raise sufficient concern among the public to be unsustainable.

This seems to be the case largely because of an equally strong concern manifest in public opinion with the danger of nuclear war. The intensity of this concern has diminished or increased over the years in response to international circumstances and their implications for the saliency of war, but has never been very far from the surface. The sudden emergence of the anti-nuclear movement as an important force in American politics during 1982 and its continuing impact, particularly on the maneuvers and positions of Democratic political aspirants, suggests that future American policies will of necessity continue to try to accommodate the inherent contradiction between the dictates of a tough anti-Soviet posture and the need to ease the public concern about nuclear risks; any such policy almost by definition will be unstable. One suspects that only if the 1984 presidential and congressional elections result in a clear mandate for a candidate and party distinctly committed to a certain type of relationship with the USSR would this ambivalence be resolved. And even then, as was demonstrated during the past three years, the newly elected administration's ability to sustain its preferred policy would not be certain.

On the Soviet side, future policies and their implications for weapon decisions are equally unpredictable. Although General-Secretary Andropov continued to consolidate his hold on the party and government apparatus during 1983, important questions remained open as to the future of the present regime and its policies—not least of which concerns Mr. Andropov's health. The failure of Soviet policy in Western Europe, manifest in the victories of the CDU in the German elections in March, of the most strongly "Atlantic" of the smaller Italian parties in June, and of the Conservatives in the British election in June, and the subsequent successful initiation of Pershing and cruise missile deployment, may induce a reconsideration of Soviet policy toward the United States and its NATO allies.

The fulcrum through which these events will have the most manifest effect on the relative nuclear capabilities of the two sides will be the negotiations in Geneva for limitations on intermediate-range and central nuclear forces. Although these talks must grapple with the purely technical difficulties of placing mutual limitations on weapons, their pace has always depended most critically on politics. If both sides perceive important incentives to reach agreement—owing to budgetary pressures, the needs of allies, or domestic pressures to improve their mutual relationship—then technical issues prove soluble. When such incentives are not present, however, the most creative technical minds prove inadequate to the task before them.

There are thus important uncertainties in the projections which have been presented in this section, uncertainties which will be resolved one way or another at the Geneva negotiating tables, even though the latter will reflect much broader economic and political considerations.

If the INF talks were to resume, the most likely agreement in the INF talks would permit only a relatively small number of intermediate-range missiles on each side in Europe, and place collateral constraints on comparable missiles deployed elsewhere and on certain classes of nuclear-capable aircraft. It would certainly require the USSR to phase out all its older SS-4 and SS-5 missiles (something which is being done in any case), and almost certainly specify a sharp reduction in the number of newer SS-20s already deployed. On the US side, an INF agreement would require drastic reductions in planned deployments of both ground-launched cruise missiles and Pershing intermediate-range ballistic missiles. Predicting the character of any INF agreement that might occur, however, is a great deal easier than predicting when, if ever, there might be such an agreement. Certainly, there was no reason at the end of 1983 to expect that a treaty would be concluded anytime soon.

Forecasting the results of the INF talks seems simple, however, compared to the difficulties of predicting what, if any, agreements might eventually result from the START negotiations. The two sides are substantively even further apart in these latter negotiations—so much so that drastic revisions would be required in one or the other's basic approach if an agreement were to result.

In Tables 9 and 10, we have arrayed data describing what the

TABLE 9   Illustrative Soviet Force Postures, 1990

Weapon System	START Agreement		Soviet START Proposal		US START Proposal	
	Launchers	Weapons	Launchers	Weapons	Launchers	Weapons
ICBM						
SS-11	520	520	188	188	450	450
SS-13	0	0	0	0	0	0
SS-17	150	600	0	0	0	0
SS-18	308	3080	800	800	0	0
SS-19	360	2160	360	2160	100	600
SS-X-24	240	2400	240	2400	110	1100
SS-X-25	240	240	240	240	240	240
Subtotal	1818	9000	1108	5788	900	2390
SLBM						
SS-N-6	272	272	0	0	0	0
SS-N-8	292	292	236	236	0	0
SS-N-17	12	12	0	0	0	0
SS-N-18	256	1792	256	1792	160	1120
SS-N-20	140	1260	140	1260	140	1260
Subtotal	972	3628	632	3288	300	2380
Bombers						
Bear	0	0	0	0	0	0
Bison	0	0	0	0	0	0
Backfire	410	1640	0	0	340	1360
Blackjack	60	1200	60	1200	60	1200
Subtotal	470	2840	60	1200	400	2560
TOTAL:	3260	15 468	1800	10 276	1600	7330

TABLE 10   *Illustrative US Forces Postures, 1990*

Weapon System	No Arms Control		Soviet START Proposal		US START Proposal	
	Launchers	Weapons	Launchers	Weapons	Launchers	Weapons
ICBM						
Minuteman II	450	450	368	368	450	450
Minuteman III/ Mark 12	250	750	200	600	0	0
Minuteman III/ Mark 12A	300	900	300	900	100	300
MX	100	1000	100	1000	100	1000
Midgetman	0	0	0	0	0	0
Subtotal	1100	3100	968	2868	650	1750
SLBM						
Poseidon C-3	304	3040	0	0	0	0
Trident I C-4	384	3072	384	3072	352	2816
Trident II D-5	48	432	48	432	48	432
Subtotal	736	6544	432	3504	400	3248
Bombers						
FB-111	62	124	62	124	62	124
B-52 D/E/F (storage)	302	1812	170	1020	43	258
B-52/ALCM	195	3900	68	1360	195	3900
B-1B	100	2000	100	2000	100	2000
ATB	0	0	0	0	0	0
Subtotal	659	7836	400	4504	400	6282
TOTAL	2495	17 490	1800	12 876	1450	11 280

two sides' central strategic forces might look like in 1990 under three alternative assumptions: (1) no START agreement; (2) an agreement as proposed by Soviet negotiators; and (3) an agreement as proposed by President Reagan.

In the absence of negotiated restraints on nuclear forces, both US and Soviet forces could grow substantially during the course of the decade. Given the already large size of the two forces, their relative capabilities are unlikely to change substantially. The total number of weapons in Soviet central forces could nearly double, with nearly half of the gain originating in deployments of the SS-X-24 ICBM, and most of the remainder associated with air-launched cruise missiles on the Blackjack and SS-N-20 missiles on *Typhoon-*

class submarines. The number of US weapons could increase by more than 70 percent during the same period; as the US submarine-launched ballistic missile force is already MIRVed, most of this increase would originate with deployments of cruise missiles on bombers. None of these figures accounts for the qualitative advances in accuracy, reliability, survivability, and other characteristics also incorporated in new weapon systems, of course.

The Soviet START position would trim this growth substantially in all classes of weapons. The two sides' forces would be precisely equal in number of launchers and, in all probability, nearly equal in number of weapons. These weapons would continue to be distributed among the different force components asymmetrically, as the Soviet proposal would not require either side to change its force structure. As a consequence, the USSR would retain its present advantage in equivalent megatonnage—a lead which some observers believe could be used to deploy much larger numbers of weapons suddenly upon abrogating the treaty (or covertly without abrogation) and used to threaten US strategic forces with barrage attacks.

The US START proposal would require much deeper cuts in the number of missile launchers and weapons on the two sides, but would not place restrictions on bombers. This would suggest a sizable US lead in weapons at the end of the decade, at least until the Soviet Union had an opportunity to expand its own bomber force. The US proposal would also require a substantial shift in Soviet missile assets from land-based missiles to submarines.

THIRD COUNTRY NUCLEAR FORCES

The British, French and Chinese nuclear forces are estimated in Table 11.

These forces will continue to grow at a steady pace over the next decade, even at the expense of each country's conventional capabilities, and could have an important impact on regional nuclear balances, particularly in Europe. By the end of the decade, in addition to the procurement of substantial numbers of nuclear-capable F-16s and Tornados by other Western European countries, more than 400 new nuclear-capable tactical aircraft will be built by Britain and France. In addition, both nations are planning substantial increases in the number of nuclear warheads on their missile forces. Chinese forces, on the other hand, continue to grow at only a slow rate.

Britain. The British sea-based strategic force, now consisting of 64 Polaris A-3 missiles deployed on four *Resolution*-class submarines,

TABLE 11   Third Country Nuclear Forces

Type of Launcher	United Kingdom			France			China[a]	
	1983	1984	1990	1983	1984	1990	1983	1984
ICBMs	0	0	0	0	0	0	2	4
IRBMs	0	0	0	18	18	18	60	80
MRBMs	0	0	0	0	0	0	50	50
SRBMs	0	0	0	30	30	30	0	0
SLBMs	64	64	64	80	80	96	0	0
Bombers	12	0	0	34	34	18	90	90
Nuclear-Capable Tactical Aircraft	170	192	305	146	146	201	0	0
Total delivery systems	246	256	369	308	308	363	202	224
Total warheads	500	619	689	379	379	794	202	224

[a] = There is too much uncertainty about Chinese nuclear programs to project its force structure in 1990.

is being upgraded. The Chevaline program will convert each missile to carry six 200-kiloton independently targetable warheads as compared to the current payload of three 200-kiloton warheads which are able to strike only a single large target. A primary reason for deploying the new warhead has been concern about possible improvements to the Soviet ballistic missile system around Moscow. (The British as well as the French strategic forces, because of their small size, are reported to be targeted primarily on Moscow and other large cities.)

British aircraft capable of delivering nuclear weapons are also beginning to be modernized extensively. By early 1983, all British Vulcan B-2 bombers, introduced in 1960, had been retired or converted to tankers. They are being replaced by the Panavia Tornado, an all-weather strike fighter, expected to survive in even highly demanding combat environments. At the end of 1983, three 12-aircraft squadrons were operational, two of which entered active duty during the year. By 1989, 220 Tornado fighter-bombers should be operational, allowing the British to retire their 20-year-old Buccaneer bombers from active service.

Over the long term, Britain intends to spend $13.9 billion to modernize its sea-based strategic force. Four new submarines are to be built to replace the Resolution-class boats, each large enough to carry sixteen D-5 (Trident II) missiles purchased from the United States. Deployments are scheduled to begin by the early 1990s. Initially, each submarine will carry only 12 missiles, each armed with 8 warheads, for a total of 384 warheads, but the force may eventually be expanded to include 512 more warheads. The Trident program exerts considerable pressure on the British defense budget, however, and could squeeze out funds for conventional forces. It has consequently become controversial, even among conservative segments of opinion, and may thus never be fully implemented.

France. A number of French initiatives designed to maintain a credible nuclear force into the next decade are either underway or planned. The French sea-based strategic force, now consisting of five submarines, each armed with sixteen M-20 missiles fitted with a single warhead, continue to receive the highest priority. After undergoing its second refit since entering service ten years ago, the fifth boat, *Le Terrible*, returned to active service in 1983, allowing France to maintain three submarines continuously at sea, a policy begun by the present government in 1981. Also in 1983, procurement of 71 Super Etendards, carrier-based nuclear-capable strike aircraft, was completed. Only 36 to 45 aircraft can be deployed at sea at any one time, however.

Beginning in 1985, several new French nuclear systems should enter active service. A sixth ballistic missile submarine, *L'Inflexible*, launched in June 1982, will become operational. This submarine will carry 16 M-4 missiles with a MIRVed system of six 150 kiloton warheads. Four of the five older boats will be converted to carry the M-4 missile as well, beginning in 1987 and ending in 1990. The six-boat force (five armed with the M-4) will thus eventually include 96 launchers with 496 warheads. A new type of missile-carrying submarine is planned to be launched in 1990 and become operational in 1994. The submarine is to carry a new missile, currently being studied, the M-S.

France's nuclear-capable aircraft are planned to be modernized extensively beginning in the mid-1980s. Eighteen of 34 aging Mirage IV bombers are being modified to carry a nuclear-armed, medium-range, stand-off missile able to destroy hard targets; the remaining sixteen planes will be retired. Similar to the American short-range attack missiles deployed on B-52s, the Air-Son á Moyenne Portée (ASMP) will carry a single 100- to 150-kiloton warhead to a range of 50 to 100 kilometers. Full-scale flight tests began in June and initial deployments on Mirage IVs will begin in 1987–88. Fifty Super Etendards will also be converted to carry the ASMP, beginning in 1984. In 1988, the French will begin to operate the

Mirage 2000N, a tactical aircraft equipped to operate under all weather conditions at low altitudes. The first Mirage 2000N was flight tested in February of 1983 and the second in the summer. As these new planes enter the force, the 30 nuclear-capable Mirage IIIEs now in the inventory will be phased out. Up to 200 Mirage 2000Ns may eventually be procured; each will carry the ASMP.

Production of French enhanced radiation (neutron) weapons could begin by the mid-1980s and certainly by the next decade. (The French have been testing neutron devices at their Pacific test sites since the mid-1970s.) The new French five-year defense plan preserves the option for deployment on the Hades short-range ballistic missile.

While developments beyond 1990 are uncertain, modernization of land-based missiles appears to be an important priority. The Hades is planned to replace the 30 Pluton nuclear-armed, short-range ballistic missile, perhaps on a greater than one-to-one basis, with the first regiment scheduled for deployment after 1992. Hades will have greater range and improved accuracy as compared to Pluton, and will be capable of striking enemy forces on the inter-German border from bases in France.

France's eighteen intermediate-range ballistic missiles are now based in fixed silos and thus vulnerable to attack, but a mobile replacement, the S-X, is being studied. The new missile would carry a single 150-kiloton warhead and be transported on trucks, which normally would be stationed on military bases. The S-X was expected to enter service in 1996, at which time the remaining 18 Mirage IV aircraft would be retired, but the program has been delayed.

People's Republic of China. In early 1983, Defense Minister Zhang asserted that China should concentrate on the production of nuclear weapons. While by no means certain, this position may reflect a decision by Chinese leaders to place increased emphasis on improving nuclear forces as a substitute for the far greater expense of modernizing conventional capabilities. A number of other developments point to the future diversification and growth of Chinese nuclear forces, though it remains difficult to make specific projections. The Chinese for years have moved much more slowly in deploying nuclear delivery systems than many Westerners had projected.

A new ICBM, the CSS-4, with a range of 13,000 kilometers, has now entered service, with four missiles believed to be operational by the end of 1983. There are no signs as yet that the missile has entered serial production, although, according to US intelligence estimates reported publicly, 15 missiles are likely to be deployed by the end of the 1980s. Likewise, there are no indications that the CSS-4 is equipped with multiple warheads, although deployment of missiles with multiple warheads remains a distinct possibility. A missile carrying three space research satellites was launched at the end of 1982, leading some experts to believe the Chinese now have such a capability.

Developments over the past few years indicate some progress in Chinese sea-based strategic forces, although the public reports of this activity are contradictory and uncertain. The first Chinese-built, nuclear-powered, ballistic missile submarine, with 8 to 12 missile tubes, was reported to have been launched in April 1981 and could enter active service by the mid-1980s; other reports indicate that it, and even a second submarine, said to have been launched in 1982, may have become operational in 1983. (The Chinese also own a single, 1950s vintage, Soviet-designed *Golf*-class submarine, which is used for developmental purposes.) In any event, by the end of the decade, as many as four Chinese SSBNs could be operational.

The Chinese have announced that they successfully fired their first submarine-launched ballistic missile in October 1982—a step obviously necessary for an operational SSBN force. It is not clear, however, whether the test was conducted from a submerged submarine or from one operating on or near the surface, and whether the new class or the ancient *Golf*-class was used. No further tests were reported in 1983, in any event.

Western sources believe that when operational, Chinese missile submarines will be stationed with the North Sea Fleet within range of Siberia and the Soviet Far East. By the end of the decade, patrol areas could be expanded to include Arctic waters within range of European Russia and the northwestern United States.

The Chinese also may be developing tactical nuclear weapons. In June 1982, the Chinese exploded a nuclear weapon for the first time during a military exercise near the Mongolian border. The device, apparently delivered by an aircraft, was used against a simulated Soviet force. The threat of using tactical nuclear weapons against Soviet invasion forces is an attractive option given the Chinese lack of credible counter-city options, and the territory along much of the Sino-Soviet border, which is only thinly populated. There is no evidence, however, that the Chinese have produced a substantial number of these weapons.

10

CHAPTER

A HISTORICAL PRECEDENT:
THE ROMANS IN DACIA

*I*n our own disordered times, it is natural to look back for comfort and instruction to the experience of Roman imperial statecraft. No analogies are possible in the economic, social, or political spheres of life, but in the realm of strategy there are instructive similarities. For the Romans, the two essential requirements of an evolving civilization were a sound material base and adequate security. For the Romans, the elusive goal of strategic statecraft was to provide security for the civilization without prejudicing the vitality of its economic base and without compromising the stability of an evolving political order. The historic success of the Roman Empire, manifest in its unique endurance, reflected the high degree to which these conflicting imperatives were reconciled. It was certainly not battlefield achievements alone that ensured for so long the tranquility of vast territories, lands that have been in turmoil ever since.

The superiority of the empire, and it was vast, was of an altogether more subtle order: it derived from the whole complex of ideas and traditions that informed the organization of Roman military force and harnessed the armed power of the empire to political purpose. The firm subordination of tactical priorities, martial ideals, and warlike instincts to political goals was the essential condition of the strategic success of the empire.

The general principles of the Roman imperial strategy were applicable to the whole scale of the Empire although each frontier sector had its own particularities imposed by different enemies or geographic situation.

In this chapter we will deal only with one—and somehow limited—pattern of this strategical principle, and this was Dacia and Lower Danubian territories.

At the death of Augustus, in A.D. 14, the territories subject to direct or indirect imperial control comprised the coastal lands of the entire Mediterranean basin, the whole of the Iberian peninsula, continental Europe inland to the Rhine and Danube, Anatolia, and, more loosely, the Bosporan Kingdom on the northern shores of the Black Sea. Control over this vast territory was effectively ensured by a small army, whose size was originally determined at the beginning of the principate and only sightly increased thereafter.

There was as yet no demarcated imperial frontier and no system of fixed frontier defenses, nor were the legions in permanent stone fortresses as they were to be in the future.[1] Uninvolved in major wars of conquest between A.D. 6 and A.D. 43 (Britain), the salient function of the army was necessarily defensive, i.e., providing security against the sudden emergence of unforeseen threats.

These threats were primarily internal. Aside from the sporadic transborder incursions of Germans, Dacians, and later, Sarmatians, and the conflict with Parthia over the Armenian investiture, Rome's major security problems were the result of native revolts within the empire.

Under Augustus, the Dacian problem was alleviated, but not solved, by punitive expeditions and reprisal operations.[2] Roman diplomacy, especially during the principate of Tiberius, also established an "invisible frontier" of client relationships with the more primitive peoples beyond the Rhine and Danube.[3] Under Tiberius,

[1] C. M. Wells, The German Policy of Augustus: An Examination of the Archaeological Evidence (Oxford: Clarendon Press, 1972).
[2] A. Alföldi in CAH 11:84–85.
[3] The phrase is Ernst Kornemann's, from the title of his lecture "Die unsichtbaren brenzen des römischen Kaiserreichs," reprinted in Staaten-Völker-Männer. Aus der Geschichte des Altertums (Leipzig: Dieterich, 1934), pp. 99–116.

diplomacy was tried, but the Dacians could not be turned into reliable clients (perhaps because they had gold of their own).[4] The Romans therefore used the Sarmatian Iazyges, installed between the Tisza (Theiss) and Danube, to keep Dacian power away from that stretch of the river.[5] Simultaneously a client state with severe internal and external security problems was installed in Thrace, whose ruler, Rhoemetalces I (and later his quarreling successors), had to be repeatedly assisted against the Thracian tribe of the Bessi.[6]

However, the Romans could not simply ignore the peoples living beyond the Rhine and Danube. These peoples, both great and little, represented too powerful a force to be left uncontrolled on the long and vulnerable perimeter of the Empire, which still had no border defenses. In answer, we must note, first of all, that in Europe the river frontiers of the Rhine and Danube were not protected by linear barriers. Instead, watchtowers and signal stations were complemented by riverine patrol fleets like Classis Moesica on the Danube.[7]

The security policies of Vespasian and his successors, which reached a logical culmination under Hadrian and his successors, may be seen as an attempt to transform the empire into a marching camp writ large. The metaphor is perfectly applicable: the network of imperial border defenses created under these policies, like those of the marching camp, were intended to serve not as total barriers but rather as the one fixed element in a mobile strategy of imperial defense.

By the time of the Flavians, the Roxolani, another Sarmatian people (i.e., of Iranian stock), occupied the plains along the lower course of the Danube. Tacitus records their ill-fated raid of A.D. 69 across the Danube and into Moesia, in which 9000 mounted warriors were intercepted by the legion III Gallica and cut to pieces as they were retreating, laden with booty.[8]

In A.D. 85/86, under Domitian, the Romans again had to fight the Dacians, who had recentralized under the rule of Decebalus. After

[4] *Daicoviciu*, La Transilvanie, *pp. 52–54.*
[5] *Lee John Harmatta, "The Sarmatians in Hungary"* in Studies in the History of the Sarmatians, *Magyar-Görög Tanulmányok, 30 (Budapest: Pázmány Péter Tudományegegyetemi Görög Filológiai Intézet, 1950), pp. 45–46.*
[6] *Ronald Syme, CAH 10:356.*
[7] *Chester G. Starr, Jr.,* The Roman Imperial Navy, 31 BC–AD 32. *Cornell Studies in Classical Philology, vol. 26 (Ithaca: Cornell University Press, 1941), pp. 135–37.*
[8] *Tacitus,* Histories, *I, 79.*

driving the Dacians back across the Danube following yet another incursion into Moesia, the Romans pursued them, but suffered a serious defeat; in A.D. 88 this was avenged by a successful strategic offensive, which culminated in a great victory at Tapae, in the plain beyond Turnu Severin.[9] Perhaps Domitian intended to follow up this victory in the field with an advance on Sarmizegethusa, the seat of Decebalus and his court, but the revolt of Antonius Saturninus, legate of upper Germany, intervened in January, A.D. 89. By then, however, the client system on the Danube sector was crumbling, and this drastically restricted the strategic options open to the Romans.

The Romans faced three major tribal agglomerations in the region, which had been under a loose but effective form of diplomatic control since the time of Tiberius: the Marcomanni, the Quadi (centered in the general area opposite Vienna), and the Iazyges. There is no evidence that these peoples had helped Domitian's forces in the campaigns of A.D. 85 and A.D. 88 against Decebalus. But neither had they hindered it, for the Romans could not have mounted simultaneous offensives across the 600 miles of the Danube border from Dacia to the Marcomannis territory west of the Elbe. The acquiescence of these powerful neighbors was essential for any strategic offensive against Dacia, just as the acquiescence of the Dacians was essential for any strategic offensive against the Marcomanni, Quadi, or Iazyges. Thus, when the Marcomanni, Quadi, and Iazyges all threatened war,[10] Domitian was forced to make peace with Decebalus on the basis of the status quo ante (and a technical aid program);[11] for the next several years there was inconclusive war against Germans and Sarmatians upstream from Dacian territory, which itself remained at peace.[12]

It is in this context that Trajan's wars with Decebalus and his ultimate conquest of Dacia must be seen. It once was de rigueur to contrast Trajan's heedless adventurism with Hadrian's peaceful disposition. Across the Danube, as across the Euphrates, Trajan supposedly left deep salients that marked his grandiose conquests but lengthened the imperial perimeter needlessly. Trajan's annexation

---

[9] Syme, CAH 11:168–72; and Demougeot, La Formation de l'Europe et les invasions barbares: Des Origines germaniques à l'avènement de Dioclétien (Paris: Aubier, 1969), pp. 162–64.

[10] Syme, CAH 11:175–76, based on fragmentary information (Dio LXVII.7.1).

[11] Ibid., p. 176; Demougeot, La Formation, pp. 162–64.

[12] Syme, CAH 11:176–77; Demougeot, La Formation, pp. 162–64.

of Dacia has also been explained as a throwback to the days of predatory imperialism and unlimited expansionism.[13]

Decebalus, ruler of Dacia, could have been transformed into a highly useful client in the wake of Trajan's first and victorious Dacian war (A.D. 101–2).[14] Defeated but still powerful a Dacian client state could have assumed responsibility for preventing infiltration and raids on the Daco-Roman frontier and for interdicting Sarmatian attacks. The relationship between a client Decebalus and Rome under the earlier system of empire would have been shaped by the realities of power: Decebalus, kept in subjection by the ultimate threat of war and deposition, could have complied overtly with Roman security desiderata without fear of domestic opposition. Confronted with the worse alternative of direct imperial rule, the Dacians would have a powerful incentive to obey a ruler who himself obeyed Rome. Not so in the new strategic environment. Faced with an empire that could concentrate superior forces on the Dacian sector only with visible difficulty,[15] and more important, which was obviously reluctant to expand (as shown to all by the failure to annex Dacia in the wake of Trajan's first war), Decebalus was

---

[13] Jérôme Carcopino argues this, under the title "Un retour à l'imperialisme de conquête: L'Or des Daces" (1934), in Les Etapes de l'imperialisme roumain (Paris: Hachette, 1961), pp. 106–17. See, contra, Lepper, Trajan's Parthian War, p. 107, in which he describes Trajan's Dacian policy as "Domitianic." The strength of Trajan's army (twelve to thirteen legions) in both wars shows how powerful a state Decebalus had organized. An economic frontier strategy on that sector was incompatible with the survival of so strong a neighbor. There is also the evidence of Pliny's "Panegyric" which invokes no visions of grandiose conquest ("non times bella hec provocas"). Albino Garzetti, Problemi dell'Età Traianea: Sommario e testi (Genova: Fratelli Bozzi, 1971), pp. 51–52, briefly states the arguments: that Trajan concluded his first Dacian war (A.D. 101–2) with another attempt to convert Dacia into a client state, refraining from conquest; that Decebalus himself provoked the second war (A.D. 105–6) by breaking the terms of the treaty of A.D. 102; that the second war was not followed by total conquest, since only Transylvania was provincialized, while the lands on either side were left to the Sarmatians. See the recent survey of the debate in Kenneth Hugh Waters, "The Reign of Trajan and Its Place in Contemporary Scholarship," ANRW, pt. 2, vol. 2, pp. 417–22.

[14] Lemosse, Relations internationales, p. 117, n. 250.

[15] Domitian massed a force of nine legions against the Dacians in A.D. 87 (Parker, Roman Legions, p. 158), of which one, V Alaudae, may have been lost in the fighting; Lee Watson, Roman Soldier, pp. 23–43, for an abbreviated discussion of the issue. In his first Dacian war, Trajan had a force of twelve legions on the Danube (Parker, Roman Legions, p. 156), and he may have had a total of thirteen for the second war (ibid., p. 157). Cf. Longden, CAH 11:231.

insufficiently intimidated to act as a satisfactory client.[16] And even if he personally had been willing to obey Rome, it is likely that others in Dacia would have demanded a more independent policy. Thus it can be argued that Dacia had to be annexed, paradoxically enough, because the empire had become visibly defencist, and its rulers reluctant to annex. In other words, Trajan had to destroy Dacian independence because the option of indirect rule was no longer open to the empire.[17]

It is certainly true that once Dacia was conquered, after Trajan's second war against Decebalus in A.D. 106, the frontiers of the new province of Dacia formed a deep wedge centered on the Sarmize-gethusa-Apulum axis, eventually adding more than 370 miles to the length of the imperial perimeter.[18] In fact on the map the new province presents a classic profile of vulnerability. This impression is strengthened by the nature of the military deployment left in place once the campaigns were over. The salient's center of gravity was not at its base, but toward the apex, since the legionary base at Apulum in the Maros valley was nearer to the northern edge of the Carpathians than to the Danube. Neither then nor later was the Dacian limes as a whole enclosed with a wall system; it remained organized as a network of independent strong-points astride the main invasion routes, guarding the major lines of communication.[19]

This new frontier, which makes so little sense in the light of the superficial strategy of small-scale maps, becomes highly rational in the light of the hierarchy of priorities of Roman policy: the elimination of Dacia's independent power provided the necessary conditions for a restoration of Roman diplomatic control over the Germans and Sarmatians of the entire region. Both deterrence and positive inducements (i.e., subsidies) would be needed to keep Marcomanni, Iazyges, and Roxolani from raiding the Danube lands; and as long as Decebalus remained in defiant independence, the deterrent arm of the policy would be fatally weakened. As a province, Dacia was not worth having, but as a strategic shield for the region as a whole it was very valuable indeed.

---

[16] *Ibid.* See also Gordon, "Subsidization of Border Peoples," p. 41.
[17] *Lemosse,* Relations internationales, p. 119.
[18] *Szilágy,* "Les Variations," p. 205, estimates the length of the imperial perimeter, including Dacia, at 10,200 kilometers, and without it, at 9600 kilometers.
[19] The limes is described in Daicoviciu, La Transilvanie, pp. 89–99; for an updated account of the Trajanic settlement in Dacia, see idem., "Dacica" in Hommages à Albert Grenier, ed. Marcel Renard, 3 vols., Collection Latomus, vol. 58 (Brussels: Latomus, 1962), vol. 1, pp. 462–71.

Following Sarmatian attacks of A.D. 116–19, the flanks of the Dacian salient were narrowed through the evacuation of the western Banat to the north and Muntenia to the south. By A.D. 124–26 Dacia had been divided into three provinces (Malvensis, Porolissensis, and Apulensis), and at least sixty-five separate outposts were built to provide a defense-in-depth of Dacia Porolissensis. This Limes Porolissensis formed the outer shield of the entire system of Danubian defense, with rear support provided by the legion XI Gemina, stationed in Apulum. On either side of the Dacian salient were the plains occupied by the subsidized Sarmatians: Iazyges to the west and Roxolani to the east. Had Rome been weak and the Sarmatians strong, the Dacian provinces would have been vulnerable to encirclement (across the neck of the peninsula of Roman territory on the Danube); but with Rome as strong as it then was, the Dacian frontier effectively separated the Sarmatians on either side and weakened their combined power. Though subsidies might still be required, the strong auxiliary garrisons of Dacia Malvensis (on the Danube) and Dacia Porolissensis (on the Carpathians) as well as the legion in Dacia Apulensis would suffice to complement the inducements with the threat of retaliation for any transborder raiding.[20]

The elimination of the Dacian threat provided security for the Dobruja and all the Danube lands up to Vienna; with security, there came, first, agricultural prosperity and, then, urbanization: the coastal Greek cities of the Dobruja recovered swiftly from the effects of insecurity, while new cities emerged in the entire region, from Thrace to Carnuntum (Deutschaltenburg). The legionary bases at Ratiaria and Oescus on the lower Danube were left in the deep rear by the conquest of Dacia, and the legions were withdrawn since the sector was no longer of military significance. But the two localities did not wither away. Instead they became civilian settlements, with the high status of colonia.[21] Once the scene of raid and counter-raid, the Danube valley could begin after Trajan's conquest to contribute to the human and material resources of the empire, augmenting its fundamental strength.

The only priority of Roman frontier policy that the Dacian fron-

---

[20] For Dacia's role in the overall Danubian strategy, see Vasile Christescu, Istoria Militara a Daciei Romane. (Bucharest: Fundatia Regele Carol I, 1937), pp. 36–42. For a survey of the evidence, see Donald W. Wade, "The Roman Auxiliary Units and Camps in Dacia" (Ph.D. dissertation, University of North Carolina, 1969).

[21] Frova, "The Danubian Limes," pp. 28–29.

tier did not satisfy was the lowest tactical priority since the perimeter was lengthened rather than shortened. This did not, of course, affect imperial communications, which could now follow routes just as short but much more secure. Nor is the impression of vulnerability given by the map of the Dacian frontier justified. Aside from its obvious topographic advantage the Limes Porolissensis was a salient only in purely military terms: its flanks east and west were not open invasion axes, for they were occupied by peoples under Roman diplomatic control.[22]

Though the conquest of Dacia thus reinforced Rome's strategic and diplomatic control of the entire Danube frontier, the Limes Porolissensis was still something of an outpost, or rather a whole series of outposts centered on the XIII Gemina at Apulum, the only legion left in place once the frontier was organized.[23] As is true of any outpost, as long as the sector as a whole was securely held, the Dacian salient added to this security. Far from being vulnerable to encirclement, the salient itself could be used as a base to encircle the Iazyges to the west or the Roxolani to the east: Roman forces could advance on the Drobeta-Apulum highway and then turn to attack the Sarmatian in the rear.[24]

Because the Romans had developed a comprehensive system of perimeter defense in the second century, their response to the first serious penetrations of the imperial perimeter, which took place under Marcus Aurelius (ca. 166), was incremental and remedial. Neither a system of elastic defense nor one of defense-in-depth was adopted. Instead, on the most vulnerable tracts of the perimeter, border fortifications were strengthened and garrisons were augmented.

It was only after the chaotic breakdown of imperial defenses in the great crisis of the mid-third century that definite action was

---

[22] Lepper, Trajan's Parthian War, pp. 109–10. For the subsidization of the Sarmatians, see Colin D. Gordon, "The Subsidization of Border Peoples as a Roman Policy of Imperial Defense" (Ph.D. dissertation, University of Michigan, 1948), p. 44.

[23] Parker, Roman Legions, p. 157. On auxiliary units (including numeri) see Giovani Forni, "Contributo alla storia della Dacia Romana," Athenaeum, n.s., vol. 36 (1958–59): 3–29 (fasc. 1–2) and 193–218 (fasc. 3), especially 206. See also Christescu, Istoria Militara, pp. 42–46 (on troops) and 47–52 (on fortifications).

[24] The salient was used this way when the forces of C. Velius Rufus seemingly attacked the Iazyges in the rear after an advance north of the Danube and west across the river Tisza (Theiss), c.a. A.D. 89; R. P. Longden, CAH 11: p. 176.

taken to adopt a new strategy. When and where frontier defenses
were totally overrun, remedial strategies could only take the form
of elastic defense, but to the extent that deliberate choice was possible, the strategy that emerged had the character of a defense-in-
depth based on a combination of static frontier forces and mobile
field armies.

The Antonine system of preclusive security had always been vulnerable to simultaneous attacks from different directions and in 162
the Parthian invasion of Armenia initiated a whole series of conflicts
that were to last, with short intervals, until the death of Marcus
Aurelius in 180.[25] The threat on the Danubian and (to a lesser
extent) the Rhine sectors was permanent. As the expeditionary
forces were returning from the east, bringing a devastating plague
with them, Quadi, Marcomanni, and Iazyges crossed the Danube
over much of its length, evaded or defeated the weak frontier garrisons, and advanced in bands large and small deep into the empire.[26]
The SHA speaks of a barbarian "conspiracy," but even without coordination the opportunity must have been simultaneously apparent to all.[27] By 172 the Marcomanni had been driven out of the
Empire, and a peace was imposed on them; two years later the
Quadi were suppressed, and in 175 it was the turn of the Sarmatians.[28] When Quadi and Marcomanni renewed hostilities in 177,
the outcome was a great Roman victory on the Danube in 179.[29]
Marcus Aurelius had supposedly planned a trans-Danubian operation to conquer the homeland of the Marcomanni, and much else
besides, but this project, if it was in fact seriously contemplated,
was abandoned by his son Commodus upon the emperor's death
in 180.[30]

[25] *The sources on this subject are exceedingly poor; see the recent summary
in Anthony R. Birley,* Marcus Aurelius *(London: Eyre and Spottiswoode,
1966), pp. 223–45, 283–86.*
[26] Émilienne Demougeot, La Formation, *pp. 215–29; J. Fitz, "A Military History of Pannonia from the Marcomann Wars to the Death of Alexander Seve-
rus (180–235),"* Acta Archaeologica Academiae Scientiarum Hungariae *14
(1962): 32–36; Pavel Oliva,* Pannonia and the Onset of the Crisis in the Roman Empire *(Prague: Ceskoslovenské Akademie Věd, 1962), pp. 260–78.*
[27] SHA, Vita Marci, XXII.1.
[28] Demougeot, La Formation, *pp. 220–24; Birley,* Marcus Aurelius, *pp.
233–45.*
[29] Demougeot, La Formation, *pp. 224–27; Birley,* Marcus Aurelius, *pp. 272–86,
passim.*
[30] *See Oliva,* Pannonia and the Onset of Crisis, *pp. 299–304. This contradicts
sources as cited, including SHA, Vita Marci, XXIV.5. Cf. Wilhelm Weber in
CAH 11:355, 362.*

Fortunately, there is no need to quantify the change in order to establish that the overall threat faced by the Empire during and after the third century was much greater than that of the two preceding centuries. The narrative sources provide enough evidence to show that the East German Goths, whose westward attacks had reached Tyras on the Dniester by 238, and who crossed the Danube delta four years later, were a much more formidable enemy than the Carpi and Sarmatians, who had been until then the major enemy in Lower Moesia.[31]

There was a perceptible two-way interaction, intentional or otherwise, between the rhythm of Gothic attacks on land and at sea and the intensification of Persian pressures in the East. In 250 the emperor Decius set out to reestablish the lower Danubian frontier, and after driving the Carpi from Dacia Malvensis, his forces engaged the Goths who had penetrated into Thrace and forced them to raise the siege of Nicopolis.[32] A war of strategic maneuver followed, in which the Goths were eventually forced to withdraw northward into the Dobruja. It seems that a catastrophic tactical defeat then reversed an apparent strategic victory: the Roman field army under Decius was destroyed at Abrittus (in the central Dobruja) in 251.[33] In 252 Shapur opened a major offensive in the East. In the next four years came the deluge: Dacia was submerged by invaders, the Goths reached Salonika, sea raiders ravaged the coasts, and Shapur's armies conquered territory as far away as Antioch, while in the West, Franks and Alamanni were subjecting the entire-Rhine frontier and the upper Danube to almost constant pressure.[34]

New federations of old neighbors of the empire, like the Franks and Alamanni, relatively new arrivals in the immediate vicinity of the limites, like Gepids, Goths, Heruli, and Vandals (the Asdings opposite Pannonia, the Silings on the Main), and old established

[31] Demougeot, La Formation, p. 395. On Gothic attacks in general, see ibid., pp. 393–433, and John B. Bury, The Invasion of Europe by the Barbarians (1928); reprinted (New York: Russel and Russel, 1963), pp. 3–22.

[32] On the Carpi, see Demougeot, La Formation, pp. 437–39. On the Goths in general see the recent summary in Lucien Musset, Les Invasions: Les vagues germaniques, Nouvelle Clio no. 12 (Paris: Presses universitaires de France, 1965), pp. 80–82. On the sequence of events, see Demougeot, La Formation, pp. 409–11.

[33] Demougeot, La Formation, p. 412.

[34] On Dacia, see ibid., pp. 434–42; on Gothic victories and raids after 250, see ibid., pp. 416–25; on the emergence of the Frankish federation and its attacks until ca. 260, see ibid., pp. 465–89 passim; on Shapur's threat to eastern Anatolia, see Besnier, L'Empire romain de l'avènement des Sévères, p. 178.

enemies like the Carpi and Sarmatians may have jointly constituted a threat greater than that of their predecessors.

The new seaborne incursions of Franks and Saxons in the Channel and of the Goths, Heruli, and associated peoples in the Black Sea and the eastern Mediterranean were qualitatively different: from about 253 until about 269 Goths and Heruli ravaged, first, the Black Sea coasts and, later, the Aegean in a crescendo of raiding expeditions, often leaving their boats to penetrate deep inland. In the process, productive lands were devastated, and many important cities were attacked, sacked, and sometimes utterly destroyed.[35] After almost a decade of lesser attacks, in 266 and 267 Goths, Heruli, and their allies again raided Thrace, Macedonia, Greece, and Asia Minor in large combined expeditions at sea, while attacks also continued on land.[36]

The narrative sources give inordinately high figures for the size of the raiding armadas and warrior armies of the Goths and their allies. We hear of 2000 ships in the Goth expedition of 267 and of 320,000 warriors advancing on land (across the modern Dobruja).[37] Naturally, modern historiography does not accept the accuracy of such estimates, though it is usually conceded that the dimensions of the threat were unusually large—much the largest facing Rome in the third century.[38]

Strategic rationality for the central authorities of the Empire and the best interests of the provincials were two very different things, however, and this disparity was to have grave political consequences. The nexus between the multiple invasions of the third century and the multiple successions in Britain, Gaul, Egypt, and North Africa was direct. Provincial security had been sacrificed for the security of the empire as a whole, and the provincials can be excused for their failure to accept the logic of the system.

This was the case of Dacia, whose military worth as an outpost declines and finally becomes a liability as the security of the baseline diminishes. Thus, in the great crisis of the third century, when Rome lost control of the Sarmatians on either side of the salient, the Limes Porolissensis did become a vulnerable salient liable to be cut off, as well as a drain on the resources of the sector as a whole. It was finally abandoned during (or just after) the reign of Aurelian

---

[35] Demougeot, La Formation, p. 419.
[36] A. Alföldi, CAH 11:148–49.
[37] SHA, Vita Claudii, VIII, 1 and VI, 4.
[38] A. Alföldi, CAH 12:149. Bury, The Invasions of Europe, p. 22, merely remarks that the figures are grossly exaggerated.

(A.D. 270–75),[39] the frontier being reverted to the pre-Trajanic line of the river. Until then, however, the Dacian limes had been the highly cost-effective military instrument that ensured Rome's military and diplomatic control over the entire region.

The reorganization of frontier defenses during and after the third century was therefore a realistic adaptation of system to resources. Although these territorial losses reflected in large measure the force of circumstances, the tetrarchic reorganization of the frontiers also presents the unmistakable signs of a deliberate policy. In the case of Dacia with Carpi and Visigoths established in the Transylvanian highlands and in Wallachia, the Taifali in Oltenia, and the Sarmatians still in the Banat (but under pressure from the Asding Vandals established in what is now eastern Hungary),[40] it would undoubtedly have been very difficult to reestablish Roman control over Dacia (i.e., Transylvania and the Oltenia land bridge). But a strategic disincentive was operating here: the tetrarchic form of defense-in-depth was shallow, and it did not require advanced salients. The legions and cavalry units of each province reinforced, if need be, by expeditionary forces, were to defend provincial territory on a provincial scale. In contrast, the earlier "forward defense" system hinged on Dacia had been regional in scale, with the Dacian provinces forming a defended salient from which lateral counter-offensives into the Banat to the west and Wallachia to the east were possible. Whether or not the new strategy was the right one to adopt from a conceptual standpoint, it is clear that its adoption would considerably reduce the military value of the Dacian salient.[41]

[39] Numismatic evidence proves that Roman power was successfully maintained in the Dacia Malvensis until then (i.e., in Transylvania west of the river Olt): Eugenio Manni, L'Impero di Gallieno: Contributo alla storia dell III secolo (Rome: Angelo Signorelli, 1949), p. 29. The loss of Dacia was progressive, with the earlier abandonment of the Severan Limes Transalutanus. See Demougeot, La Formation, pp. 434–42, 452–57; and C. Daicoviciu, La Transilvanie dans l'antiquité (Bucharest: 1945), pp. 165–87. On the responsibility for the loss, see Eugenio Manni, L'impero di Gallieno, pp. 26–31, where each phase is distinguished.

[40] E. A. Thompson, The Visigoths in the Time of Ulfila (Oxford: Clarendon Press, 1966), pp. 3–6.

[41] Under Constantine, who resumed an aggressive strategy of forward defense, a bridge across the Danube was built in 328 to provide access into the Olt valley. This trans-Danubian bridge head was used, as Dacia as a whole had been used, as a base for lateral attacks. In 332 the Visigoths (then attacking the client Sarmatians in the Banat) were taken in the flank by a Roman force coming from the Olt Valley and suffered a shattering defeat; see Thompson The Visigoths, pp. 10–12; on the strategy, see Stein, Histoire du Bas-Empire, pp. 128–29.

11

CHAPTER

A RECORD OF FAILURE

Zbigniew Brzezinski's *Power and Principle: Memoirs of the National Security Adviser, 1977–1981* is an honest and well-written account which will be valuable to historians and attractive to many readers. Inevitably, it is also a record of failure—not his own personal failure, of course, and not necessarily the failure of the nation's foreign policy either (for it is only in the retrospect of decades that the ultimate results of the doings and undoings of a world power can truly be known) but certainly the political failure of the Carter administration, in whose 1980 defeat at the polls foreign affairs played a most unusually large part.

The National Security Adviser's major role is to protect the President's interest in the conduct of external affairs. What may seem desirable to the State Department, the Arms Control Agency, the Pentagon, or to an "inter-agency" committee of all three may still be damaging to the President, and it is the National Security Adviser who is supposed to protect him in such circumstances; in addition, the National Security Adviser can also attempt to protect the President from himself—as Henry Kissinger apparently did with some frequency especially in the last phases of Richard Nixon's presidency.

Brzezinski as National Security Adviser obviously failed to protect Jimmy Carter. Without manifesting a resentful disloyalty to the man who placed him so high, without perhaps being fully conscious of doing so, Brzezinski explains throughout the book why Carter could not be protected from the departments, notably State, and why above all he could not be protected from himself.

A classic example of a very clever but basically unintelligent man, Carter was incapable of understanding the fundamentals of international affairs even while acquiring much detailed knowledge of their mechanics and surface manifestations; and since he never realized how much he was in need of help, he would not let Brzezinski guide him, either. Nixon, when driven by violent emotions, would sometimes want to do foolish things; but if his orders were simply ignored for a brief interval by Kissinger, no harm would follow because his rational judgment would reassert itself as soon as he calmed down. Carter was much better at controlling his emotions but unwisdom was his permanent condition, revealed in foreign affairs as soon as he chose Cyrus R. Vance as his Secretary of State and finally exposed in full view by the Iranian crisis.

One example will suffice. On November 10, 1979, there was a meeting (without the President) at the National Security Council to discuss the possibility of expelling the Shah from the United States. Vance and Vice President Walter Mondale favored expulsion, while Defense Secretary Harold Brown suggested that the Shah be prevailed upon to announce his intention to leave once he recovered from his illness. Brzezinski opposed this concession to the "students" who had seized the U.S. embassy and its staff in Teheran the week before. He quotes himself at the meeting: "A month ago we backed down to the Soviets and the Cubans after declaring that we found the status quo [the presence of a Soviet brigade in Cuba] unacceptable. Now we shall back down again. What will this mean for our international role as a global power? Who will find us credible hereafter?" When the question was referred to the President, he "flatly" pronounced against expulsion.

In making this decision Carter had apparently showed that he understood the foreign-policy content of the issue—that is to say, the worldwide loss of American authority which an expulsion would entail. But not at all. In a matter of days (on November 14) Carter reversed himself, and decided that Mexico should once more be asked to receive the Shah. The Mexicans, reflecting in their conduct the very loss of American authority which Carter's decision brought about, naturally refused to accept the Shah (who was eventually consigned to the extortionist Omar Torrijos of Panama).

Brzezinski does not report why Carter had earlier "flatly" rejected expulsion. It cannot have been because he truly understood what was at stake, for then he could not possibly have changed his mind so soon (no new relevant facts had intervened). Carter's reasons must have been of a lesser order, perhaps personal pique at being bullied by the Teheran "students" or misplaced optimism concerning the early release of the hostages.

In any event, in a pattern that was repeated incessantly in his administration, Carter made himself an expert on all the details of the hostage question, while failing to grasp the fundamentals, namely, that a world power must always consider the worldwide effects of its action in any particular setting. In the circumstances, this meant that the Teheran anti-Americans had to be confronted, not appeased.

• • •

In one case, to be sure, the peculiar defects of Carter and his foreign-policy team had a most productive outcome: had it not been for the evident intention of the Carter administration in 1977 to reconvene the Geneva conference on the Middle East under joint American and Soviet sponsorship, President Sadat would never have decided to go to Jerusalem. The Egyptian president had risked his neck to get the Soviet Union out of Egypt; he had built his entire policy on a deliberate rejection of the Soviet alliance and on a reassertion of Egypt's national identity (as opposed to Nasser's pan-Arab fantasies). When Sadat discovered that the Americans, of all people, wanted to cast Egypt back into the Arab fold, and under the patronage of the Soviet Union as co-chairman of the Geneva conference, he had the courage and inspiration to break out by creating his own context of negotiation, directly with Israel. The risks of going to Jerusalem were great, but the spectacular unwisdom of American policy entailed even greater dangers: at Geneva, Egypt could only expect to find itself outflanked by the Syrians and blackmailed by the Russians.

Then came the prolonged bilateral and trilateral negotiations which eventually resulted in the peace treaty between Israel and Egypt. Cyrus Vance's contribution to these negotiations, which Brzezinski generously stresses—his treatment of Vance spells out all their differences, but in a most gentlemanly fashion—owed a great deal precisely to the quality that made Vance unfit for his office. The kindly man who in dealings with Iran would not sanction the

use of force to protect American interests, was kind to Egyptians
and Israelis alike, infinitely attentive to all the nuances of their interests. As always he concentrated relentlessly on the single issue
at hand, always searching for every possible avenue of accommodation, treating Egypt and Israel as if they were two well-paying
clients of his law firm, and never as client-states of the United States
of America.

As for Carter, he most certainly deserved a Nobel Prize for at-
tending so assiduously to the negotiations which he had so strongly
promoted. Both the Egyptians and the Israelis were astonished to
discover that Carter was willing, over a very extended period, to
immerse himself in the most minute negotiating details. It would be
churlish to deny Carter's deep-seated commitment to peace, but it
is also plain that his attitude to the negotiations owed much to the
fact that once again he never understood the fundamentals. Carter
saw himself throughout in the role of a mediator. Yet it was not his
diplomatic abilities that the Egyptians and Israelis wanted but rather
his commitment of American prestige and resources—which would
greatly add to each side's "take" from the negotiations. Sadat and
the Israelis could have made peace on their own, but they would
have been foolish to do so: each impasse in the negotiation was resolved as much by American contributions as by reciprocal concessions.

• • •

Brzezinski writes a great deal in this book about the "policy process." Again we are reminded of the extent to which the elaborate
machinery of policy making, which is supposed to coordinate the
large and undisciplined departments of the executive, produces
paralysis or confusion as its most natural result. The Constitution
calls for a separation of powers between the branches of government; it cannot be blamed for the "checks and balances" which
have arisen *within* the Executive as a consequence of luxuriant bureaucratic growth, Brzezinski notes, for example, that the normal
consequence of overruling the State Department was a hostile leak,
a very effective, if certainly improper, "check." Kissinger simply accepted that the "process" did not work, and that it had to be circumvented if serious initiatives were to be launched. Brzezinski could
not or would not emulate his predecessor. Hence his impact on the
making of policy was small.

One instance of confusion is worthy of special mention. In January 1979, with the Shah still in Teheran and the Bakhtiar government about to be formed, General Huyser was to be sent to Iran to

make direct contact with the military chiefs. A meeting was convened on January 3 to decide what instructions Huyser should be given. Vance, Deputy Secretary of State Warren Christopher, and Mondale insisted that the military chiefs should be warned against a coup. Brzezinski agreed but argued that Huyser should also encourage them to stage a coup "in the likely event that Bakhtiar should fail." In practice, therefore, Huyser received directly contradictory instructions. The predictable effect was to paralyze the Iranian military, the one group that might yet have saved the situation.

The next day, Brzezinski met with the President in Guadeloupe, where a four-power summit was being held. The scene was characteristic: Carter in a bathing suit in his cottage, sitting on an icebox, Hamilton Jordan also in a bathing suit, sprawled on a sofa. (Such scenes, which occur frequently in the book, can easily persuade one that formal attire has its uses after all.) Vance was on the phone, in "considerable agitation" because the Iranian military had told U.S. Ambassador William Sullivan that they wanted to keep the Shah in Teheran and suppress the rebellion in full force, with as much bloodshed as it would take. Vance and Mondale wanted permission to tell the military chiefs that the United States would oppose their use of force. Brzezinski joined in the argument, which "lasted a long time." Finally, he records: ". . . much to my satisfaction . . . the President took a very firm line. He told Cy that he did not wish to change General Huyser's instructions."

This "decision," however, merely reaffirmed the earlier contradictory instruction, Huyser's yes/no to a coup. Obviously, the Iranian military chiefs had not approached Sullivan because they were in need of conversation. With mobs on the rampage and the Soviet Union in malevolent proximity, they were seeking a firm and unequivocal U.S. endorsement of a dangerous but potentially decisive act. To add the impact of military choreography to mere words, U.S. aircraft carriers could have been sent into the Gulf, military supplies (needed or not) could have been airlifted. Instead, there came from Washington only conditional statements, full of ifs and buts.

Even in retrospect, Brzezinski does not seem to recognize what had to be done to implement the policy which he so eloquently promoted. For after the Guadeloupe episode he notes, with apparent surprise, "Alas, nothing happened. Vance conveyed the instructions orally to Sullivan, and I have no doubt that he did so faithfully. At the other end, the military . . . simply procrastinated."

• • •

Toward the end of this book, Brzezinski produces a formal list of what he loyally defines as President Carter's accomplishments in the areas of foreign policy and defense. The list encapsulates the entire problem of the administration, and of this book. Naturally, it includes the Camp David peace agreements and the Panama Canal treaty, along with the post-Afghanistan "Carter Doctrine," and so on. But the first item on the list is the Carter human-rights policy, which as it happens left the Soviet Union more repressive than ever while doing in a number of friendly rulers, and the last item is the SALT II agreement, which remained unratified. In many ways, and not only in its honesty, this is an innocent book.

12

C H A P T E R

OF BOMBS AND MEN

The Wizards of Armageddon: Strategists of the Nuclear Age, by Fred Kaplan, an account of the evolution of American strategic thought in the nuclear age, begins in a promising fashion, with the first attempts to understand how the atomic bomb could be used, or rather kept unused, to keep the peace. Among the first to study the matter were the classical economist Jacob Viner, the equally classical political philosopher Arnold Wolfers, and the young Bernard Brodie, already well known as a naval historian. Brodie soon transcended his elders because, unlike them, he was deeply interested in the technical aspect of the new weapons; he understood, for example, that the fission bomb of those days could destroy cities far more easily than armies in the field, especially if they were tank armies.

The quest for new ideas was soon encouraged and supported by the most progressive military figures of the day, the generals of the army air corps and emergent air force, notably Henry Arnold and Curtis LeMay. They were responsible for the creation of Rand, the first of the nonprofit government-funded "think tanks." Rand was launched as an air force project for the explicit purpose of providing a permanent peacetime home for the sort of civilian scientists and "operational analysts" who had been found so useful in the war just ended. To attract talented minds who would not want to remain in the peacetime civil service, Rand was designed to combine the virtues of a non-bureaucratic research institute with the long-term funding and secret information which only the government could provide.

It was in those earliest years of the nuclear age that the ancient idea of deterrence (already explicit and indeed prominent in Roman times) was given its modern role, at the very center of strategy. Here Kaplan has good material in the doings and sayings of interesting and talented men, and he uses it well. Yet there is also a curious omission: Kaplan does not feel it necessary to describe, even in a single phrase, what it was that the American deterrent was to deter, namely Stalin's Soviet Union, which was even then being sealed off from the outside world more fully than ever before, which was subjecting Eastern Europe to novel political brutalities, and which was probing for expansion most energetically from Norway to Iran.

Nor does Kaplan think it interesting to ask why it was that seemingly not a thought was given to the possibility of extracting concessions from the Soviet Union by the threat of using the bomb, then still an American monopoly. As a matter of fact, Kaplan does not record even the modest defensive benefit the bomb did bring merely by its existence: the tacit rules of conduct that allowed the United States to protect key interests in spite of the superior might of the Soviet army, as most notably in the first Berlin crisis. It was only because of the invisible protection of the bomb that the Soviet land blockade could be circumvented by entirely vulnerable American transport aircraft which landed safely in West Berlin right over Soviet anti-aircraft guns.

It is obvious enough why the atomic monopoly served only passively to protect American interests from further aggressions, and not to force Stalin back from Central Europe, as Czar Alexander I had been forced to withdraw after Napoleon's defeat. The reason was that an American society which had so recently refused to fight until forced to do so, would not now even contemplate the deliberate use of the bomb for a diplomacy of coercion. But why did military men, sometimes depicted as downright bloodthirsty, not even try to argue the merits of an American *pax atomica?* Would Stalin have shown similar restraint had the atomic monopoly been his?

This most fundamental difference between the Soviet Union and the United States is the central truth of the strategic contention between the two: the United States is most reluctant to use such power as it has, whereas in the Soviet system there is compulsion, partly ideological and partly bureaucratic, to use power to the very limit. But it is precisely this truth that Kaplan avoids, for, as one soon discovers, what he is trying to do is to show American intellectuals and military men collaborating mostly to promote the "arms race." So too he avoids all reference to the purely defensive benefits which the bomb did bring in the 1945–49 period of U.S. monopoly, because it is now *de rigueur* to insist not merely on the dangers of nuclear weapons, but also on their complete uselessness for the purposes of statecraft.

• • •

But the trouble with Kaplan's book does not become fully apparent until one reaches page 74 and the chapter on the role of the Rand men in the decision to develop the thermonuclear "super-bomb." There was of course a fierce controversy, supposedly scientific but actually political: in a malpractice that was to become habitual, scientists who actually opposed the weapon for political reasons usurped their scientific authority to argue that such a bomb was not technically feasible (the current rendition of this practice is aimed at President Reagan's new strategic-defense initiatives). Kaplan makes much of Edward Teller's personality in explaining why it was that the H-bomb was developed at all. Teller, he writes, was "an almost fanatical anti-Communist with a particular loathing for the Soviet Union." In contrast to a wise and almost saintly J. Robert Oppenheimer, who did not want to build the H-bomb, Teller is described as "furious, driven," and obsessive.

Kaplan, judging by his citations, went to great lengths to uncover obscure unpublished sources and to extract documents from the Pentagon by using the Freedom of Information Act. All this activity must have interfered with the plain reading of widely available printed books. Had he consulted Dean Acheson's *Present at the Creation,* he would have discovered that the H-bomb decision was not the product of Teller's individual character and supposed political beliefs but rather followed from lawyerly deliberations on two key questions: could it be built? and could the Soviet Union build one soon? Acheson and his aides (chiefly Paul Nitze) examined the evidence and decided that the answer to both questions was yes. That made the decision to build the weapon inevitable.

Kaplan ends the H-bomb chapter with a little anecdote calculated to depict Teller as a unfeeling monster. When the H-bomb device, code-named "Mike," duly exploded in the first test, Teller "in a fit of joy" sent a telegram to the director of the Los Alamos laboratory: "It's a boy." It is only some thirty pages later, and then by tangential reference in a chapter devoted to Albert Wohlstetter and his pervasively influential basing study (which inaugurated the centrality of force vulnerability in American strategic-nuclear thought), that Kaplan casually mentions the fact that the Soviet H-bomb was detonated in August 1953, a mere eleven months after the American test. And it is still some pages after that, in discussing Rand's role in instigating the development of the ICBM, that Kaplan refers, again tangentially, to the fact that the Soviet H-bomb employed lithium. This was no small matter: it meant that the Soviet H-bomb was in fact a *bomb*, a practical weapon, deliverable by an aircraft or even a missile. "Mike," by contrast, had only been an experimental device made huge and nondeliverable by a refrigeration apparatus. Now Rand's influence and Teller's supposed obsessions seem not so important after all. Seriously delayed by Oppenheimer's opposition, the American decision to build the H-bomb had come just in time.

Obviously, the Soviet H-bomb could not have been the product of the "action-reaction" phenomenon that supposedly drives the arms race. The Soviet Union's test of a bomb in August 1953 suggests a decision made by 1948 or even earlier, certainly long before Dean Acheson arbitrated between the contending scientists. Kaplan is writing about Americans, and the evolution of American thinking about the strategic questions of the nuclear age, but given his depiction of Teller, and his description of the Rand crowd as "collaborators" in the awful deed of building the H-bomb, we should ask ourselves how it was that the Soviet Union, quite Randless, started to build the H-bomb even earlier. Who was the Soviet Teller? Was he perhaps Hungarian too? Did he also have bushy eyebrows, and was he "an almost fanatical anti-capitalist with a particular loathing for the United States"?

Nor does Kaplan pause to consider the profound and sinister implications of the fact that the Soviet H-bomb decision was made so early. For the circumstances of the Soviet Union would easily have justified a long delay in acquiring the weapon. A wealthy United States, far more advanced scientifically but very weak in military power of the conventional sort (in 1950 American forces could scarcely cope with the North Koreans), could easily obtain the bomb and also had a great need of it, then as now to contain the far superior armies of the Soviet Union. For the latter, by contrast, the H-bomb was a far greater sacrifice of far smaller utility. Nevertheless, in a Soviet Union where the war's destruction had compounded colossal mismanagement to bring back a harsh poverty of miserable overcrowding, ragged clothes, and sheer hunger, the decision to build the H-bomb was made even earlier than in the United States.

That uncovers the second central truth of the strategic contention between the two sides so misleadingly equated in the very term "superpowers," and it too is a truth ignored by Kaplan. It is that there is no symmetry of effort between Americans who so reluctantly use a small fraction of their vast wealth to acquire military power and a Soviet regime which imposes enormous sacrifices on its own people and colonizes others in order to increase its military power.

• • •

With the entire strategic reality of the Soviet Union thus excluded from the picture, Kaplan is off and running. In writing of Paul Nitze and his role in NSC-68 (the plan for conventional rearmament prompted by the Soviet A-bomb in 1949 but implemented only in part, and then only after the North Korean invasion); in describing the Gaither committee and the ballistic-missile decisions it advocated (in the wake of the Sputnik shock); and in discussing the Rand thinkers, Kaplan combines a lucid exposition of ideas and procedures with the insistent suggestion that Nitze and the rest were afflicted by almost hysterical fears or, worse, that they consciously manipulated the evidence to arouse groundless fears.

With not a word about the Gulag, Budapest 1956, or Khrushchev's threats of nuclear bombardment against Paris and London in that same year (on the occasion of the Suez invasion), and above all with nothing whatever said about the Soviet army, we are invited to contemplate arrogant and yet weak American minds relentlessly threatening the Soviet Union with unnecessary arms.

In the same vein, when Kaplan writes of the Strategic Air Command, Curtis LeMay, and the persistence of a rigid, all-out bombing plan (which anticipated and outlasted the policy of "massive retaliation"), the text is again well informed and informative about all the detailed aspects and yet simultaneously tendentious in the extreme. Now Kaplan offers us the spectacle of men cold-bloodedly planning the destruction of Soviet cities but he gives no serious consideration to the strategic predicament which was the source of it all: to protect Western Europe from intimidation if not attack, the

United States had acquired all the attributes of a European Great Power except the most important, a great army.

The thinking and operational studies of Bernard Brodie, Herbert Goldhammer, Herman Kahn, William Kaufmann, Nathan Leites, Andrew Marshall, Henry Rowen, Albert Wohlstetter, and other Rand strategists; the planning and building of the military establishment and notably the Strategic Air Command; and the policy advocacy of Paul Nitze, Robert Sprague (the true author of the influential report named for Rowan H. Gaither), and a good many others since, including the Committee on the Present Danger, have all been prompted and shaped by the great asymmetry between the Soviet Union's powerful ground forces and their changing but always inadequate Western counterparts. To keep a tolerable overall military balance that would protect its more exposed allies even in conditions of non-nuclear inferiority, thus allowing them to resist Soviet intimidation—and also to dissuade the proliferation of national nuclear forces—the United States has had to extend the scope of its nuclear deterrence to cover its allies as well. If it were not for that, if the only requirement were the deterrence of a nuclear attack upon the United States itself, then indeed all the labors of Rand, all the advocacy of additional strategic-nuclear strength, and a great part of the nuclear weapons themselves would always have been unnecessary.

By leaving the Soviet army out of the picture, and by constantly pretending that American nuclear weapons serve only to deter a most improbable Soviet nuclear attack upon the United States, it is easy enough to make the thinking of the nuclear strategists seem nothing more than self-serving, even mercenary over-elaboration. By leaving out the Soviet army and its armored divisions equipped, trained, and deployed to threaten invasion, one can ridicule any and every measure of nuclear force-building as useless and dangerous "overkill," a word which suggests an absurd excess measured by matching the many American nuclear warheads with the small number of Soviet cities—as if American nuclear warheads were in fact targeted upon Soviet cities to any important extent, and as if the United States could plausibly deter attacks upon other countries, and attacks not necessarily nuclear, by the desperate and unbelievable threat of destroying the cities of the Soviet Union. By leaving out the Soviet army, one can depict SAC and the rest of the military as mad bombers, forever wanting to burden the planet with more and more nuclear weapons, for no better reason than bureaucratic self-interest, or even for the profit of the contractors. Kaplan avoids

such explicitly crude characterizations, and yet he implies them by
his omission of any sustained and serious discussion of the non-
nuclear imbalance of forces.

• • •

In reality, all the significant thinking of the Rand men and their
many emulators, and almost all the building of new nuclear weapons, have been motivated by the very opposite of a quest for "overkill." Far from seeking to obtain more destructive power against the
peoples of the Soviet Union, the aim rather has been to uncover
ways and means of making retaliatory threats more selective, more
flexible, and much less destructive—threats which could in turn
plausibly deter Soviet threats themselves less catastrophic than the
all-out nuclear attack upon America which is indeed most easily
dissuaded by a very small nuclear force. As soon as it becomes
necessary to do more, everything becomes far more difficult, and
many more weapons far more accurate and resilient are needed.

Thus, for example, if the Minuteman missiles served only to deter
a nuclear attack upon our own cities, then we should not be concerned by their vulnerability to attack. Even if the Soviet Union
could destroy 90 percent of them with its own larger missile force,
the remaining 10 percent would still be ample to destroy every Soviet city worth destroying—thereby still inhibiting any Soviet attack
upon our cities.

But that is not the exclusive or even predominant purpose of the
Minuteman force. It serves rather to add an element of deterrence
to inadequate non-nuclear defenses. These land-based missiles, the
most controllable of all long-range nuclear weapons, can best extend deterrence because they can be used selectively, perhaps in
twos or threes, to threaten not Moscow or Kiev but military facilities relevant to the invasion to be deterred, facilities perhaps remote
from any large civilian population.

Now the vulnerability of the Minuteman force does reduce its
deterrent value. For how can the threat of using a *few* of the missiles be plausible when the Soviet Union can threaten just as plausibly to destroy all of them if any are used? Thus, ironically, to
threaten less one needs more.

Those who flatly assert that the Soviet Union would promptly
launch an all-out assault if it ever became the target of any nuclear
attack at all, even one provoked by a massive invasion of Europe,
are merely echoing a transparent Soviet attempt to inhibit the extension of deterrence. Of them we should ask whether the Soviet
Union, having unleashed an invasion, would add the cataclysm too

if, say, a single airfield were destroyed by a single warhead. And if not, what of two warheads and two airfields? And so on, in a reversal of "salami tactics."

Those, by contrast, who merely note that nuclear weapons are so destructive that any "selectivity" is dubious, and therefore exceedingly dangerous, have a far simpler and more impressive argument. But so long as they offer no better defense against the Soviet army than loose talk of new anti-tank weapons (the Syrians had thousands in the Bekaa against Israel last year), and still looser talk about the drunkenness of Soviet officers (drunk they fought, and drunk they won, in 1945 as in 1812), the only alternatives to the decline of Western security will continue to be nuclear forces resilient enough and powerful enough to extend deterrence, or else the enormous increases in defense spending that a truly adequate conventional deterrent would require.

• • •

When Kaplan reaches the "missile-gap" episode at the end of the Eisenhower era (yes, we meet yet again an avuncular Eisenhower, firm or almost so in resisting military demands), he becomes even more tendentious. We now encounter air force Intelligence enlivened by General George Keegan—the same Keegan who many years later introduced the entire rubric of beam weapons into our public debate, only to be branded as a fantasist by the Carter administration, which was soon enough to fund those very weapons to the tune of hundreds of millions of dollars.

Kaplan recounts the fierce paper battles of the air force with the CIA experts who began to doubt, and later flatly denied, that there was any missile gap at all. Kaplan has a good time in contrasting the frightening air force estimates of a hundred Soviet ICBMs by 1960 (and five hundred soon thereafter) with the tens forecast by CIA, and the *four* actually known to have been deployed. But consider the circumstances: first, there was in 1957 the shock of the Soviet launch of Sputnik, the first manmade space vehicle; second, there was the plain fact that the booster which had launched Sputnik into orbit could more easily launch a nuclear warhead at the United States, thereby functioning as an ICBM—at a time when the United States had no such weapon; third, there was the carefully orchestrated Soviet propaganda campaign designed precisely to persuade the world that the Soviet Union was in fact producing ICBMs in quantity; fourth, there was the absence of reliable and comprehensive intelligence from inside the Soviet Union until the first satellite photography became available in 1960 (the earlier U-2 photography had been unable to bring back pictures from some of the most likely missile locations).

And then there was one more fact, the most significant of all, which Kaplan as it happens does mention, but only in passing and in another context, long after he has had his fun with Keegan and the air force. Although there was a controversy over the number of Soviet missiles of intercontinental range, there was *no* controversy about the medium-range ballistic missiles of which the Soviet Union had hundreds at the time. Thus the reader is invited on page 167 to ridicule Keegan's early estimate of hundreds of Soviet ICBMs, only to be casually informed on page 301 that the Soviet Union did indeed have hundreds of ballistic missiles, though not of intercontinental range.

To be sure, there was an absolute difference between the two classes of weapons so far as the vulnerability of American-based nuclear forces was concerned. But the ability to build medium-range missiles certainly suggested a parallel ability to build equivalent weapons of intercontinental range, and the air force was thus being only prudent in estimating that what could be built would be built.

Moreover, in the broader context of strategy, the difference between Soviet medium-range missiles aimed at Europe and ICBMs aimed at the United States was not all that great, given the fact that the purpose of American nuclear forces was (and is) primarily to protect Europe by deterrence. Obviously Soviet medium-range missiles that could destroy any European city diminished the assurance that American protection could confer.

• • •

The missile gap was indeed a myth, if only because the Soviet Union was overambitious and tried to deploy too quickly a huge and most impractical first ICBM. But a myth has also been created about the myth—that the missile-gap overestimate was the result of unreasoned, groundless hysteria or even deliberate fabrication. In fact, it was induced by elementary prudence, for once misapplied. And there is worse, much worse: the missile-gap myth lasted only for three years, but the myth about the myth endures still. As do its evil consequences.

One such consequence is simply the inclination to disbelieve even the strongest evidence of increases in Soviet military power in any form. Another was confined to the inner world of the intelligence men themselves, but its effects were broad indeed, effects with

OF BOMBS AND MEN

which we must now live, at great cost and some added risk: the systematic *underestimation* of the Soviet ICBM force from the mid-1960s onward. The same group of CIA analysts who exposed the overestimate of the 1957–60 period, and who thereby gained authority over the combined (or "national") estimates, systematically proceeded to underestimate the quality of new Soviet ICBMs and their rate of deployment, continuing to make the same gross error year after year until the mid-1970s. It is odd that Kaplan does not feel it necessary to censure error in the direction of imprudent optimism, though this was an error that persisted for many more years than the missile-gap error did, and which was altogether less excusable given the availability of satellite photography throughout the period.

It was on the basis of such profoundly misleading but ardently welcome estimates that Secretary of Defense Robert McNamara—traumatized by the Cuban missile crisis—cut off any major innovation in the American nuclear arsenal after 1963. Kaplan follows the fashion by celebrating the post-1963 McNamara as the man who stood up to a voracious military and especially the air force (which wanted to build not only a new bomber but also the WS-120—just the sort of large ICBM that the Soviet Union now has in its SS-18). Kaplan's account eventually extends to the McNamara of delicate personal agonies about Vietnam who was to expiate his sins by serving as the unlikely preacher for the poor at the World Bank. But there is one aspect of McNamara's doings that Kaplan does not choose to discuss, namely, that his openly declared policy of one-sided restraint was based on a gross miscalculation of the Soviet response—an error of epic proportions, unambiguously documented in the successive Annual Defense Reports for Fiscal Year 1964, 1965, 1966, and 1967.

In fact, the systematic underestimation of Soviet armaments went far beyond the ICBMs alone and lasted long beyond McNamara's tenure at the Pentagon, serving as the foundation for policies of arms control and non-deployment which might have worked well if only our antagonist were Great Britain or perhaps Sweden. It was those policies which engendered the predicament of today, in which a weapon as unsatisfactory as the MX is nevertheless a greatly belated necessity, and in which nuclear weapons must awkwardly be deployed in the crowded setting of Europe to serve as costly, inadequate, but essential substitutes for the intercontinental nuclear advantage that was so frivolously surrendered.

• • •

Kaplan concludes his book by proclaiming that "the bomb" remains "a device of sheer mayhem, a weapon of cataclysmic powers no one really had the faintest idea how to control. The nuclear strategists had come to impose order—but in the end, chaos still prevailed." If this were said in order to call for more thought and better planning, for further refinements of engineering and for new and better policies, then the matter might be debated on its merits. But that is not at all the case. Kaplan relishes the chaos he has placed in prospect, and insists on the futility of any remedy.

And yet it is a fact most easily documented—without recourse to the Freedom of Information Act—that today's nuclear weapons are far less destructive and far more reliably controlled than those of twenty years ago; and it is a fact that needs no documentation at all that we have lived since 1945 without another world war precisely because rational minds did not surrender to unreason but rather devised the plans and procedures, the deployment modes and the policies that extracted a durable peace from the very terror of nuclear weapons.

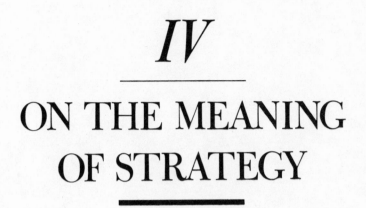

IV

ON THE MEANING
OF STRATEGY

13

ON THE MEANING OF STRATEGY... FOR THE UNITED STATES IN THE 1980s

As a nation, Americans are pragmatic problem-solvers rather than systematic or long-range thinkers. Our whole experience tells us that it is best to narrow down complicated matters to isolate the practical problem at hand, and then to get on with finding a solution. Strategy by contrast is the one practical pursuit that requires a contrary method: to connect the diverse issues into a systematic pattern of things; then to craft plans—often long range—for dealing with the whole. In the life of this nation it has not been strategy but rather pragmatic problem-solving that has created a society wealthier than most—and now also more just than virtually all others—and it has not been long-range planning but rather the impatient dynamism of a hard-working people that has allowed so many to pursue happiness as well.

That is why it is now so very difficult for Americans to accept the ineluctable fact that to achieve even moderate success the nation's external policy must be guided by the alien rules of strategy.

BASES OF PAST U.S. POLICY

It was not always so. Until the beginning of this century, the United States enjoyed the classic prerogatives of the great sea powers of history: it could take as much or as little of the world's affairs as it wanted. Neither a powerful navy nor broad oceanic borders assured this fortunate state. Rather was it the power of Great Britain, a nation then itself exquisitely strategical, that secured for the Americans all they really needed of the outside world. Even in intermittent discord there was shared interest in all the fundamentals. To keep others busy with large land armies and thus themselves supreme at sea, the British used both diplomacy and force to maintain the warlike equilibrium called the "Balance of Power"; hence the Americans had the Great Powers balanced for them and kept from their door.

The British kept trade open for all in order to keep trade open for their own industry. The Americans thus had their trade as free as they desired and still as protected as they chose. Above all, to maintain their own moral economy the British pursued idealism too; hence the suppression of slavery, the punishments of the czars for their pogroms, and the pervasive teaching of decent practices in international life, sometimes by Mr. Gladstone's sermons and sometimes by Lord Palmerston's cannonades. Thus the Americans could look out on a world steadily advancing in the manners of civilization and in the legalities of international transactions.

Since the British made their greater decisions in the privacy of country houses and London clubs and since they were in the habit of using pragmatic and reticent language, the fact that their affairs of state were guided by a coherent strategy relentlessly pursued was not at all evident. The discretion is understandable. Maintenance of the Balance of Power was a harsh business not at all confined to the beating down of bullies; it required also favoring the Turk against Christian powers—and a Greece that Byron chose to die for—and it meant opposing the unification of Europe, no matter how progressive the union might have been. Until 1945 the Americans were merely called to war, and that briefly. It was the British who set the strategy and who chose our enemies for us.

Even after 1945 the Americans needed no strategy merely to keep on an even keel. There was an economy so powerful that others could scarcely keep their own, resources so abundant that the world's oil price was set by "Gulf plus freight"—that being the Texan shore and not the Persian. Then there were war industries so amply productive that any enemy would ignore the dissolution of the armies after the victory over Japan, seeing in prospect those thousands and thousands of aircraft and tanks ready to pour from the production lines. On top of all, there was the nuclear weapon—first the fission bomb and then the thermonuclear—that others could perhaps emulate in sample numbers but which only the United States could really use on a large scale, and scale still counted in the days when the total number of weapons was still small.

And so it was that the simplest of strategies, "containment," could be triumphantly successful. Europe, Japan, and their appendages duly recovered from the ravages of war safe behind the shield of American power. The task was made easier—and perhaps even made possible—by the great weakness of the Soviet Union. Behind Stalin's 6 million men in arms there was a desert of war destruction in all the Russias west of Moscow, with cities in ruins and agriculture beaten down to a level medieval; even east of Moscow, in the lands that had remained beyond the reach of the Germans, the population was exhausted and greatly lacking in men. Stalin and then his first heirs desperately tried to keep the only true secret of those most secretive times: that behind those 6 million men in arms there was not the capacity to sustain their fighting. And they were successful. By any calculus of power that cold-blooded men might have made, Stalin did not have the strength to keep the large part of Europe that Russian arms had won. After all, the czar had danced in Paris after Waterloo, yet the British had their Russians driven back all the way to eastern Poland very soon after the music stopped.

With "containment" the Americans pursued what the British had once pursued for them—until Vietnam. Then it was not only the wisdom of policy that broke down in the enervation of an elite; it was not only the competent pursuit of war that collapsed under the weight of a luxuriant military bureaucracy indifferent to the earnest study of the true phenomena of warfare. It was the very notion of strategy that waned, even that largely passive strategy of containment which required merely that we react.

But still, even after the final defeat—which brought with it not merely a totalitarian rule but also one far bloodier than even war at its worst, even after we had consigned millions who had pledged trust with us to Hanoi's brutalities and Pol Pot's autogenocide—even after that defeat, Americans could nevertheless think that the discipline of strategy remained unnecessary. There was still a slim margin in our favor in the "strategic-nuclear" balance (the very term a reminder of the degraded meaning of "strategic" in our discourse), and even if all who desired could very easily project the advent of unambiguous inferiority in the 1980s, most could still imagine that all was well, since few desired to project. And by then we had the Strategic Arms Limitation Talks (SALT) whereby, as we are even now reminded, the great strength accumulated by the steady effort of the Russians would be negated, at low cost and at no risk, through the drafting of legal documents. In that atmosphere it was an easy matter for the instrument—arms control—to displace the purpose, for only a national strategy could define the purpose and we had no national strategy. Hence the pursuit of SALT as an end in itself, the only real test of each proposal being its negotiability and the only test of that being the Russians' acceptance.

SALT, NATO, AND THE MILITARY

Aside from SALT, most of our defense policy was defined by the North Atlantic Treaty Organization's (NATO's) real or fancied needs. That was not at all a strategic choice, but rather a political compromise. Those who had wanted America "to come home" and those who were still residually internationalist could find a compromise in an all-for-NATO defense policy. Thus two acronyms substituted between them for the difficult business of constructing a national strategy responsive to our needs at home and cognizant of the dangers abroad—SALT and NATO, NATO and SALT. Too bad that a defense policy that made NATO its only real focus under the slogan "No more Vietnams" would mean that we would be enhancing stability only in the one segment of the perimeter of our interests that was already rather stable; too bad that we would be adding strength only where our weakness is least—these being procedures that no self-respecting junior officer would use in defending a company perimeter. But NATO and SALT, SALT and NATO had to do duty for the thought, the plan, the consensual strategy that was absent.

It was perhaps inevitable that sooner or later some ineffable figure innocent of strategy but taught in the arts of public relations should think of mating the acronyms; and so we had the experience, in its own way memorable, of being told insistently that NATO would not survive without SALT. The moment in which Cyrus Vance, secretary of state, chose to hesitate theatrically in open hearings before saying "I don't know" to a senatorial query on whether NATO could withstand a rejection of SALT II shall undoubtedly be recorded as the nadir of America's unstrategical decade. Such a gross defection from the duties of statecraft demonstrated how far policy could stray without the anchor of strategical priorities. To Mr. Vance, the SALT II accords were merely his brief; the hearing, his court; and the White House, his client. Our allies had much reason to be shocked. It is not that SALT is incompatible with strategy. It could and indeed should be: in the context of a coherent strategy, SALT could be a most powerful instrument of policy. But the good ingredient unbalanced makes bad medicine—in this case, of the narcotic variety.

In the absence of strategy, it is substrategical impulses that govern what we do. Thus the weapons we design, develop, and eventually build reflect the technical ambitions of the engineers as well as the ideal forms of our bureaucrats in uniform. Only tactical logic is absent from the process. The army, having failed for two decades to obtain a new battle tank, insists nevertheless on having its new XM-1 tank propelled by a gas turbine—at high cost and greater risk of failure. Such propulsion adds nothing whatever of combat value to the XM-1 but it satisfies the technological urge, and there is no tactical logic to satisfy anyway. After all, tactics must be derived from the operational method of warfare—be it *Blitzkrieg* or defense-in-depth, the hold-and-counterpunch or the agile defense. There can be no operational method of warfare unless it is derived from *theater strategy*, and that in turn cannot be framed except within a national strategy. No wonder that an unguided technical ambition dominates the scene. Nor is it surprising that in the War Colleges our officers study much about management but not at all about the Art of War. Far better to muster those techniques so useful in civilian life than to study war—a painful process since the "data base" is merely the library of military history and some books are even in languages other than English.

What the army has done in trying to develop armored fighting vehicles is a subject already notorious: the ten-year program that failed to yield an infantry combat carrier (a thing already achieved even by the Yugoslavs), the billion-dollar program that could not produce a scout car (as even the Brazilians have). The story is always the same. Without the discipline of strategy and of its tactical needs, luxuriant technicity yielded machines of legendary technical attainments and of unattainable cost. And so also it has been, though perhaps in less bloated form, with the other armed services. Technicity is a wonderful servant and a disastrous master.

In the absence of strategy, it is substrategical choices that govern the form of the armed forces we deploy. In war, two great phenomena contend: maneuver, made of circumventing action, to bypass the barrier, to outflank the thrust, and to evade the main strength of the enemy in all things from weapon design to grand strategy. Such maneuver is the product of surprise, deception, and above all agility in thought, planning, and action. And then there is the other great phenomenon: firepower, assayed by volume, by accuracy, by lethality, and made of industrial strength, transportation, and efficient logistic distribution. Throughout the history of war, blends of maneuver and firepower have contended in a thousand forms. Maneuver has generally been less costly in blood and treasure, but firepower was always the safer course and demanded merely an outright superiority in means. But even in the face of superior firepower and superior resources, maneuver in all its forms—tactical, operational, theater-strategic, and developmental, as well as the higher maneuver of grand strategy—has always held its own and often has elegantly prevailed.

THE IMPACT OF TECHNOLOGY

But that was before maneuver finally met its match in the figure of the American "systems' analyst." When this new apparition came to take its place alongside the Great Captains of history, the long line of men from Mauricius the Emperor to Manstein of the Donetz, from Marius of the legions to the colonel who planned the Entebbe raid, then and only then was maneuver finally undone. Its fatal defect was that no numerical index can be attached to surprise, deception, or the outmaneuvering action. Thus no criterion of effectiveness stated in numbers can be defined for the purposes of systems' analytical computation. Firepower, by contrast, is very easily measurable, volume being tonnage, accuracy being hit probability, and lethality being a known factor. In countless mathematical models the "combat value" of forces is thus measured exclusively by their firepower. The "simulations" now widely used to define what weapon characteristics are needed, what type and size of forces are to be deployed, and even to assess what passes by the name of tactics, are all in fact firepower-exchange computations.

All this may seem excessively recondite. But it is of the essence. For many years now, the weapons we build and the forces we deploy have been heavily influenced by mathematical criteria of choice that do not capture a most important dimension of warfare. That is one reason why our army, half as large in numbers as the Soviets', has only 16 divisions to their 168—ours being heavy in logistics to sustain firepower, producing it by methods of industrial style. That is a main reason why our aircraft must be so large and costly, since there is apparent efficiency in the economies-to-scale of the large vehicle. One pilot produces more firepower with the larger aircraft—and never mind that numbers give flexibility for action, and never mind also that the large fighter is seen by the smaller one before the smaller one is seen by the larger one. And that is why our navy is shaped by the logic of bigness on one side—as if ballistic-missile submarines were firepower factories—and by prejudice against "offensive" warships on the other, as if the nation that has no effective navy is thereby made moral by the impotence that results.

Yet the logic of strategy in such things begins precisely with the rejection of the logic of civil efficiency. The large thing is often more efficient in producing the unit of firepower. But in war the very objective must be to mingle in the fight, and then the large thing is often almost as vulnerable as the small thing of which more can be had. In civil life one builds the bridge over the river using trusted formulae to construct the safely engineered solution; but in strategy there is perpetual contention and the fixed solution is merely out-maneuvered. No natural river will deliberately set out to evade the span that would bridge its banks, but that is quite the normal thing in the realm of strategy.

There is thus a fundamental opposition between (civil) efficiency and (military) effectiveness, almost entirely ignored because instead of strategists we have only bookkeepers of cost and effectiveness. And where are our generals and admirals who will rise to protest such methods, who will expose their falsehoods, and, if needs be, resign? They are busy supervising their own "systems' analysts" who make their own suitably rigged calculations with the same misleading criteria of choice. Already themselves far too removed from the true study of war to uphold its endless unquantifiable complexities, these are not the men who will remind us that the force with the greater firepower has lost more often than not in the record of war. They are not the ones who will insist that maneuver as well as civil efficiency be the criteria of choice. It is so much easier to bend to the fashion of the day and to fill endless rolls of computer printout with "simulations" that will serve to advocate what their bureaucracies want. Thus a nation which spends much too little for its armed strength anyway receives even less than it pays for.

THE CURRENT SITUATION

In the absence of strategy, it is substrategical perspectives that govern our understanding of what confronts us. Over a period of several months in the years 1978–79 Americans debated, first, the meaning of the supply of Russian submarines to Cuba; then the meaning of the arrival of new high-performance MiG–23s with Russian pilots; then the discovery in Cuba of modern air-defense weapons for battlefield use; and finally the revelation that a Soviet armored brigade was stationed on the island. Each episode was separated from the next by a few weeks or months, and that interval proved long enough to ensure that each episode would be viewed in isolation.

Of the submarines, it could be said—by those eager for inaction—that they were non-nuclear and thus harmless. Of the MiG–23s, the question was merely asked if they were fitted with provisions for nuclear bombs. Of the air-defense weapons, nothing was said at all, the questions of why and where being too recondite to answer. Cubans in Africa had no need for such weapons; Cubans to be sent to Arabia might well need them, but Arabia is far from Cuba and to connect the two distant places would require a strategic mind. Of the brigade, it was asked only—and foolishly enough—whether it might invade the United States of America. The president eventually proclaimed, as the Russians had claimed all along, that the brigade was in Cuba only to train and not to fight. With that revelation the matter was then simply dropped, and the question of why the Cubans needed armored-warfare training—useless in Black Africa but essential in Arabia—was not asked at all. Since it is only within the framework of strategical understanding that diverse things may be connected to form a view of the whole, the genuine profile of the danger—that is to say, not the submarines as such, not the MiG–23s on their own, not just the air defense, not merely the brigade but rather the entire transformation of Cuba into a first-class military power—never emerged at all. That indeed was the one issue not debated, even while hawks and doves spoke and wrote millions of words on each fragment of the whole that was never even recognized as such.

Until the later years of the 1970s there were still residues of power, or at least residual delusions that the United States could prosper even in weakness. Only now, as of this writing, is the long holiday finally over—at long last and so late, so very late. The agencies of our education were several: the relentless exposure of the most intricate details of our "strategic-nuclear" weakness engendered by the Senate hearings on the SALT II accords, the growing realization that a NATO-only defense policy meant a fatal passivity in the face of a Soviet strategy that creates bases of power between us and some of our most vital interests, and then finally—at the hands of the mobs of Iran—a belated education in the all-too-concrete value of the intangibles of prestige and authority. Of course, deep emotional resistance is not so easily overcome. As of this writing at the end of the year 1979, the United States was still refusing to behave as a Great Power must in its dealings with Iran. But at least the mood of the people has changed, and profoundly, and the need to enhance the nation's armed strength has been very widely accepted.

The time has finally come when the acknowledgment of weakness and the understanding of its unacceptable price has educated us all in the need for strength and for a national strategy that can use it wisely. Its shape must be dictated in many lesser decisions made over time by executive and legislature, but the broad rules are the same for all nations, and we too must frame our desires within them:

• Never deal with the single crisis, or the single matter of any kind, in isolation. When, for example, Soviet power intervenes to decide the outcome of war in Ethiopia, do not look at Ethiopia alone but rather at the consequences of action or inaction for the whole of East Africa, for the Middle East, for the world.

• Do not seek partial solutions without considering their effect on the general equilibrium of power. If SALT offers a "parity" of strategic-nuclear weapons, ask if there is also "parity" in theater-nuclear weapons, in non-nuclear weapons and forces, and in other means too—clandestine-military and covert-political action, and then also in the constructive instruments of aid and trade, in that order. Otherwise a guaranteed parity in one class of weapons alone may seal inferiority overall. The partial solution may still be desirable, and practical solutions will almost always be partial solutions but they cannot be framed in a partial view. If there is a national strategy, there may well be need of SALT negotiating tactics also, but let not those tactics usurp the place of strategy.

• Do not confront strength but maneuver around it; do not allow the enemy to exploit every area of weakness without acting to do likewise, for otherwise there is no hope of success. If it is the Soviet policy to separate the alliance, active measures of alliance solidarity are essential, but they must be complemented by a relentless campaign to embarrass the Soviet Union in Eastern Europe: it is neither useful nor moral to incite Hungarian children to confront Russian tanks, but it is merely appeasement to have our officials speak of "socialist" countries when we should speak only of Russia and of captive nations. More substantially, if it is the Soviet policy to conspire against us in Iran, let us reciprocate in Afghanistan where, as of this writing, Russian armed helicopters are decimating—for want of a few portable anti-aircraft missiles—the warriors ranged against them.

• Do not confuse ethics and aesthetics. Ethics must reflect the moral calculus of least human suffering. Aesthetics merely reflect the superficial appearance of things. If the Organization of Petroleum Exporting Countries uses the market strength of a cartel to inflict inconvenience upon us, poverty increases in such countries as Turkey and Brazil. When the marginal countries suffer impoverishment, Asian peasants actually starve for want of crops—that is to say, for want of water for their crops; that is to say, for want of diesel oil for their tube wells. And so let armed power be brought in to balance market power, for our own good and for that of many others.

• Do not make of others what they refuse to be. The Soviet Union is the vehicle for the aggrandizement of the Russians, the one truly imperial nation left on this earth. The Russians have a strategy, and it is an imperial strategy of classic form: to protect Muscovy, the Ukraine and Byelorussia must be held; to protect the latter, a further cordon of non-Russian lands from Estonia to Moldavia must be annexed to the Soviet Union; to protect the latter, the states of Eastern Europe too must come under Russian power lest their freedom inspire revolt in the non-Russian fringe. But Eastern Europe will remain restless so long as the countries of Western Europe parade their liberties and prosperity before its peoples—thus Western Europe must be tamed if Eastern Europe is to become permanently obedient so that the non-Russian fringe lands will be obedient also, so that the cordon will be safe, so that Moscow will remain powerful over all.

But Western Europe will never be tamed as long as American protection intervenes to allow its elected leaders to defy Moscow's demands for obedience. And so the Soviet Union's imperial strategy relentlessly pursues the struggle to diminish American power and to separate Europeans and Americans. Now the new prospect of achieving both great objectives by acting against a third, the Persian Gulf, has opened vast new possibilities for Moscow. Let us defend the perimeters directly under threat, but that cannot possibly suffice. Hence the need to maneuver and articulate power where opportunity offers scope and in East Asia in particular. The best defense for Europe is most probably located somewhere between Outer Mongolia and the banks of the Ussuri. Thus the folly of a "Eurocentric" strategy, precisely because Europe is justifiably held to be most important for us.

• And then finally, and above all, we need tenacity. That is not a quality as easily admirable as creativity or compassion. But it is the one quality that strategy unalterably requires. That is not quite the same thing as calling for more virtue or preaching "motherhood," as the saying goes. No doubt we shall find that many of our elite institutions will have to be rebuilt with new people who do not share the paralyzing enervation that nowadays passes for sober restraint, who do not fundamentally believe that the United States should be weak, for if strong it must be recklessly destructive or at least the upholder of an unjust order of things. After all, just as strength without strategy yields very little, strategy and strength combined will not avail if both are in the hands of an elite that prefers retreat over the advancement of power and which, in its worst moments, has a positive longing for the humiliations of defeat, believing that . . .

Οἱ ανθρωποι αντοι ησαν μιὰ κάποια λνσις.

("... the Barbarians, after all, were some sort of solution.")

14

CHAPTER

AFTER AFGHANISTAN, WHAT?

*T*hose of us who have been warning for some years that the military balance was shifting in favor of the Soviet Union, and that the consequences would unfailingly become manifest in harsh reality, have been sufficiently vindicated by events to resist the temptation of celebrating successful prediction—especially since we failed to prevail over the counsels of passivity soon enough to avert our present, sinister, predicament.

It is worth recalling the stages of the debate. In the years of paralysis and confusion of the early 1970s two arguments were advanced by the respectable to oppose the upkeep of American military strength and the restoration of a foreign policy that would actively resist Soviet power. The first, especially popular in academic circles, was that military power as such had become ineffectual for both the Soviet Union and the United States: the two could not fight each other without suicidal results, and neither could they usefully employ force against others in a world of aroused nationalisms. Armed conflict, then, was simply passé in a world characterized by "interdependence." When presented in the full-dress jargon of contemporary American political science, such contentions acquired much academic authority, and indeed they still remain lodged in the textbooks that are employed in many of our universities.

The policy prescription derived from this line of argument was simple: since the Soviet Union was merely trying to establish a symbolic parity in arms, the United States need not compete with it. And if nevertheless the Russians foolishly persisted in adding to their armed power beyond that point, the United States would lose nothing thereby, since the Soviet Union would merely ascend to a more costly plateau of impotence.

The second argument was heard from a whole variety of voices, ranging from the eminent retired diplomat George F. Kennan to plainly self-seeking businessmen. On the authority of their personal acquaintance with the country and its leaders, such men declared that the Soviet Union had at long last become a status-quo power, satisfied with what it had, and that the Kremlin leaders were "moderate" men, essentially peaceful. By the suggestion that Soviet intentions were not in any case aggressive, the argument that the growth in Soviet capabilities would be harmless was much reinforced. (In Kennan's view, this meant that only American military power would be harmful, to the national economy and to the conduct of our foreign policy—which a powerful defense establishment would seek to "militarize.") Here also the policy prescription was self-evident, and devastatingly influential if only because of the eager deference with which such views were publicized in the quality press.

Once the Soviet Union began in 1975 to act in warlike fashion, relying on its new strategic-nuclear strength to provide cover for the whole array of naval forces, long-range air transport, and weapons shipments that sustained the direct combat of Cubans and Vietnamese, both arguments were undone at once. Plainly, the leaders in the Kremlin had not lost the ambition to reshape the world by military force as opportunity allowed. At the same time, their evident ability to use force successfully to decide the outcome of the conflicts in Angola, Ethiopia, and Indochina swiftly demolished the academic theory that held military force to be useless in our time.

By the later 1970s it had become obvious that behind the two arguments with all their claims and elaborations there was nothing more substantial than one crude generalization, and one inexcusable delusion. In the former, the American defeat in Vietnam was misunderstood to mean that all would fail everywhere, including the

Soviet Union in the Third World. In the latter, men claiming great expertise in Soviet affairs had somehow come to believe that the processes of ruthless power accumulation through which party men gained promotion step by step would produce leaders at the top who would be uninterested in power and its increase.

• • •

Sustained by their resilient authority in the media and the institutions of learning—an authority which owed much to their legitimization of the easy course of abdication and retreat—the advocates of passivity overcame the complete collapse of their arguments with remarkable ease. Leaving the conclusions unchanged, they merely put forward new arguments. Instead of offering us theories of supposedly universal validity, and propositions about the fundamental nature of the Soviet Union, they now admonished us to avoid the superpower provincialism that would relate everything to the East-West conflict: it was *local* circumstances and *local* forces that were shaping the contentions of the day. Soviet military power, we were told, was at bottom irrelevant to what happened in Angola, Ethiopia, or Indochina; only the superficial would allow their attention to be detained by the Soviet airlifts and the inflow of Soviet weapons that accompanied such episodes. Actually it was the locals who were truly in control of the action, and the Russians were merely providing the instruments. And we were even invited to speculate on the possibility that Cuban expeditionary forces were actually fighting for the cause of Castro's revolutionary idealism rather than serving as tools of Soviet policy; the Russians were merely arming, training, and delivering Castro's men, but for Castro's purposes and not their own.

Once the argument was thus translated from a strategic into a purely local perspective, the rest was easy. Why should the United States object to what was happening in Angola, etc., when the outcome of each conflict was so positively desirable from our own point of view? In Angola itself, a regime approved by both the Congressional Black Caucus and the Gulf Oil Company had prevailed over rivals tainted by their association with a corrupt Mobutu and, worse, the South Africans. In Ethiopia, the multinational force commanded by Colonel-General Petrov had merely restored the universally recognized boundaries of that country, violated by the Somali invasion and regionalist uprisings. Even in Indochina, where a country's sovereignty was terminated, the Pol Pot regime thereby displaced was of such outright murderousness that no protest was admissible. Since in each case the effect of the Soviet action was actually constructive from our own point of view, it was foolish vanity to oppose the outcome merely because the issue was decided in Moscow rather than Washington. So we were told.

All this was very persuasive, except that it was a little too obvious that equally persuasive explanations would have attended any other outcome brought about by Soviet power. In Angola, any faction supported by the Soviet Union would *ipso facto* have become "progressive" and would therefore have gained the support of the Congressional Black Caucus, just as it would have received the endorsement of the Gulf Oil Company because it would have won. With the United States paralyzed, that outcome was inevitable, as was the fact that only the South Africans would remain to support the other side—further proof that the Soviet-backed faction was "progressive." In the case of Ethiopia, had the Russians chosen to arm and reinforce the Somalis, we would have been told that the "Wilsonian" principle of national self-determination should prevail over the suspect legality of colonial boundaries. The same voices that deplored our refusal to celebrate the restoration of Ethiopian sovereignty over the Ogaden achieved by Soviet power, would have reminded us that the region is inhabited by ethnic Somalis, and they would have asked in rhetorical style why the United States was so obdurate as to stand in the way of nationalism, the strongest (most "progressive"?) force in today's world. In the case of Indochina, if the Chinese had obtained Hanoi as their own client, the Russians would have emerged as the protectors of Cambodia and Laos, and those who in the event found themselves applauding the downfall of Pol Pot would then have invited us to give due credit to Moscow's support of the independence of small nations.

Those who for one reason or another refuse to resist power unfailingly find some convenient principle whereby virtue may be seen in the result. Indeed, one consequence of adverse changes in the balance of power is precisely to reshape men's conceptions of what is tolerable, acceptable, and even desirable. It is precisely by such mental conditioning that military power can earn its keep even without war.

• • •

Thus in the later 1970s an old story was repeated. Why object if Hitler reoccupies the Rhineland, an integral part of Germany, universally recognized as such? By what right can outsiders object if Austro-Germans and German-Germans are at last reunited in a national state? Why should men in the enlightened 1930s be bound by the vengeful restrictions fossilized in the Versailles Treaty? Why should a war be fought to suppress the national aspirations of the Germans of the Sudetenland?

In the 1930s neither great stupidity nor malevolence was needed to embrace the principles that would comfortably justify inaction in the face of power manifest and growing: it sufficed that there be no consistent, that is ideological, objection to totalitarian government. Once the ideological aspect was ignored, perhaps because of a lack of faith in the democratic alternative, it was easy enough to see merit in the results brought about by the growth of German power.

In our own times, the antagonist is very different from Hitler's Germany, and the conditioning process—the insidious influence of the balance of power on our minds—much more pervasively effective. For one thing, the Soviet Union is much more powerful than Hitler's Germany, both relatively and absolutely: relatively because there is now no quiescent continental power behind the United States ready to restore a shattered balance, as the United States itself once stood behind an England and a France directly challenged by Hitler; absolutely, because Hitler's Germany lacked the self-sufficiency of materials and the world-destroying weapons that characterize Soviet power today. And then also, the Soviet Union does not actively dissuade defeatist propensities as much as Hitler did by selective persecutions and flagrant gangsterism. The Russians, even now, are still bound by certain hypocrisies of conduct and by the dim residues of a humanitarian conception which remains lodged in the official ideology. Thus both the greater power and also the less obvious bestiality of the Soviet Union conspire to dull our perceptions.

What on the other hand does recall the 1930s is that once again it has become distinctly unfashionable to insist that totalitarianism itself must be resisted, and not merely such of its episodic manifestations as are brought to our attention in the travails of famous dissidents. Even many of those who are entirely unsympathetic to the Soviet Union nevertheless much prefer to stress practical motives and tangible interests in arguing the need to resist its expansion—and then of course China becomes part of the solution, instead of being recognized as a variant of the very same problem. Moreover, we have some in this country—a group varied enough to include both Andrew Young and Senator Edward Kennedy—who honestly seem to find it very difficult to concentrate their minds on the permanent evil of totalitarianism, even while being enthusiastic in their condemnation of pro-American but authoritarian states whose very substantial residual liberties they take for granted even when it is those very liberties that allow us to hear the opposition voices which (quite properly) complain of political repression. In any case, to ignore the ideological dimension of the East-West struggle in the attempt to contend directly with the "reality of power" condemns us to a misperception of that very reality. Far from being an impediment to our understanding of the practical strategic problems that confront us, a constant attention to the ideological struggle is indispensable if we are to assay correctly the balance of military power, and the predicament that the present imbalance has created.

• • •

All this by way of warning. The time allowed us to hesitate before launching broad action to restore our strength has fully expired, and yet even now, in the aftermath of the Soviet invasion of Afghanistan, newly minted arguments have emerged which minimize the scope of what has happened—arguments which by implication deny the need to restore our military strength and reactivate a foreign policy of broad resistance to the Soviet Union.

The most important of the post-invasion arguments offered by the advocates of passivity is that the Soviet Union acted only in self-protection. Faced with the risk that a fanatically Islamic regime would come to power in Kabul, fearful that such a regime would inspire widespread dissidence among the Muslim populations of Soviet Central Asia, the Kremlin was forced to send its own troops to suppress an "Islamic rebellion" which the Afghan forces loyal to the Soviet-controlled regime could not do themselves. And because the Afghan President actually in power was unwilling to cooperate with an outright occupation (even though he himself was a Soviet client), or perhaps simply because he was judged ineffectual by the Kremlin's experts, the Afghans had also to be provided with a new President, who was duly delivered in the baggage of the invading Soviet army.

What this theory suggests, of course, is that the Soviet invasion of Afghanistan is not evidence of a shift in the balance of power but rather merely a symptom of Soviet insecurity. It is thus implied that no further acts of aggression need be feared: the Soviet move, an "essentially defensive reaction," is inherently limited in scope.

Superficially plausible in its conjunction of the undoubted fact that Soviet Central Asia is full of Muslims with the recent and spectacular outbreaks of Muslim fanaticism in Iran and elsewhere, this theory nevertheless rests on a whole chain of increasingly demanding assumptions: that the Kremlin is afraid of Muslim dissidence in

Central Asia (very likely indeed); that the Muslim populations of the USSR could be seriously influenced by events in Afghanistan even though they regard themselves as culturally much superior (doubtful: Portuguese may imitate the revolutions of the French, but not vice versa); that the prospective Muslim regime in Kabul would be perceptibly more militant and inflammatory than the Muslim regime already established in Teheran (very hard to believe); and finally that the Kremlin would consider that the best way of insulating Soviet Muslims from Afghan Muslims was to send tens of thousands of the former to invade the country of the latter, with all the official and unofficial contacts that this must entail (a thing almost impossible to believe).

Add two further facts and what is left of the plausibility of the theory entirely dissolves. First, until now no Islamic government has made any significant effort to arouse the religious sentiments of the Muslims of Central Asia; now, however, several may do so, and the Kremlin must have anticipated the possibility. Second, we have no evidence at all that there is any significant Muslim dissidence in Soviet Central Asia. Nor should that be surprising, since Central Asia is the only portion of the whole empire that actually obtains material benefit from the Soviet system. While the vast majority of the other non-Russian populations of the Soviet Union see that fellow ethnics and kindred folk lucky enough to be outside the U.S.S.R. enjoy a higher standard of living than themselves, the Muslims of Central Asia are materially far better off than the Muslims of Afghanistan, Iran, and Turkey, not to speak of the Muslims of Chinese Turkestan (Sinkiang).

Yet even if one accepts the theory that the Soviet Union invaded Afghanistan for defensive reasons, it should give no comfort to any not wholly deluded. As the power of empires increases, new layers of insecurity that must be remedied by further expansion are invariably found. Thus Rome conquered the Latium to shield the city itself, Italy to shield Latium, Gaul by stages to shield first Italy and then prior layers of conquest in Gaul, and finally Britain because Western Gaul could not be secured if Gaulish Druids and other dissidents could find ready shelter among their fellows across the channel. In other words, the "defensive" characterization of the Soviet invasion offers no certain security for any country less remote than New Zealand (and considering potential rivalry over the Antarctic, even that is not a safe presumption). Once we dismiss such last-ditch attempts to minimize the import of what has happened, we can begin to confront the crucial question before us: why did the

Soviet Union employ its growing power to invade Afghanistan? Obviously, if we knew the strategic purpose of the move, we could usefully anticipate any further moves that might now follow.

• • •

By reason of geographic proximity the Afghanistan-Persian Gulf nexus has an immediate plausibility. In purely military terms, the occupation of Afghanistan has the effect of bringing the Gulf of Oman, which forms the entrance to the Persian Gulf, within the *tactical* reach of Soviet military power. Operating from bases in southern Afghanistan, Soviet fighter-bombers could now interdict at will the vital traffic of oil tankers entering and leaving the Gulf; they could attack warships too, of course; and, more importantly, Soviet land-based aircraft could now neutralize the air-power superiority that the United States would otherwise enjoy in the immediate area by virtue of its naval aviation on board the great aircraft carriers. Since the navy air wings on board the carriers represent our one last major military advantage in the whole spectrum of non-nuclear forces, any reduction in their freedom of action amounts to a very serious loss in American strength overall.

Still in a purely military context, a Soviet overland drive to the sea could much more easily be accomplished by setting out from bases in southern Afghanistan to cross the deserts of Baluchistan (on the Iranian or Pakistani side, or both) than by way of the 1000-kilometer route that separates the Soviet border in the Caucasus from the nearest shore of the Persian Gulf. The very great advantage of the Baluchistan route is that the area in question is almost devoid of population, while by contrast the Caucasus route cuts across lands inhabited by 50 million Turks, Kurds, Persians, and Arabs. In both cases, poor roads in difficult terrain greatly restrict transit capacity, but against the feeble opposition that would meet them, Soviet forces could afford to travel light, using the roads for troop convoys to create the *fait accompli* of an occupation of the shore rather than for the heavy loads of ammunition that would be needed for serious warfare.

Along with the direct military advantages, the Soviet Union obtains a diplomatic advantage fully manifest even in the absence of conflict: its ability to intimidate the countries of the area has greatly increased now that the threat of direct Soviet military attack has become so vivid. Certainly it is not by accident, as *Pravda* would put it, that all the Soviet embassies in the region stand intact. It seems that one is not dealing with blind fanaticism after all: the mob is inclined to attack those who advertise their refusal to defend themselves or to punish such violations—and this is an inclination shared by the local governments which have the choice of controlling the mob or else letting it work its will. While hatred of the Soviet Union has no doubt increased, so has fear, and great military empires do not ordinarily seek love but rather the anxious respect that fear can best inspire.

These, then, would be the incentives of the invasion if its purpose were further to enhance the Soviet Union's military and diplomatic power over the Persian Gulf. Given the all too obvious importance of the region's oil resources, the prospect of gaining bases in Afghanistan—either to start war operations of its own, or to oppose an American intervention, or merely to strengthen the hand of its own diplomacy—was certainly a sufficient incentive for the Soviet invasion.

But before we accept this explanation and leave it at that, some objections should be seriously considered. First, how valuable in fact are the Afghan air bases in the light of the already great pre-invasion potential of Soviet air power? To be sure, it is useful for the Russians to have fighter aircraft positioned so close to the shores of the Gulf of Oman. But we must also remember that both the tanker traffic and warship movements in and out of the Persian Gulf could be interdicted even before the invasion, by Soviet medium bombers operating from bases inside the USSR. American aircraft carriers too were vulnerable to the large fleet of Soviet medium bombers and indeed any attacks upon the carriers would most likely rely on anti-shipping missiles, weapons too large to be launched from fighter-class aircraft but standard equipment on the Soviet navy's 300-odd medium bombers.

Secondly, what is the net value of the overland route to the sea that the invasion of Afghanistan has virtually opened to the Soviet Union? Certainly, it is better than the direct Caucasus-Gulf route and offers a choice of violations between Persian and Pakistani Baluchistan. But it also has the great defect of leading not to, but away from, the major oil fields, which are clustered around the head of the Gulf a long way from the Baluchi coast, and moreover on the opposite shore. And why employ overland routes anyway? Against the very weak forces of the Saudis and the Sheikdoms, Soviet air-delivered infantry with a few light-armor vehicles (mainly for show) should do very nicely; and even against an American expeditionary force, Soviet airborne divisions would suffice for the position-taking exercise that a Soviet-American confrontation would mainly entail, neither side being at all likely to open fire upon the other.

Thus while the expansion of the Soviet empire into Afghanistan does enhance its power over the Persian Gulf and the whole region around it, these objections are sufficiently weighty to justify a search for alternative explanations of the Soviet move.

To do this our field of view must first be widened, and very considerably: it is the entire strategic picture that we have to consider and not merely the regional circumstances to Afghanistan and the surrounding areas.

• • •

For some time now, there has been talk of a Soviet "window of opportunity"—a period of several years in which the Soviet Union could count on a net advantage over the United States in strategic-nuclear forces. American obstinacy in pursuing arms control by unilateral restraint in the deployment of strategic-nuclear weapons, along with the energetic Soviet production of those weapons, has now brought this unhappy circumstance upon us.

Certainly the United States can no longer rely on a strategic-nuclear advantage to offset weakness in theater forces, and that, among other things, opens vast doubts about the security of the NATO alliance, whose very foundation is the American nuclear guarantee. It is, however, quite wrong to view the U.S.–Soviet strategic-nuclear balance in isolation. In fact, the Soviet armed forces have achieved or are about to achieve superiority not only in strategic-nuclear weapons, and not only over those of the United States, but rather in military capabilities overall, nuclear and not, and against the forces of Western Europe *and* China as well as those of the United States.

By perverse coincidence, the period 1968–75, in which the United States failed to build up its military forces (first because of vast expenditures in Vietnam and then because of budget cuts), was also a time in which Western Europe reduced defense *investment* for growth (partly because manpower costs greatly increased). Moreover, this was also, more or less, the period of the "Cultural Revolution" (1966–77) in China, when the ascendancy of the anti-bureaucratic faction (the "Gang of Four") greatly restricted the flow of new equipment for the Chinese armed forces.

During those same years the Soviet Union continued to invest steadily in the growth and qualitative improvement of its forces, adding each year to its expenditure at a rate usually stated as 4 percent (real growth). This undramatic but constant increase, kept up year after year, has had its cumulative effects: in detail, the result is manifest in the mass deployment of new aircraft, armored vehicles, warships, strategic weapons, and in the whole connective tissue of supporting and ancillary forces, and also infrastructures; *in toto* the result is manifest in the fact that the Soviet Union could greatly increase its relative strength as compared to the West even *after* building a whole new panoply of forces and infrastructures to achieve a net superiority over a China transformed from ally to antagonist.

By any standards, the Soviet achievement has been a very great one, even if much facilitated by the sheer bad luck that made our own misconduct of the Vietnam War (and more foolish anti-war reaction) concurrent with the outbreak of adolescent fury that turned Mao's disenchantment with the Communist party of China into a force strong enough to disrupt the lives of 900 million people. That NATO–Europe then failed to assay the adverse trend, that it failed to recognize the task left to its own statecraft, that it failed to offset American weakness by applying some fraction of its growing wealth to military investment—all this was not of course bad luck, except insofar as the willful descent of entire national elites into self-satisfied provincialism may be so described. In any case, our own military decline was not offset by the growth in the strength of others also ranged against the Soviet Union.

The perverse circumstances that allowed the Russians to gain military superiority over a collection of countries much richer and more populous than themselves now shapes the worldwide military balance. Because of the delay of several years that intervenes between military expenditures and the actual deployment of armed forces, the fruits of the uncontested Soviet effort did not fully emerge until quite recently, and the Soviet advantage will continue to increase for some years almost regardless of what we, Western Europe, and the Chinese might all now set out to do.

Had the United States, Western Europe, and China simply continued to underinvest through the later 1970s and beyond, the 1980s would have been characterized by a growing and *open-ended* Soviet military advantage. Had things turned out that way, the pressure of Soviet intimidation on Western Europeans and Chinese would of course have steadily increased. But on the other hand, we could all have been assured of a time of tranquility, albeit dismal and doomed, since then the Soviet Union could have looked forward with confidence to a period of wholly decisive and uncontested military advantage during the later 1980s and beyond. Peace would thus have been assured today and over the next few years at the cost of an assured Soviet domination thereafter.

• • •

However, this is not to be. Again by coincidence, the gradual recovery of American realism about the outside world after 1975, the death of Mao and the fall of the Gang of Four in 1976, and the first stirrings of belated alarm in Western Europe have all created circumstances in which the decline in the military effort of each side has been reversed, so that a modest but accelerating recovery is now under way. Even at a net annual growth that is in reality well short of the much-publicized 3 percent U.S.–NATO budget target, the trend has now become adverse for the Soviet Union. With a combined economic capacity so much larger than that of the Soviet Union, even a sacrifice so slight does produce results for Americans and Europeans; with armed forces so backward, and arsenals so obsolete as those of the Chinese, even a modest flow of new equipment has an amplified impact on real capabilities.

Thus, instead of being free to expect an open-ended period of growing military advantage, the Soviet Union is now confronted with a *transitory* period of superiority that will end—on present trends—in the later 1980s, when the efforts of today and of the next few years will mature in the reality of American and other military forces armed, trained, deployed, and ready.

The lineaments of great danger are easily recognizable in this situation: if an edge in military power can normally be expected to encourage activism (but also make it less necessary since others will pay power its due in their diplomatic concessions), a transitory advantage is apt to make action positively urgent. Since the elements of military power are mostly rather perishable, equipment becoming obsolete and training dulled in a matter of years, the Soviet Union needs a great effort merely to maintain the high quality of its present forces, which have been made much more ambitious in quality as well as somewhat larger in size over the last fifteen years or so. To do more than maintain the relative advantage of today would require a greater effort still, and with roughly one-eighth of the Soviet national product already given over for defense, the Soviet leaders cannot easily offset the reawakening of their competitors by simply imposing a greater sacrifice on their population—whose existence is already a shoddy one, by standards of comparison which they themselves recognize.

Still, even so, one could not go beyond the assessment that there is a danger of war to predict its virtual certainty, if it were not for yet another perverse coincidence that now intervenes: the time period in which the "window" of Soviet military advantage is projected to close happens to coincide with the advent in full force of a restriction on the Soviet economy whose first signs are already with us. It is well known that the Soviet economy is not growing as fast as it used to do,[1] and the unfavorable estimate is that its growth will decline to very little or cease altogether by the mid-1980s, so that Soviet military growth can continue only if its share of the total product is increased pro rata.

One may cheerfully disregard the prognostications of economists, but this one actually reflects the prediction of demographers, and as such it is an altogether more serious matter. Apparently, the European population of the Soviet Union is not growing and is therefore aging; thus a rising proportion of those who enter the labor force are Central Asians and Transcaucasians, mostly Muslim and backward;[2] with this, worker productivity will decline, and much new investment will be needed just to maintain production levels rather than to increase them.

For the first time ever—if these projections turn out to be as accurate as they are persuasive—the leaders of the Soviet Union will not be able to look forward to the future with optimism as far as the productive capacity of the Soviet economy is concerned. And given the demographic cause of their economic problem, the Kremlin leaders must also be pessimistic about the socio-political future of the Soviet Union, that too being an unprecedented state of affairs. Russian nationalism made a neat replacement for a Communist ideology of waning appeal during World War II and even more so during its victorious aftermath. But it is scarcely a solid foundation for a Soviet regime whose subjects will increasingly be non-Russian, and indeed peoples that were conquered by Russians, often recently enough for the humiliation and sufferings to live on vividly in ethnic memory.

There is, moreover, the primary effect of ideological decline: el-

[1] CIA "synthetic growth index" (total industry): 1961–65: 6.6; 1966–70: 6.3; 1971–75: 5.9; 1976–78: 3.8 (average annual growth percentages) in F. Douglas Whitehouse and Ray Converse, Soviet Economy in a Time of Change, Vol. I, Joint Economic Committee, U.S. Congress, October 10, 1979, p. 406.

[2] In 1970–79, out of 23.8 million net entrants to the work force, 10.5 million originated in the Russian Republic (RSFSR) and 8.6 million in backward areas. In 1980–89, out of 6.3 million projected net entrants, all but 0.4 million will be from backward areas, with the RSFSR work force actually declining by 1.2 million. Ibid., p. 417.

derly leaders, still living with a close recollection of the triumph of Bolshevism, nowadays find their own grandchildren thinking more of Gucci and Pucci than of Marx or Engels. That too cannot inspire much optimism about the future of the Soviet regime, even if it were true that the highest leaders are unaware of the cycle of nepotism, cynicism, and pervasive corruption that is now characteristic of Soviet life by all creditable accounts.

• • •

Once these factors are admitted into the overall picture, the danger of conflict is greatly heightened. If military advantage prompts activism, in the search for ways of exploiting power otherwise perishable, and if a transitory advantage adds the urgency of a time limit to that intent, the combination of a short-lived military optimism with a long-term regime pessimism is a most powerful impulse to war—in the attempt to change an unfavorable future by forceful action.

Thus if, by war, the Soviet Union could achieve a permanent enhancement of its position in some decisive map-changing way, all would become easier in the future, even the possibility of reduced military expenditures being imaginable. Alternatively, successful warfare might seize valuable resources for the Soviet state, and then the advantage of such resources might serve to modify the future that now looms so unfavorable.

Either way, it is obvious enough that there is no more certain driving force to deliberate war than the conjunction of short-term military optimism and long-term national (or regime) pessimism. That indeed was the classic mechanism that brought war in 1914, when the Hapsburg army and court elites could see in war the only salvation against ethnic separatism; in war, they believed, all the plain folk would rally around emperor and army—the only multi-ethnic institutions of the empire—abandoning the journalists, teachers, and publicists who were preaching the cause of the Southern Slavs, of Czechs and Slovaks, of united Italy, and of all-Germany. And in 1941, that same conjunction persuaded the rulers of imperial Japan to act, men who obviously had great confidence in their navy but very little in Japan's ability to hold its empire against a resurgent America that had just begun to build warships and aircraft on an American scale.

Even so, the impulse to go to war might be resisted if the leaders of the Soviet Union lacked *operational confidence* in their armed forces. Such confidence is not at all the same thing as a generic sense of military superiority. In a pattern of expectations greatly reinforced by the experiences of World War II but in fact very much older, the rulers of Russia could retain faith in their country's ability to win wars even without having any great operational confidence in their armed forces. The enemy would attack and invade; Russian generals would then be revealed as incompetent, Russian plans irrelevant; ambitious new weapons would not work, and whole Russian armies would be lost. But by its own victorious advance the enemy would then be stretched out across the vast Russian lands, and rains and snow and ice would come to paralyze him; and then through rivers of blood, war-created Russian armies, newly formed, commanded by new battle-educated leaders, using methods newly learned from the enemy, would drive out the invader—and then advance the borders beyond the initial starting line. By such means has Russia expanded in its recent history.

This particular conception of its military strength, which closely paralleled a certain cultural self-image of the Russian as less accomplished but stronger in spirit than the West European, was not one that would incline Russian political leaders to use their military forces in a deliberate search for advantage. (All this indeed applies mainly to war in the West. In the East, against Central Asians and Chinese if not the Japanese, the Russian experience and Russian expectations have been quite different.)

Very different was the German conception of 1914, or the Japanese in 1941. The political leaders of the two countries plainly regarded their armed forces as sharp instruments of precision, which could be trusted to execute military operations just as they were planned, to achieve results set in advance to gain some great, war-winning advantage. It was not on a generic superiority of military resources that the Germans counted in 1914—indeed they saw themselves as inferior in resources overall—but rather on the ability of their forces to encircle and destroy the French armies in one great swift turning move that would require action entirely precise, regulated by marching plans exceedingly intricate. And the Japanese, with far greater eventual success, also trusted their naval aviators to execute an attack of very great difficulty, in extremely demanding conditions. In both cases, the necessary condition of the acceptance of war was, precisely, the operational confidence of leaders in their armed forces, trusting them to deliver what was promised—which was a great deal.

• • •

Until quite recently, such confidence and trust could not be for Russians: *their* kind of military power, even if massive, had a blundering and uncontrollable quality that would disqualify it as a useful instrument of aggression, deliberate, precise, and purposeful. It was this military fact rather than any innate moderation that endowed Soviet conduct with a degree of prudence—a prudence much exaggerated and altogether misinterpreted by the Kennans of this world who saw as a chosen restraint of ends what was only an imposed restraint of means. It is most unfortunate that this powerful, peace-preserving inhibition upon Soviet conduct has now been removed.

The first clear sign of this undoubtedly momentous but largely overlooked change was manifest in 1977, when the Soviet Union stepped in to decide the outcome of the Ethiopian war. Colonel-General Petrov, *de facto* commander in chief of the defense of Ethiopia, embodied in his own person the advent of Soviet operational confidence as he elegantly orchestrated the whole array of local Amhari militias, Cuban armored units, East European technicians, the Soviet airlift, and Soviet arms to achieve the winning combination in that war.

To be sure, Soviet troops were not then directly involved, but Soviet prestige undoubtedly was, and in a most important way. For the Kremlin leaders were obviously out to prove that they, unlike the Americans, would effectively defend those to whom their protection was granted. Admittedly, too, the Somali invasion forces, the regional rebels, and the Eritrean secessionists facing Petrov were not quite up to the standards of the *Waffen SS Panzer Korps* in its best days. But it must be remembered that when the Russians staked their reputation on the outcome, they were going in to defend a shrinking enclave on the high Ethiopian plateau, whose only land link to the outside world was a single rail line to the sea interrupted by Eritrean sabotage twice a day. One has the uncomfortable feeling that if our own Joint Chiefs had been directed to help the Ethiopians, they would have demanded large forces and prolonged preparations to mount a slow-moving reconquest, to secure first the coast, then the land link, and finally the enclave for a major buildup of forces and logistic stocks prior to any counteroffensive. Petrov, by contrast, was flown in with a small staff to command an improvised multinational force, without having any possibility whatever to redeem failure in the manner traditional to the Russians, by throwing masses of divisions into the fray.

• • •

In Ethiopia we caught only a glimpse, but in Afghanistan the picture was fully revealed. The surprise airborne descent on Kabul, the special operations (including the use of deception and sabotage to paralyze the Afghan forces that might have been hostile), the willingness to rely on the swift follow-up of mechanized forces through narrow roads with many vulnerable tunnels and bridges—all present a familiar aspect, but one not at all Russian in style. It is rather the style of the German conquest of Oslo by a handful of men, of the seizure of the great Belgian fort of Eben Emael by glider troops landed directly on its roof, of the airborne conquest of Crete, of Rommel in Cyrenaica—it is quintessentially the style of the self-confident who mean to prevail over victim forces (perhaps much larger) by swift, bold action and a simulated omnipresence that paralyzes the will to resist.

The Kremlin leaders who sent such forces into action to use such high-risk methods very obviously had acquired an operational confidence in them and their leaders that they had lacked as recently as 1968, when unresisting Czechoslovakia was flooded with invasion forces in numbers so large that the Soviet logistic system broke down at many points. Such an over-allocation went beyond all the normal bounds of prudence, and was a clear sign of a lack of confidence.

Of course the Afghans were thoroughly penetrated before the invasion by Soviet operatives, to the extent that the whole Afghan air force was seemingly in the Soviet service. Of course the Soviet Union had the capital advantage of territorial contiguity with its latest victim-land. But to assay the significance of the new phenomenon before us—of Soviet military forces not only self-confident but fully trusted to deliver by their political masters—it suffices to note one single tactical fact: it is reliably reported that an Afghan tank division was actually garrisoned in the environs of Kabul quite near the airport where the Soviet airborne troops were to land. A divisional force of full-weight battle tanks, even if very poorly handled, can wreck an airborne descent very easily, merely by driving onto the airfield and shooting at anything that moves. The Russians apparently relied on surprise, deception, and special-purpose covert action to immobilize the Afghan armor—they could certainly not count on being able to defeat it with the small number of light fighting vehicles that were flown in with the troops. To rely on such high-risk means to defeat a threat so inherently formidable to an operation so inherently fragile, denotes self-confidence of a high order, obviously matched by trust equally broad on the part of the leaders who sent in the troops.

If any would scoff at this, let them compare what happened in

Kabul to the doings of the British at Suez in 1956, when the whole venture was crippled by the slow and visible preparation of a cumbersome full-scale expeditionary force, and this because of the insistence that all due precautions be taken to protect the British troops dropped by parachute against Egyptian armored forces—and this was armor much more remote from the landing zones than in the Afghan case, available in far smaller numbers, and mostly so newly delivered that Egyptian crews had hardly begun to train with the new Soviet equipment.

And if the British of 1956 are not accepted as a fair test, then let our own military men be interrogated: would they be willing to fly in an airborne division—of necessity lightly armed—in the immediate presence of a potentially hostile armored division? The answer would be a categorical negative, no matter how poorly one could rate the skill, motivation, and readiness of that armored force; it is simply the case that fifty-ton battle tanks can overrun foot infantry and their light air-delivered vehicles almost effortlessly if they catch them in the open spaces of an airfield as they are disembarking. And let our political leaders be interrogated: would they sanction the risk?

• • •

Thus we are now facing a Soviet Union that has changed in a way most ominous. The Soviet Union of ceaseless opportunism that would fill any local vacuum as a sneak thief in a hotel tries every door, but which would *not* deliberately go to war for fear that its forces would make a mess of things, has now evolved into a different kind of enemy, one that is plainly willing to add direct warfare to its abundant array of expansionist instruments: proxy forces, not only Cuban; arms supplies meant to upset regional balances rather than preserve them; political warfare by all possible means, from forgery to assassination, as well as propaganda, black, gray, and white; and of course a tireless diplomacy of threats and blandishments of punishment and reward—a diplomacy much more coherent than our own in recent years. Even before the new instrument of direct war was added we could scarcely cope with the sheer tenacity of the Soviet policy. Now we face the prospect of war as well.

It might seem, nevertheless, that the great sanction of nuclear destruction would still intervene to avert war. After all, even if the economic and political future, which Soviet leaders must now foresee is bleak—and one should not underestimate the system's ability to retain control even in very unfavorable circumstances—the consequences of nuclear war must be rated as infinitely more catastrophic.

ON THE MEANING OF VICTORY

To be sure, the Soviet Union's military superiority is sufficiently pronounced in the nuclear categories, from the "strategic" (intercontinental) to the tactical, to ensure that others cannot rely on nuclear means to offset non-nuclear defeat, but its superiority is still not absolute. It does not ensure immunity from nuclear retaliation. In technical terms, the Soviet Union does not now have, and cannot soon acquire, a *disarming* counterforce capability. This being so, one may straightaway rule out a deliberate Soviet war upon the United States directly, and also against NATO in Europe. There is no doubt that the American nuclear guarantee is no longer the reliable protector it used to be, as Henry Kissinger for one has noted. But in the NATO lands there are still many thousands of nuclear weapons large and small, and they are usefully scattered about in different countries: the very fragility of NATO's non-nuclear defenses makes it more believable that they would be used in the chaos and disaster of a losing war.

Unfortunately, there are several other theaters of action where the Soviet Union could achieve the conversion of its transitory military advantage into a long-term enhancement of its position by resorting to deliberate, purposeful, and safely non-nuclear war. One possibility would be to launch swift invasion columns to cut off the vast territories of Chinese Central Asia from the rest of that country. In the arid, open terrain of the region, the tactical advantage of mechanized Soviet forces over Chinese infantry would be greatest, and the combat value of Soviet air superiority would be maximized. At the same time, the very small population and its heavily non-Chinese composition would render a guerrilla resistance insignificant, while the Russians could count on their vast nuclear superiority to inhibit any suicidal Chinese intent to resort to nuclear weapons. (And against China, the Soviet Union must have a fully disarming counterforce capability.)

The assured strategic benefit would be to shift China eastward by 1,000 kilometers, and a concurrent campaign of non-nuclear bombardment against Chinese industry could retard that country's development very seriously. One possible benefit might be to precipitate the latent regional separatisms throughout China by exposing Peking's inability to defend the national territory, thus undermining its chief claim to authority. And since the Soviet Union would under no circumstances annex the area but rather turn it into a "Turkestan People's Republic," a nominally independent client-state such as Outer Mongolia already is, the Soviet ethnic problem would not be aggravated, and might instead be alleviated, perhaps in a major way, if immigration were to develop into the new state—an outcome that large-scale Soviet investments and ethnic preference[3] might well bring about. For the same reason, the diplomatic repercussions of the venture could be much reduced: the Russians would no doubt claim credit as liberators for engendering the national self-determination of the Turkic peoples till then under Chinese domination.

• • •

Other map-changing opportunities present themselves in Korea, where a Soviet-sponsored unification would greatly facilitate the long-standing Soviet attempt to pressure Japan out of the American alliance and into a weak neutralism. This would be most useful to the Soviet Union even if Japan is too large in population and too recondite in culture to be Finlandized. At the very least, a weak, neutral Japan could be induced to invest heavily in Siberian development, while avoiding investment in China.

As for Pakistan, map-changing could take the easier form of playing anvil to India's hammer to destroy that country's independence. As an alternative to the Turkestan scheme—and the two would be incompatible—a unified India would *ipso facto* be greatly advantageous to the Soviet Union, since then it would be an effective strategic counterweight to China.

And then of course there are the various possibilities in and around the Persian Gulf, from the seizure of Iran's northern provinces to something on a wider scale; or else, starting from the Soviet base in Yemen, south-to-north political-military action, to change political structures in Arabia, if not the map.

• • •

To predict which course of action will have the most appeal for the leaders of the Soviet Union is not the object here. What we for our part must now recognize once and for all is that such possibilities have now become actual Soviet options. That, finally, is the inevitable consequence of the imbalance of power through which we must now survive. Afghanistan was merely the weakest and least protected of the countries unfortunate enough to be directly adjacent to the Soviet Union. Now the others wait their turn, facing a Soviet military empire once again on the move.

[3] *In the Sinkiang there are some 5 million Uighurs and .7 million Kazakhs; the Soviet Union has 5.3 million Kazakhs and 173,000 Uighurs. They, as well as the Kirgiz (1.4 million), might find a Turkic state attractive; in theory the Soviet Union could extrude more of its minority population by donating territory to the new state.*

As for us, now that the military advantages of the Soviet Union can no longer be concealed by delusionary or perhaps cynical claims that we are still "number one"; now that the transitory nature of that advantage creates a fixed urgency to convert perishable power into long-lasting results by decisive map-changing war, it is very important that we recognize the full significance of the new phenomenon before us. Never in their recent history have the Russians had this quality of operational confidence in their armed forces, and its emergence now completes the matrix that will lead to war unless we are very much luckier than we deserve to be.

15

INTERVENTION
AND ACCESS TO
NATURAL RESOURCES

*N*othing is gained by considering the general when it is in truth the particular that defines the matter: oil *is* a special case, indeed unique—at least for a while. For another decade quite certainly, and perhaps for two, the economic well-being and therefore the social stability and thus the political equilibrium of a hundred countries around the world both large and small will continue to depend on secure and sufficient supplies of oil. All manner of raw materials are freely traded on the world market, and those who would try to control the supply of any one—as the Organization of Petroleum-Exporting Countries has done—soon discover that the fluidity of substitution which modern industrial techniques allow limits the gain to a brief interval. And such gain is soon transformed into permanent loss: once a costly synthetic plant or a new non-cartel mine comes into existence, even a prompt reduction in the price of the original product will not easily recapture the lost market.

Under this dispensation, recondite materials now produced by only a handful of countries, and thus seemingly capable of easy cartelization, remain available to consumers at reasonable prices, along with rare metals and common ores, foods and fibers, coal and virtually every other raw material. Oil is different, not because it is a "noble" product as the late Shah was fond of saying, but rather because it is so commonly used in such enormous quantities even while its supply is greatly concentrated. It is one thing to develop a tolerable *ersatz* for tantalum or columbium needed by the pound or the hundredweight; quite another to replace oil by the million ton. Thus the ease with which the supply of oil has been controlled by the cartel, and its colossal extortion, which since 1974, and more acutely since 1978, has greatly impoverished the world economy.

The cartel does not of course operate with electronic precision. Because there is as yet no substitute for oil on the requisite scale, it is the ability of the world economy to absorb its exactions that serves as the sole limit to the price-setting power of the cartel. Confidence in the will and ability of the cartel to act according to its long-term ("enlightened") self-interest has been the crucial ingredient in the optimism of the bankers and economists who have been so active in minimizing the consequences of high oil prices. The cartel would not increase prices excessively, we were told by Robert S. McNamara in his World Bank incarnation and by dozens of others claiming similar authority, because to do so would cause a global economic depression, which would in turn reduce demand for oil—and thus diminish the revenues of the oil exporters. Everything would of course depend on the estimation of very complicated differential elasticities—but for some peculiar reason it was believed that the finest of such calculations would be made in Riyadh, apparently the new seat of higher economic wisdom in place of Cambridge, England, and Cambridge, Massachusetts (Oxford's farsighted disdain for that dubious discipline now stands *fully* vindicated).

Naturally the optimists were wrong, and as of now the cartel is suffering a loss in total revenues since its over-extortion (the "second oil shock") has damaged the world economy excessively. Thus, as of this writing, prices are somewhat reduced so that the barrel of oil which used to sell for less than two dollars in 1972, and which is supposed to be sold for thirty-four dollars by the cartel's order, may actually be purchased for a mere thirty. Consequently, the oil-exporting countries have suffered a loss of income which reflects in miniature, and no doubt temporarily, the huge losses inflicted on the world economy ever since 1974, which have been manifest in the form of diminished growth and financial imbalance, along with their attendant consequences: unemployment for those who go out to work and impoverishment for those who do not—the peasants and craftsmen of the poorer countries that have no oil.

One recalls the soothing estimates offered by assorted experts when oil prices began to multiply: scarcely anything would be lost; they claimed growth would be reduced by a percentage point or two for a year or two, and "recycling," they said, would overcome all the disequilibria in international payments. In the United States especially, many positively welcomed the change: thinking no doubt of Nigeria or Ecuador as the beneficiaries, and of affluent suburbanites as the contributors, the promoters of international economic equality saw the cartel as a most fortunate device that would make the rich a little poorer and the poor a little richer. As for the new but most articulate band of ecologists, they looked forward with pleasurable anticipation to the demise of the eight-cylinder automobiles of vulgar working-class Americans and saw no great loss in a reduced rate of growth that would arrest the spread of mills, satanic or electronic. And if fears were expressed for the financial stability of all the many countries large and small that would suddenly have to pay tribute to the cartel measured in tens and then hundreds of billions of dollars, no less a figure than Robert S. McNamara, head of the World Bank, stood ready to explain with great patience how everything would work out just fine.

What followed of course was the abrupt interruption in the ascent of the poorest in the poor countries to the modest prosperity that tube wells (with diesel pumps) and fertilizers (oil-based) could provide; the deceleration in the high-growth economies of the hardworking that were reshaping millions of lives for the better in such diverse countries as Brazil, Korea, and Turkey; the recessions and depressions of the highly developed in Europe, North America, and East Asia, and more generally the end of the economic optimism that had propelled the progress of the world economy since the Second World War. While the limousines of the bankers that reassured us back then remain polished and well fueled, millions have suffered unemployment if not outright impoverishment in the centers of the automobile industry in Europe and North America; while the professional anti-growth ecologists remain no doubt well funded, the "green revolution" has come to an end in the crowded countryside of Asia.

And what great purpose has been served by the change? Certainly the search for oil has been broadened and deepened (literally so) in many of the newer wells, and certainly much progress has been made in energy conservation. But it seems that these adjustments and also the technological quest for alternative energy sources would have taken place anyway, and altogether less painfully and much more economically had it been only the increasing natural scarcity of oil that would have set the pace of substitution: "crash" programs are never efficient even if effective.

As a matter of fact, the very origin of the price increases retarded the process of conversion to other sources of energy. When oil that costs perhaps a dollar to produce in Arabia (by the most inflated estimate) is sold in a market artificially controlled for thirty-four dollars, the would-be investors in very costly substitution industries must hesitate, since they know that the price is rigged and may collapse if the power of the cartel were to be broken. If by contrast, oil prices had increased steadily and cumulatively in reflection of natural scarcity, oil might now be selling for much less than thirty-four dollars a barrel and yet there might be more rather than less investment in substitution, since risks and rewards could then be projected on the basis of more reliable estimates of future oil prices. The *certainty* of being able to sell substitute energy (including non-OPEC oil) for, say, twenty dollars per barrel is a more powerful incentive to investment than the possibility of fifty-dollar oil—when there is also the possibility of fifteen-dollar oil.

There is thus little merit in the insistent claim that the cartel has actually contributed to the long-term health of the world economy by "reinforcing" the price mechanism; the peculiar readiness of many commentators to find virtue in the cartel's extortion reflects more the inherent tendency to rationalize and justify evils deemed uncontrollable than any economic realities.

THE CASE FOR INTERVENTION

The easier case for intervention, by the classic definition of a "dictatorial inference in the national affairs of other states" presumes a deliberate interruption of supplies by producers that collectively control a decisive quantum of production rather than a mere increase in prices. Ever since the 1973 Arab oil embargo, the menace of another and possibly more prolonged and more complete interruption has been a factor in world politics. It is that fear which best explains the peculiar solicitude of many governments for the plight of the Palestinians—a stateless people to be sure, but one of many, and a nation many of whose members are refugees, but again the world is filled with refugees who benefit from no such eager concern. Anything that attracts sympathetic attention for any part of the large congregation of suffering humanity must be welcomed, regardless of motive, and in spite of an insincerity usually quite transparent. But insofar as the fear of another Arab oil embargo is translated into real leverage for the Arab oil producers in world affairs, the latter must expect that it will evoke countervailing leverage. What remains to be defined is the form that such countervailing leverage might take, and specifically the role of force, if other means are destined to be ineffectual. The morality, legality, feasibility, and necessity of the use of force are discussed in what follows.

THE MORAL ASPECT

There is an obvious difficulty in upholding the morality of the use of force in response to an act which comports no violence in itself. It can be said outright that no moral case can be made for the use of force in order to *retaliate* for the imposition of an embargo; there is an obvious disproportion between the resort to deadly violence and the denial of supplies which are not directly and immediately essential for survival. But that is not the circumstance before us: force would not be used to punish the countries that would impose an embargo but rather to undo its results by seizing oil fields to restore production.

Thus the moral issue is defined by a comparison between two sets of consequences: what will humanity suffer if the hypothetical embargo is simply allowed to continue, and what will be the suffering inflicted by an act of intervention designed to restore production and supply? That an embargo both comprehensive and prolonged would inflict great suffering is clear; the catastrophic disruptions that would be manifest in the wealthier economies would translate eventually into increased death rates in poorer countries. When millions of workers become unemployed in the highly industrialized oil-importing countries, thereafter surviving in varying degrees of comfort at public expense and by exhausting private savings, many more millions in "middle-income" economies will have to survive unemployment without public assistance and with scant savings destined to be soon exhausted; and then in turn the poorer countries, where the very concept of unemployment is irrelevant, will be dragged down from poverty into a worse situation.

It is only by a science yet more dismal than economics that one could arrive at some precise estimate of the deaths that would eventually follow an embargo both comprehensive and prolonged. It is clear, however, that if the oil of Arabia is removed from the market, prices of one hundred dollars per barrel may reasonably be expected for remaining supplies, and that would mean that hundreds of millions of people would remain without the fuel that they need to pump water for their crops, to heat themselves in the coldest weather, to boil water for safe drinking, and to cook food that cannot otherwise be eaten. In the additional malnourishment and sickness that would follow, millions of deaths would undoubtedly result.

As against that, it may be estimated very safely that an intervention conducted in the empty lands where oil is produced in the greatest amount, where local military forces are feeble, and where no popular resistance is to be expected at all, might result in a few hundred deaths or at most a few thousand, and even that requires the heroic assumption that an intervention completely staged would evoke serious resistance.

What makes such calculations quite safe is that the combined number of those who would be exposed to life-threatening hardship all over the world must be a hundred times greater than total population of the countries and mini-states that a forcible intervention would affect. The fact that the first and very large casualty toll would be caused indirectly by a denial of supplies, while the second and much smaller toll would have been inflicted by the weapons of war is morally irrelevant: that distinction is a matter of aesthetics, not ethics.

In the above, the consequences of an oil embargo (comprehensive and prolonged) have, of course, been depicted in the context of the present economic world order. But to argue that none need starve if the hypothetical embargo is immediately followed by a drastic restructuring of the world economy and by appropriately huge transfers of food, medicine and so on from the rich countries to the poor, defines theoretical possibility to be sure, but not a feasible alternative, and neither does it affect the moral calculus. The complex of traditions and institutions, the distributions of skills and capital that condition the functioning of the world economy are not anyone's deliberate creation but rather the inherited results of centuries and millennia of divergent development in different parts of the world. To argue that the deadly consequences of oil denial should rather be undone by demolishing and remaking the entire economic structure of international society is equivalent to the argument that theft should be prevented by abolishing private property. To do that would certainly abolish theft, but equally it would soon enough have the secondary result of abolishing property as well, since none would have the reason to bring it into existence by work, accumulation, and saving. Similarly, the attempt to transfer food and the rest on the scale that would be required to undo the deadly secondary consequences of the hypothetical oil embargo would soon enough diminish the supply to the point where a sufficient transfer would be unfeasible.

In any case, moral questions are not to be resolved by the *ad hoc* creation of artificial worlds which transform the terms of the answer. It is within the present world that the injury of oil denial must be compared to the injury of intervention—and by any calculus of suffering, the latter must be an injury far smaller.

THE LEGAL ASPECT

I will not attempt to address legalistically the question of legality, preferring to do so instead jurisprudentially. The former course would require an investigation of precedents and conventions as well as an appropriate interpretation of the U.N. Charter; the latter by contrast requires us to consider the very meaning of legality as it may apply to the case at hand.

It is possible no doubt to construct an argument whereby any and all use of force between states is deemed *ipso facto* illegal, as is already the case for private force in municipal law (wherein the exception of self-defense implies a prior illegality). It is understood, of course, that the illegality of force in municipal law presumes the existence of alternative methods of relief against injustice. In their absence, to prohibit the use of force without prohibiting the exploitation of all non-forcible instruments of power and control must mean that the world is made safe for all such injustice as such instruments can cumulatively engender. Just as within the municipal sphere, the protection of private property without any restraints on its accumulation brings the population to a state of *de facto* serfdom, except for a relative handful of monopolists and latifundists, so also (in the absence of any other restraint upon the cartel) the latter would be free to inflict economic damage without any possibility of relief if the use of force is ruled out *ab initio*. In practice of course relief is available in the form of additional substitution and conservation measures that would be initiated or accelerated by the advent of an embargo—especially if it is to be prolonged and this were known from the start. Thus it is not the interruption of oil supplies per se that creates the injustice that requires redress but rather its abrupt character: if the oil exporters were to announce their intention of restricting or terminating oil sales on some date in the future (several years removed), then substantive remedies could have timely effect, and no unredressed grievance would remain to justify the use of force.

One can scarcely conceive of circumstances in which the oil exporters would want to impose an embargo so greatly deferred, and the case has no practical significance, but it does serve to bring out to the surface the underlying legal principle that defines the offense and can justify the use of force to reverse its consequences if other means are ineffectual. In selling oil over a long period of time in conditions where no adequate alternative sources of energy are available, the exporters inherently assume the obligation of continuing to sell their oil unless *force majeure* intervenes. The monopolistic seller enters into an implicit contract as well as the explicit contract that attends each transaction. While the latter is negotiated each time anew, the former is latent and fixed, but it still carries an obligation. If, for example, all the food consumed on some remote island is sold by only one shopkeeper, and if the latter were abruptly to refuse further sales without some compelling reason, the islanders would not be judged guilty by any court if they kept themselves supplied by forcibly taking what they needed (against customary payment) until such time as the arrival of other supplies would terminate their need for self-help. The cognizant monopolist (or cartel) tacitly assumes an obligation merely by operating in that contest; if the obligation is evaded, an offense results against which force may justifiably be used when no other remedy exists.

That surely is the principle that applies to an embargo. If Arab oil producers were to attempt to use the "oil weapon," weapons of the ordinary sort may justifiably be used to seize, secure, and operate the oil fields and loading facilities so long as: (1) the embargo would actually deny supplies that could be deemed essential, for which there is no substitute; (2) notwithstanding the intervention, customary payment would continue to be made to the appropriate recipients; (3) the development of alternative energy sources would be pursued as rapidly as possible; and, (4) the intervention would come to an end as soon as the oil supplies it makes available can no longer be deemed essential.

In practice of course there are all sorts of further difficulties that mainly arise from the fact that those most capable of intervention are also the countries that are least likely to suffer deadly consequences from the denial of Arab oil supplies. Obviously, to remain legally justifiable, an intervention would have to be followed by the establishment of distribution arrangements which would reflect the different intensities of oil dependence. (Just as in our example the forcible seizure of the only shop on the island would have to be followed by the equitable distribution of its supplies.) This condition does not, however, raise any great difficulty. The most likely interventionist power, the United States, imports only a fraction of its needs from Arab oil exporters in normal conditions; more generally, the conditions of over-capacity created by the cartel's pricing policy entail the possibility of greatly increasing total availability after an intervention. Specifically, the arithmetic of distribution would have to be worked out in a post-intervention context where some oil previously flowing would probably be cut off (i.e., production from Arab countries that had abstained from the embargo) and where rapidly increasing supplies would be available from the seized oil fields.

In a study entitled "Oil Fields as Military Objectives" prepared by the Congressional Research Service of the Library of Congress, issued on August 21, 1975, a study whose evident purpose was to depict an intervention as undesirable and unfeasible, the authors cite the U.N. Charter of Economic Rights and Duties ("no consideration of whatever nature . . . may serve as a justification for aggression") as well as the U.N. Charter itself, the War Powers Resolution of 1973, and the U.N. Resolution on Nonintervention, to argue the illegality of an intervention. But in fact, as the authors of the study admit, no conclusive case can be established which would deny the opportunity for legal justification. Thus, for example, the Economic Charter also specifically prohibits the use of economic denial for coercive purposes (Ch. IV. Art. 32); and neither does the U.N. Charter preclude intervention if self-preservation is at stake (hence the legal importance of distribution arrangements that would provide oil supplies to countries where these would avert life-threatening shortages). As for the War Powers Resolution of 1973 (to turn to municipal law), it merely defines notification requirements, and affirms the need for explicit congressional approval within sixty days of an act of war. Thus in spite of their evident desire to make a decisive finding against intervention, the authors of the study were forced to conclude ". . . [that] the legal implications of any U.S. determination to violate the sovereignty of foreign states in response to economic injuries are inconclusive" (page 9). And so they are leaving us not in a vacuum but rather with the calculus of suffering that is so decisive.

FEASIBILITY

It is understood that only the sensible objective of an embargo-breaking intervention would be the oil-producing region of eastern Arabia, a coastal strip roughly three hundred miles long from Kuwait to Oman and less than a hundred miles deep at the maximum (Ghawar). That is the total extent of territory that would have to be cleared of any active opposition; the combined extent of the areas which would actually have to be secured on a long-term basis would, of course, be much smaller—being defined by the actual dimensions of the oil fields and their associated facilities, including the major oil-loading terminals.

A crucial aspect of the problem is the Soviet reaction to an intervention. If one takes the view that the Soviet Union would react very energetically, notwithstanding its record in such matters, its lack of direct geographic access (unless Iran were to have fallen under Soviet control in the interim), and notwithstanding also its poor or nonexistent relations with the affected states, it is possible to argue that a Western intervention would be a very dangerous affair. The notion that the Soviet Union would actually attack Western forces as they went about their seize-and-hold operation cannot, however, be deemed credible in any circumstances: for a superpower to attack the forces of another (risking nuclear escalation) in response to the latter's operations against third parties which are in no sense allies is simply unimaginable. Other, and much more likely, Soviet reactions include verbal denunciations and other forms of Soviet political exploitation of the event, threatening military maneuvers and so on. Such reactions would increase tensions and evoke Western anxieties but would have no practical effect on the outcome. Similarly, it is possible to imagine that the armed forces of the affected states (Saudi Arabia, Kuwait, United Arab Emirates, and so on) would fight valiantly and well, with all the mass of highly advanced equipment that has lately been sold to them. If so, one may envisage prolonged and costly fighting in which heavy casualties would be sustained and much would be destroyed. But again, none of this is realistic. By and large, the local armed forces are simply incapable of operating their more advanced and powerful weapons without the day-to-day assistance of technicians who are mostly American and who are virtually all Western. Moreover, even when they can operate their military equipment in a technical sense, its tactical utilization is likely to be ineffectual or nearly so. The simple truth is that none of the states of the area have competent armed forces, for reasons so fundamental that they provide a virtual guarantee of immunity for an intervention force.

Finally, it may be argued that an intervention would ultimately be made futile by sabotage accomplished by local (or imported) guerrillas. If one examines the physical facilities involved, which include hundreds of scattered "Christmas Trees" at individual wellheads, almost two thousand miles of collection pipes, and the great terminal loading facilities as well as the complex separation, regeneration, and refining plants, one may easily conclude that sabotage would be highly effective in perpetuating the denial of oil following an intervention.

There is, of course, no doubt that an intervention conducted in the 1956 "Hamilcar"/"Musketeer" style, whereby a great seaborne armada slowly gathered to attack the Suez Canal area, would afford ample opportunity for systematic, pre-intervention sabotage. With weeks to do the job, and truckloads of high explosives, it would no doubt be easy to destroy so much that the facilities would in fact have to be rebuilt *ex novo;* and if so, it could take as long as two years to restore full capacity. But of course the Anglo-French invasion attempt of 1956 is a textbook case of error. Any competently planned intervention would preserve surprise till the end by masking and deception, thereafter inaugurating the proceedings with a sudden descent in commando-style at many, many separate locations. (There are, as it happens, several dozen airstrips fit for heavy transports in the area, and few of them would need to be secured by preliminary parachute assault.)

In view of the absence of serious local forces, there would be no need to prejudice surprise by attempting to send in right from the start a large multi-divisional force, complete with heavy weapons. Reinforcements and logistic-support forces would of course be eventually needed, but the latter could be provided in a distinct second phase in which it would no longer be necessary to accept preparation penalties for the sake of surprise. As for the initial wave, that should obviously consist of lightly armed elite troops contributed by the participating nations in a combined force which could be accommodated in a manageable number of heavy transport aircraft along with the few small helicopters and light vehicles actually needed right from the start.

In the context of a competent surprise intervention there would be scarcely any opportunity for preventive sabotage, and none at all for systematic destruction. The problem of post-intervention sabotage does, however, remain. Again, it is possible to make an

extremely pessimistic estimate on the assumption that oil workers
would devotedly fight for the property rights of the local rulers, or
the further assumption that they would not be replaced or restricted
to non-critical areas, and/or by assuming a major and successful effort by local and imported guerrillas. But again there is little substance to such fears. In the first place, the number of oil workers
actually needed to *work* the oil fields (as opposed to the far greater
number that are kept on the payroll for training purposes or social
reasons) is surprisingly small and does not exceed a few thousand
in all. Far from being participating members of the ruling elites,
most oil workers who actually work are foreigners, and those who
are not Western are kept in a humiliating non-citizen status, which
is seemingly deeply resented. Moreover, it would be perfectly possible to replace the totality of the workforce (and operating management) with imported personnel recruited for the purpose. Oil
workers are exceptionally mobile, they are used to working in unusual and even dangerous circumstances (at suitable wages), and
most of the skilled oil workers all over the world are Americans.

As for the guerrilla threat, it is understandable that the Vietnam-
shocked (such as the authors of the congressional study cited above)
should believe that guerrillas are inherently formidable, no matter
what the terrain or the human circumstances. In the new post-
Vietnam mythology, it seems that the mere possession of a supply of
Ché Guevara posters, obligatory AK-47 assault rifles, and other such
fashionable accessories will *ipso facto* create a guerrilla force against
which regular forces—and especially those of the United States—
must be powerless. Vietnam was full of trees and brave men, and it
was a country rather densely populated, in which large bodies of
guerrillas could find shelter and food, as well as information and
protective masking by implementing Mao's prescription. Eastern
Arabia, by contrast, has the totally open terrain of the desert, with
a very small population living in settlements extremely well delin-
eated or else easily removable (i.e., Bedouin encampments). Moreover, the local population is largely hostile to the rulers (at least in
the eastern region of Saudi Arabia) or else indifferent to their interests. In any case, even if the local population were to engage in
sabotage or assist outside guerrillas, which is a most unlikely thing,
desert conditions will suffice to make such enemies powerless against
modern guard forces with night-vision devices, helicopters, and
sensor-fences. (It was the Israeli experience that the guerrilla threat
was insignificant in the Sinai, and the rather delicate Negev facilities have been immune from sabotage.)

Nor are the oil facilities as vulnerable as they seem, not even the pipelines (small-capacity pipe is easily replaced; large-capacity pipe is hard to destroy). There is, above all, the fact that even a great increase in production from present levels would still leave much spare capacity, so that actual loadings would not decline even in the presence of much sabotage.

In the congressional study cited above, the authors offer a survey of the force requirements they deem necessary for a seizure of the oil fields. Their calculation assumes circumstances described as "favorable" (page 67) and an intervention limited to the "Saudi core area" only (defined as the four major onshore oil fields, and their associated facilities). The resulting list of requirements includes 2 airborne divisions (which require in turn 1,187 heavy-transport sorties), 1 marine division (in 48 ships), other troops for a total force of 160,000 men, a large number of tactical combat aircraft, 9 air-defense battalions, 16 aircraft carriers, 128 cruisers and destroyers, and an unspecified number of attack submarines. The "methodology" of the study is very impressive, and each of its elements is argued with a wealth of detail. If one accepts the results as valid, one is forced to conclude that an intervention—even if limited in scope to the onshore Saudi fields—would in practice be impossible. Aside from the sheer inadequacy of American capabilities (the U.S. Navy has only 13 carriers, not the 16 deemed necessary, etc.), there is the very great strategic risk of employing such a large part of the total forces available in one very remote area, thus exposing other sectors (NATO, Korea) to great risk since their reinforcement would no longer be possible. Moreover, the envisaged area of operations does not contain enough export capacity to make the intervention worthwhile, since the additional output obtainable is inferior to the non-embargo Arab supply likely to be lost following an intervention. (Traditionally, the radical states of the Arab world limit themselves to the advocacy of embargoes; their own oil exports remain unaffected and may actually increase.)

But just as one is on the verge of being persuaded, the exercise is undone by the simple procedure of applying the "methodology" of the study to military actions of the more or less recent past. And then one discovers that by such calculations D-Day would still be in preparation to allow the accumulation of the requisite number of troops, counted by the tens of millions; that the Falklands operation would have required at least six large carriers instead of two very small ones; that the Israelis would have needed a full airborne division at Entebbe, and so on. In reality, if one envisages a commando action rather than an invasion in the Armada-style, the seizure and control of the entire oil-producing region of Eastern Arabia can be considered a manageable military venture (although a risky one) for a Western coalition which would not include American participation. With it, assuming only competent planning, an intervention should be a relatively straightforward affair which would only entail a very small strategic risk in the form of Soviet counter-intervention, and tactical risks of insignificant proportions.

DESIRABILITY

The use of force cannot be desirable; it can only reluctantly be deemed acceptable in circumstances that allow no other choice. It *would* be desirable if oil were sold at prices that would allow the world economy to recover and resume the progress that the cartel's extortion has interrupted. That *desideratum,* however, is not to be achieved by force; indeed, it can be said explicitly that a price-motivated intervention would be immoral, illegal, and politically quite infeasible in any conceivable setting other than those of a denial price (a price set so high that it would be equivalent to an embargo). In the event of a political embargo, however, force would definitely become a feasible option politically, as it already is militarily; and given the conditions described above, an intervention would also be morally and legally justifiable.

16

ON THE MEANING
OF VICTORY

*T*he West has become comfortably habituated to defeat. Victory is viewed with great suspicion, if not outright hostility. After all, if the right-thinking are to achieve their great aim of abolishing war they must first persuade us that victory is futile or, better still, actually harmful. To use Stalinist language, one might say that the struggle against war requires the prior destruction of the very idea of victory. Accordingly, we are being told insistently that it is very unfortunate for the British that they have won the Falklands war: now they will have to garrison the islands at great cost, and sooner or later they will have to fight again—unless they give up their reconquest—thus making their victory futile.

Never mind that the British successfully defended their principles, and never mind the rather splendid performance of Her Majesty's forces. The right-thinking know better: principles are old men's abstractions that young men are asked to fight for, and war, they insist, is a dirty and squalid business that evokes only the worst in man and serves no purpose. It was a great pity, of course, that the cameras of our network news were not properly accommodated by the British, otherwise we would have been able to enjoy carefully edited footage showing seasick British soldiers en route to the island, and then the wounded crying out in pain and finally at Port Stanley a British child mutilated ("in bitter irony") by a British bomb. It was also most inconsiderate of the British not to allow a TV-star correspondent of ours to interrogate the Queen in proper style ("How do you feel about sending your son toward his probable death?").

But everything missing in the Falklands was abundantly provided in Lebanon. Never mind that the Palestine Liberation Organization's (PLO) pretensions to military power were swept away in a crushing defeat that finally forced Yasir Arafat's men to take refuge among the civilians of Beirut; never mind that the Syrians were soundly beaten both in the air and on the ground. Above all, let us have no cold-blooded Realpolitik. For otherwise we might recognize a rather substantial result of victory in the decline of the Soviet Union's influence in the region to its lowest point since the beginning of its great and costly enterprise in the Arab world, almost thirty years ago. Superpowers, like other institutions known to us, are in the protection business. When they cannot protect clients, they lose influence, not just locally but worldwide.

To ignore such things is easy when the right-thinking have as much to work with as they had in Lebanon: not one wounded child but a great many and, of course, all those picturesque ruins. Only the most documented experts in the Middle East's instant archaeology could have known that much of the footage showed ruins of the civil war—those so greatly photographed in Damour, in fact, dated back to the PLO's devastation of that formerly Christian city.

The casualty figures provided another reminder of antiquity: when we read in the *Historia Augusta* that the army of Claudius II killed 320,000 Goths and sunk 2,000 Gothic ships, should we believe those numbers? And what about the huge numbers in Herodotus? It was assumed that the historian's dilemma could not arise in our statistical age—until there came the reports of the *Washington Post* and the *New York Times* correspondents in Beirut. Their Herodotus was the suitably authoritative head of the Red Crescent ("the Palestinian Red Cross"), who happens to be Arafat's brother. Thus our newspapers wrote of thousands of children killed, tens of thousands of civilians wounded or dead, and hundreds of thousands made homeless by Israeli bombing. (Did the United States supply the several hundred heavy strategic bombers needed for the job? How did the Israelis hide them all these years?)

No ancient scribe fond of large numbers could have done better than our press. Armed with these most useful numbers, the right-thinking recovered the ground lost in the Falklands. But it was not enough to prove that war is hell; it was also necessary to demonstrate that victory had to be futile for the Israelis, and positively harmful to the United States. Greatly disappointed by the refusal of the Latin American governments to retaliate against the United States for siding with the British, the right-thinking were given a new and better opportunity for gloomy prognostications that would hold the principle that victory equals loss: the Arabs would be "radicalized"; i.e., they would turn to the Soviet Union for support; the Arabs would withdraw their funds from U.S. banks and the Treasury; the Arabs would impose an oil embargo. Such fears were apparently so credible that they were shared by sundry senators, and even by some senior officials in the Executive branch. Considerable gloom was thus duly distributed to dampen the unfortunate reflex of public opinion, whereby many obtained some satisfaction from the Israeli victory over Soviet arms.

But the right-thinking had to do even more; they had to persuade the Israelis to derive no benefit from victory. In part the evidence was provided by the advocates themselves. Having first produced so much film and so many photographs as well as acres of newsprint on the sufferings of the Palestinians, they could now argue quite correctly that Israel's reputation would suffer greatly from its venture; and then, of course, it could be argued persuasively that the Palestinians would only be further embittered by their defeat. Above all, it was insistently claimed that the PLO would win (or had won) a "political victory," precisely because of its military defeat. Inadvertently perhaps, some truth was thus told, inasmuch as Palestinian national ambitions must receive greater consideration to the degree that Israel's survival is less and less in serious question, owing to her military strength.

On the basis of such arguments, it could be claimed that Israel's victory was merely tactical, and eventually would be counterproductive, given its cost in blood, political support, and money. In the same vein, it has been argued most persuasively that the Allied victory in 1918 was futile because it set the stage for another World War two decades later; and that even in 1945, victory was ultimately harmful for the victors, because the British lost their economic strength in fighting that war, while the United States and the Soviet Union merely created the circumstances in which they would be locked in permanent confrontation with war-created atomic weapons and eventually with thermonuclear weapons so dangerous that they imperil the very survival of both.

The right-thinking can thus uncover evidence for the futility of victory in virtually every case that comes to mind in any period of history. That great father-figure of the right-thinking, Arnold Toynbee, wrote much to prove that the Romans were in fact ruined by their victory over Carthage, and Toynbee was perfectly consistent in his other capacity, as a Foreign Office expert: he was a very energetic supporter of appeasement during the late 1930s and indeed until the bitter end. After all, he argued in print that 1918 was a futile victory, and would perform likewise in writing of every Western victory that took place in his lifetime.

The hopelessly old-fashioned British and the aggressive Israelis remain unpersuaded. Our own vox populi has never, in fact, accepted the contention that war can yield no good result regardless of motive or circumstances. But at least our own enlightened elite, especially the media elite, knows the truth. Thus in the United States the process whereby all war is made unacceptable no matter what its purpose ("debellicization") is nowadays well advanced. For nuclear war, the work has been fully done. Any U.S. general who would dare to emulate his Soviet counterparts in asserting that nuclear weapons—if only tactical—might actually serve to win in some circumstance or other, would earn himself the classic assignment to that deskless office in the remotest corridor of the Pentagon. The right-thinking are very firm in insisting that any use of nuclear weapons must inevitably result in all-out nuclear war, in which no rational purposes can be achieved so that the very concept of victory can have no meaning. And that, of course, is the view relentlessly promoted in classrooms and lecture halls, in countless editorials, in the speeches of our worthies, in sermons from the pulpit, and in the pontifications of our superstar television announcers.

At the opposite end of the spectrum of conflict, the sheer impossibility of victory in fighting guerrillas has acquired the status of a certified truth in right-thinking circles. (Hence the further offense of the Israelis, in defeating guerrillas.) Already during the Indochina war the principle was established that victory was a non-goal. To speak of it was deemed conclusive evidence of protofascism by the media elite. More remarkably, any talk of victory was taken as a sure symptom of provincial naivete, by the very people who were

directing the fighting (Messrs. McNamara, McGeorge Bundy *et al.*).
Having established that costly and futile war as the canonical case,
the right-thinking could then argue that any active U.S. role in an
insurgency would unfailingly yield another Vietnam. The president's decision that no American may carry a rifle in San Salvador
was a true measure of the progress of debellicization.

Given the widespread acceptance of the claim that the United
States cannot hope for victory in either a guerrilla war or a nuclear
war, it is now the urgent priority of the right-thinking to close the
unfortunate gap in the middle whereby medium-sized conventional
war retains the possibility of victory. Thus their loud insistence that
the medium-sized conventional wars fought by the British and
Israelis must yield certifiably futile victories.

There is no doubt, to be sure, that victory always has its price,
and that it may be very high. Victory is often a terrible thing for the
victors. Only defeat is worse still: while it may contain some well-
hidden advantage, it usually brings not only material loss but also
demoralization in its wake. The British and Israelis both won costly
victories; the Argentines, the PLO and the Syrians suffered defeats
whose evil consequences are not truly diminished by the frenetic
attempts that others may make to denigrate victory and promote
the virtues of defeat.

The prominence of so many influential American voices in such
mystification suggests that our own society is threatened by a process of debellicization that would deny any opportunity for victory,
and thus for any purposeful resistance to aggression. Unless that
process is firmly opposed, unless we refute the counsel of impotence,
the only possible policy choices left open will be appeasement or
outright retreat.

ON LEARNING FROM WARS

It is notoriously difficult to derive valid tactical operational strategy,
or even technical lessons, from the wars that others have fought.
Misinformation and the sheer lack of information are the least of our
difficulties. Much more serious is the multiplicity of contexts and
facets in warfare. When we contemplate the most intricate of human
mass activities, we see not merely through a glass darkly but rather
through the dazzling refractions of a diamond. We see one truth
tactically and another technically, while an operational view may
yield yet another result, and the higher levels of strategy several
more.

Consider, for example, the technically superior, but tactically vulnerable, operationally useful but strategically dubious anti-tank missile. Is that a weapon that we should rely upon to contain Soviet armor in Europe? Or, in assessing a course of conduct, and its protagonist, what are we to say of Rommel, who was a tactical mediocrity, an operational genius, and the very worst of (theater) strategists? How then would we answer the question that national leaders will earnestly ask in war: is X a good general?

Far more than the usual abundance of contradictory evidence, it is the multiplicity and the divergence of the facets of war that denies any clear identification of its valid lessons. In the absence of any self-evident truths, military bureaucracies intent on suppressing unwelcome lessons can do so all too easily, and just as easily they can select out the lessons that usefully serve to confirm their established doctrines and equipment preferences.

The classic case is, of course, the Russo-Japanese War of 1904–5. Had the European general staffs appraised correctly the lessons that now seem so clear in hindsight, the fighting of 1914–16 would have been radically different; the armies of Europe would have gone to war without horses, lances, and swords receiving in exchange many more machine guns as well as heavy howitzers, trench mortars, great quantities of barbed wire, and an entrenching tool for each soldier.

But in fact the lessons of the fighting in Manchuria had scarcely made any impression at all on the armies that went to war in 1914. The ready explanation is, of course, the extreme remoteness of the Manchurian theater of war, and the somewhat exotic character of the antagonists. That is certainly a plausible explanation, but it happens to be utterly false. The events of the Russo-Japanese war were reported in the press in great detail and with much acute analysis. Beyond that, solid works of scholarly precision were soon published. Above all, several European armies (as well as our own) sent battlefield observers to the scene—an especially talented group of officers, as it happens—who wrote very detailed tactical and operational reports that may still be consulted with advantage. The evidence so clearly presented in all these sources should have been conclusive and it should promptly have induced great changes in the cognizant armies. Yet nothing happened.

The ready explanation is that the abundant information on the war was simply ignored by the general staffs, even the reports they specifically commissioned. That too may seem plausible, especially if one's estimate of the intellectual caliber of the pre-1914 general staff officers has been fashioned by Barbara Tuchman's well-known work *The Guns of August*.

Again the plausible explanation is utterly false. The military journals of the period are full of closely reasoned debates about the lessons of the Manchurian fighting, and the evidence was also very carefully reviewed in a multitude of internal staff working papers. (To read those documents is to discover just how false is the legend that portrays those men as harebrained uniformed peacocks, woodenheaded marinets, and neurotic war-lovers.) Thus it was neither the lack of information nor a willful disregard for the evidence that obscured the true lessons of the Russo-Japanese war. A far more subtle process was at work. The truths of the fighting were neither unknown nor ignored but rather subverted, by ad hoc "Manchurian" theories:

- The failure of the cavalry on both sides proved nothing, because neither side had "real" cavalry; Russian horses were mere ponies; and Japanese horses were few.
- The war was fought between two essentially weak armies, hence their immobility, and the resort to entrenchment.
- The siege operations at Port Arthur were inept on the Japanese side and hopeless on the Russian, hence the slow pace of the fighting and the old-fashioned employment of heavy howitzers and mortars.
- The Russian infantry was undisciplined and Japanese infantry physically weak, hence the failure of foot soldiers on both sides to defeat the machine gun by dashing assaults.

Thus social predisposition (in favor of the cavalry), tactical dogmatism (against the machine gun and entrenchment), technological pride (which protected the light 75mm gun of the French and its Krupp counterpart against the claims of heavier howitzers and cheaper mortars)—all played their varied roles in making persuasive the appropriate Manchurian theories of negation. Imposed change is always uncomfortable, often disruptive, and sometimes just intolerable. When there is a powerful desire to believe the untrue, we can all become very inventive in our distortions and in 1904–5 there was an exceptionally strong impulse to invent theories that would explain away what was happening in Manchuria. For that war was most unsatisfactory to all. It was not the war of great maneuvers, that being the only kind of war that the Germans could accept, because only great maneuvers would allow victory to the outnumbered. It was not the war of irresistible infantry offensives that the less-industrialized French needed to reconquer their lost province; and it was certainly not the war of small units, which was the only kind of war that the small British army could then fight. Hence the unconscious rejection of lessons that would have imposed the abandonment of cherished goals or else intolerable change. As we contemplate the record of recent wars, as we try to extract their valid lessons, we should simply assume that the established military bureaucracies will unconsciously invent all the Manchurian theories they might need to explain away unwelcome evidence.

At least for the cause of military analysis, it is fortunate that we now have two very different wars to examine. Their diverse evidence can help us to sort out valid lessons, while making it more difficult to give plausibility to "Manchurian" theories.

Thus, for example, on the most basic of issues: why did the British soldiers outmatch their enemies so greatly? Those of our bureaucrats in and out of uniform who support the perpetuation of the All-Volunteer Force, deem the answer obvious: the British troops were professionals, while their enemies were mere conscripts. But this typical attempt to select our desirable evidence is promptly undone by the other war: in Lebanon, Israeli conscripts and reservists did very nicely against professional long-service Syrian troops and full-time PLO fighters.

Of course there are some who will discount this counter-evidence, on the ground that the "Israelis fought only against Arabs," in the words of a senior U.S. general. That of course is the most comprehensive of all Manchurian thories, for it can be exploited to explain away not merely one part of the evidence but all the evidence of all the wars fought by the Israelis. That the Syrians at least are far better soldiers than the Argentinians is beyond all doubt, and it is also perfectly possible that they are better soldiers than the various enemies whom that nameless general had fought in Korea and Vietnam. If that is so, the question becomes more interesting and more directly relevant to our own concerns: why can both the British and the Israelis in their very different ways field units that are so cohesive and highly motivated, and how can they turn out so many junior officers of such quality in combat leadership?

What is it, then, that these two very different armies have in common as far as these all-important basics are concerned? As far as unit cohesion is concerned, the answer that clearly emerges is that in both armies the fighting units are not mere administrative entities through which soldiers and officers rotate in and out. They are, rather, very stable social groups, each with its own internal sense of loyalty, each with its own distinctive ethos. The soldiers who fought so well in the Falklands did not truly belong to the British army; they belonged to their regiments, in which they would serve their entire service lives in stable association with their fellow soldiers. Our newspapers described the Royal Marine Commandos as "elite" troops. But it would not be a safe procedure, in a pub conversation with one of their members, to question the elite status of the Scots Guards, or of any Guards for that matter, or of any of two dozen more regiments, not counting obvious elite troops, such as, the paratroopers, SAS, Gurkas, the Argylls, and more.

From their regimental system, the British obtain a very high elite content in their small 176,000-man army. Now that the U.S. Army is also small—very small indeed at 776,000 men and women, considering our global responsibilities—we too should seriously consider that system. The regimental mystique is not to be obtained in our case by the issue of tourist-shop badges and insignia or by playing up unfelt traditions. Instead, it is by way of a functional specialization that a real group identity can begin to arise, i.e., Arctic regiments, mountain regiments, desert regiments, tank regiments, jungle regiments, commando regiments, and so on. Needless to say, such units are unlikely to see combat in their nominal speciality, but in the meantime their strong sense of identity will have generated cohesion. Regimentalization is, of course, a very inefficient way of assigning men but, if efficiency were decisive, then surely accountants and economists should head our armed forces.

Alternatively, we might emulate the Israeli model, particularly since it might serve to redeem our National Guard and reserve forces. Their reserve units can be fully ready for war in three days or so; ours, we are told, would need three months or more, even though U.S. reservists serve on duty roughly the same number of days as the Israelis do.

The Israeli model achieves the same stability as the British: soldiers are assigned to a specific brigade and battalion, and there they remain throughout their years on active duty, and beyond that during the annual reserve call-ups as well. An initiative has been launched by the present chief of staff of the U.S. Army, General E. C. Meyer, which begins to provide a modicum of stability for our units, but the computerized manpower-management crowd strongly opposes that sort of thing because it results in "inefficiency," as some units become undermanned and others overstaffed. That is perfectly true, of course, and yet we need more, much more, of the sort of inefficiency that we have so recently seen at work on the hills around Port Stanley and in Lebanon.

Much more disruptive still would it be to accept the evidence that would lead us to recast the training of our young officers. West Point is an institution already quasi-antique and greatly respected, and even the new Air Force Academy is already sacrosant. It would be outright sacrilege to suggest that we should stop the present procedure whereby all cadets are educated to become future generals (and technically trained, bureaucratically skillful, politically sensitive generals at that) and to turn out instead junior fighting leaders.

It is precisely in our technological-managerial age that the technological-managerial education given to our young officers has become less and less useful, if not actually counterproductive. Why should four years of electrical engineering or economics prepare a young man to lead others in combat? Why not teach war and tactics instead, in a course lasting perhaps one or two years instead of the present four? And why should fighter pilots receive a full-scale university education, instead of being taught how to hunt and kill with their machines? In due course, those who remain in the military career can receive all the education they need, but only *after* they have done their junior duty in the realm of combat.

Once upon a time, when this nation was young and primitive, it made eminent sense to use West Point in order to provide skills that civil society so greatly lacked. And in a nation of pioneer farmers, urban craftsmen, and frontiersmen, it was right to believe that the status of the leader could best be assured by teaching him social graces, bourgeois manners, and book knowledge. But in our suburban society, where half the population receives some kind of higher education, it is the skills and aptitudes of war that are missing and it is those that the academies should provide.

What ensures the status of the junior officers in both the British and Israeli armies are three things of supreme importance to the soldiers he leads: his greater willingness to take personal risks in order to reduce the risks imposed on his men, his greater knowledge of the hardware and software of soldiering, and his personal store of combat tradecraft. Those, surely, are the things that junior officers should be taught, and not sociology and economics, electrical engineering, and management—especially when the figure of the long-service combat sergeant is rapidly disappearing from the scene.

Another example of a most uncongenial lesson, which classic Manchurian arguments try to obscure, is of a radically different character. The British, it will be recalled, employed North Sea car

ferries, container ships, passenger liners, and transport aircraft to
sustain the logistic demands of an operation of exceptional range.
The U.S. Navy does, of course, deploy a great deal of specialized
logistic and amphibious shipping and would not have to resort to
improvisations in order to stage an intervention on the scale of the
Falklands. Along with the air force it could sustain a much larger
operation solely with service-issue ships and aircraft but although
large, their capacity is not large enough: we have 3 marine divisions
but only enough amphibious shipping for one division and-a-bit; we
have 13 large carriers, but in a serious conflict we may need 15 or
20; and even a limited-war commitment of the Rapid Deployment
Force (RDF) could easily require more transport-aircraft capacity
than the air force now has.

It would thus be most useful to plan ahead for the use of mobilized civilian equipment, in order to survey ships and aircraft, and
then develop and build bolt-on weapon rigs, containerized radar
sets, boxed communication centers, and other such things for ships,
as well as loading gear and add-on electronics.

Unconsciously repeating all the objections that the Admiralty
raised in 1915–16 against Lloyd George's demand for a convoy system (when convoys were finally introduced the number of sinkings
declined sharply and immediately), the navy holds that civilian
ships are unusable, since their crews would be undisciplined and
their skippers would be incapable of keeping stations, while the
ships themselves would be virtually useless because of their inherent
design. And yet in the recent fighting, we saw civilian-manned
British ships operating successfully not merely in a war zone but
actually under fire; and we saw too how additional Harriers were
deployed aboard an ordinary container ship, converted within a few
days to serve as an aircraft carrier of sorts. If the British can im-
provise even an aircraft carrier, can we not at least plan ahead to
employ civilian transport ships that might be desperately needed?

Similarly, the air force now proclaims itself short of airlift capacity, and its claim is valid. The additional airlift, however, would not
be needed on a day-to-day basis, but only in rare military emergen-
cies to deliver large intervention forces. So why not rely on the great
mass of aircraft in our commercial fleets for some of that surge capability? There is already, to be sure, a program that is meant to do
just that, but the total airlift capacity involved remains quite small,
and the air force is reluctant to use its funds for the purpose. We do
need a larger fleet of airlifters of the C-5 variety, as only they can
carry the heaviest and largest weapons; but for the great bulk of our

airlift needs, civilian aircraft would be eminently suitable. The refusal of the air force to exploit fully the vast potential of the largest commercial air fleet in the world reminds us that military bureaucracies will never greatly favor arrangements that do not provide more officer slots for our overofficered armed forces.

Let Manchuria be remembered.

ACKNOWLEDGMENTS

I am grateful to the Center for Strategic and International Studies, Washington, DC, and to my co-editor, Dr. Barry M. Blechman, for permission to use material from the *International Security Yearbook 1983/84* and *1984/85*. The material on the nuclear balance was authored by Barry M. Blechman with the assistance of Joel S. Wit, associate editor of the 1983/84 yearbook. I also gratefully acknowledge permissions from the following journals, editors, and publishers.

I. HOW TO THINK ABOUT NUCLEAR WAR

1. "Ten Questions About SALT II," *Commentary*, August 1979
2. "Is There an Arms Race?" *The Washington Quarterly*, Winter 1979
3. "A New Arms Race?" *Commentary*, September 1980
4. "How to Think About Nuclear War," *Commentary*, August 1982

302   ACKNOWLEDGMENTS

II. THE POLITICS OF DEFENSE

5. "Why We Need More 'Waste, Fraud & Mismanagement' in the Pentagon," *Commentary*, February 1982
6. "Deus Ex Missiles," *The New Republic*, August 9, 1982

III. THE WIDER CONTEXT OF STRATEGY

7. "The East-West Struggle," *International Security Yearbook 1983/ 84* and *1984/85*
8. "The Economic Instrument in Statecraft," previously unpublished
9. "A Geopolitical Perspective on the US-Soviet Competition," *International Security Yearbook 1983/84*
10. "A Historical Precedent: The Romans in Dacia," previously unpublished
11. "A Record of Failure," *Commentary*, June 1983
12. "Of Bombs and Men," *Commentary*, August 1983

IV. ON THE MEANING OF STRATEGY

13. "On the Meaning of Strategy . . . for the United States in the 1980s," in W. Scott Thompson, editor, *National Security in the 1980s: From Weakness to Strength* (San Francisco: Institute for Contemporary Studies, 1980)
14. "After Afghanistan, What?" *Commentary*, April 1980
15. "Intervention and Access to Natural Resources," in Hedley Bull, editor, *Intervention in World Politics* (Oxford: Clarendon Press, 1984)
16. "On the Meaning of Victory," *The Washington Quarterly*, Winter 1982

INDEX

ABMs (anti-ballistic missiles), 194–
195
ABM-X-3, 194
ABM treaty (1972), 25, 28, 101, 102,
113, 194–95
Acheson, Dean, 232, 233
Aegis air-defense cruisers, 168
Afghanistan, 69, 85–86, 104, 126–
127, 138–39, 152, 203, 252,
259–63, 269–71, 273
Airborne Command Center, 191
aircraft carrier task forces, value of,
168–70
Air Force, U.S., 50, 51, 62, 95n, 98,
105, 111, 161, 231, 239, 299
command, control, and communications systems in, 190–91
Iranian rescue attempt and, 108
in Vietnam War, 55–56
Air Force Academy, U.S., 59, 298
Air Force bases, U.S., 179, 181, 193,
199

ALCMs (air-launched cruise mis-
siles), 27, 179, 181, 199, 201
Alexander I, Czar of Russia, 231
Alföldi, A., 213n, 222n
Andropov, Yuri, 124, 200, 204
Angola, 103, 128, 138, 255, 256, 257
Antarctica, 86, 260
anti-satellite systems, 188, 195–96
anti-ship missiles, 77, 117–19, 263
anti-tank weapons, 116–17, 119–20,
167, 171, 237
in Korean War, 50
NATO vs. Soviet, 66
in World War II, 93
Anzio, landing at, 117
Arafat, Yasir, 290
Argentina, 152, 293, 296
Arkansas, ICBMs in, 181
Armenia, 213, 220
arms:
cost of, 88–90
nuclear, see nuclear weapons

About the Author

Edward N. Luttwak is the author of *The Pentagon and the Art of War, The Grand Strategy of the Roman Empire, Coup d'Etat,* and other books. A graduate of the London School of Economics and Johns Hopkins University, he is a Senior Fellow in Strategic Studies at Georgetown University's Center for Strategic and International Studies, and serves as a consultant to the U.S. government. His articles appear regularly in *Commentary, The Times Literary Supplement,* and other journals.

5⁵⁰

EBBL